D1433660

Mutual Knowledge

Mutual Knowledge

edited by

N. V. Smith

Department of Phonetics and Linguistics
University College, London

1982

ACADEMIC PRESS

A Subsidiary of Harcourt Brace Jovanovich, Publishers

London · New York
Paris · San Diego · San Francisco
São Paulo · Sydney · Tokyo · Toronto

ACADEMIC PRESS INC. (LONDON) LTD.
24/28 Oval Road
London NW1

United States Edition published by
ACADEMIC PRESS INC.
111 Fifth Avenue
New York, New York 10003

British Library Cataloguing in Publication Data
Mutual knowledge.
 1. Psycholinguistics—Congresses
 I. Smith, N. V.
 401'.9   BF455

 ISBN 0-12-652980-9

 LCCCN 81-68979

Printed in Great Britain by
Thomson Litho Ltd, East Kilbride, Scotland

Contributors

Michael Brody   Department of Phonetics and Linguistics, University College, London *and* Department of Linguistics and Philosophy, Massachusetts Institute of Technology, Cambridge, Massachusetts

Keith Brown   Department of Linguistics, University of Edinburgh, School of Epistemics

Thomas Carlson*   Department of Psychology, Stanford University, California

Herbert Clark   Department of Psychology, Stanford University, California

Annabel Cormack   Department of Phonetics and Linguistics, University College, London *and* Department of Phonetics and Linguistics, School of Oriental and African Studies, London

Gerald Gazdar   Cognitive Studies Programme, School of Social Sciences, University of Sussex, Falmer, Brighton

David Good   Cognitive Studies Programme, School of Social Sciences, University of Sussex, Falmer, Brighton

Paul Grice   Department of Philosophy, University of California, Berkeley, California

Stephen Isard   Laboratory of Experimental Psychology, University of Sussex, Falmer, Brighton

Phil Johnson-Laird   Laboratory of Experimental Psychology, University of Sussex, Falmer, Brighton

Aravind Joshi   Department of Computer and Information Science, The Moore School of Electrical Engineering D2, University of Pennsylvania, Philadelphia

Ruth Kempson   Department of Phonetics and Linguistics, School of Oriental and African Studies, London

Rose Maclaran   Department of Phonetics and Linguistics, University College, London *and* Department of Linguistics, Cornell University, Ithaca, New York

Terence Moore   Department of Linguistics, University of Cambridge

Geoffrey Sampson   Department of Linguistics, University of Lancaster, Bailrigg, Lancaster *and* Institut Dalle Molle d'Etudes Sémantiques et Cognitives, Geneva

* Carlson was not present at the colloquium in person.
For participants with more than one affiliation, the *first* is the address for correspondence

Neil Smith   Department of Phonetics and Linguistics, University College, London

Dan Sperber   CNRS *and* Université de Paris X

Yorick Wilks   Department of Language and Linguistics, University of Essex, Colchester

Deirdre Wilson   Department of Phonetics and Linguistics, University College, London

Preface

A number of disciplines, most notably linguistics, philosophy, psychology and artificial intelligence, are preoccupied with the common task of analysing the use of language for communication. Unfortunately, the results produced in any one of these fields tend to remain unknown to workers in the others, so that insights achieved in one area are ignored in another, work is unnecessarily duplicated, and a subject ideally suited to the cross-fertilization of ideas is often left in a series of academic isolation wards.

Accordingly, when the SSRC (UK) expressed its desire to further research of a cross-disciplinary kind in areas of fundamental importance, I suggested the Colloquium on Mutual Knowledge whose proceedings appear in this volume. The intention was that there should be a clear linguistic bias to the colloquium, but that there should be representatives of the other disciplines directly involved, so that the linguists should have their horizons broadened and, hopefully, the representatives of these other disciplines should return to their respective folds with a clear idea of what linguists had to offer.

The precise choice of subject for the colloquium and the consequent selection of speakers was, in the first instance, the result of my earlier collaboration with Deirdre Wilson and my friendship with Herb Clark. In Spring 1979, I spent some weeks as a house guest of Herb and Eve Clark in Stanford and seemed to spend a considerable proportion of my time arguing (often out of my depth) about problems of mutual knowledge. Convinced that Clark's ideas should be confronted with better opposition than my own breakfast ramblings, and that the ideal solution would be some kind of constructive interpenetration of his theory and that of Sperber and Wilson, I organized the conference around these two papers. We thus had the ensured participation of a distinguished psychologist, Clark (working jointly with a fellow psychologist, Carlson), and of a leading linguist, Wilson, collaborating with perhaps the foremost cognitive anthropologist in Europe, Dan Sperber. The choice of the other main speakers was then not difficult. Aravind Joshi is widely known for his work on question–answering systems in artificial intelligence, but he also has a reputation for his research on the formal properties of grammars and hence could be trusted to bridge the gap whose existence was partial motivation for the conference in the first place. Paul Grice is the doyen of philosophers of language and the fountainhead of much that is good in modern pragmatics. His presence at the colloquium was an incomparable asset. Misi Brody is as yet relatively unknown, but he is an outstanding theoretical linguist who I knew could be guaranteed to contribute to the core of the discipline.

The choice of rapporteurs was made easy by the willingness of so many distinguished scholars from a range of disciplines (though again with a linguistic bias) to participate.

The major papers were distributed to the participants before the colloquium and slightly revised in the light of the discussants' comments thereafter. These comments themselves were, in general, written up after the colloquium, taking account of the changes made to the main speakers' original drafts. To avoid the incipient infinite regress that threatened to intervene, the main speakers were allowed a brief *final* rejoinder if they wished. Each paper had two rapporteurs, but in some cases, other participants have also contributed comments on their colleagues' papers.

I am grateful to all the speakers, not only for participating, but also for meeting all the deadlines and bearing my unprovoked demands with cheerful fortitude.

The colloquium was held at the University of Surrey at Guildford immediately after the autumn meeting of the Linguistics Association of Great Britain. I am grateful to the LAGB for allowing me to use their facilities, and I am particularly indebted to Stephen Barbour whose work as local organizer was invaluable.

I am also grateful to the Social Science Research Council (UK) which not only financed the colloquium (under grant no. HG 40/6/1) but which, in the persons of Keith Brown and Anne Kauder, gave me help and guidance in the organization. My thanks are due also to the staff of Academic Press for their editorial advice and helpfulness; and to Judith Halliwell and Alison Jarvis of University College, London for their cheerful efficiency in the face of adversity.

My deepest debt is, not for the first time, to Deirdre Wilson, *sine qua non*.

October, 1981   N. V. Smith

Introduction*

Such knowledge is too wonderful and excellent for me:
I cannot attain unto it   Psalms 139.v

Linguistic research over the last quarter century has been pursued overwhelmingly within the Chomskyan paradigm, which places the *competence* or tacit knowledge of the native speaker at the centre of investigation. It is undeniable that this framework has been extremely successful (cf. Newmeyer 1980; Smith and Wilson 1979). It is equally undeniable that an approach which concentrates on competence to the exclusion of the complementary notion *performance* leaves questions of fundamental importance about how this knowledge is exploited unanswered. The failure by most transformationalists to address problems of language use seriously had led some to suspect that the theory was approaching bankruptcy. Within the last few years, however, there has developed a coherent field of pragmatics, stemming from work both in linguistics and in the related fields of philosophy, psychology and artificial intelligence, which presupposes a competence theory of language and incorporates it into a more general theory of language use.

Pragmatics, defined as a theory of utterance interpretation, confronts problems which are common to all the disciplines mentioned above: how to determine what entities are referred to by NPs in the sentences uttered, how to disambiguate structurally or lexically ambiguous sentences, how to identify the time of the event specified in the utterance, how to interpret appropriately utterances whose content is superficially irrelevant to their context, and so on. In all these cases, a crucial consideration concerns what one's interlocutor knows. To take a simple example, there is little point in asking someone the score if they have no

* I am grateful to Rose Maclaran for her comments on a draft of this introduction.

means of determining which game one is talking about. Moreover, to do this, they need to know the interests or immediate preoccupations of the speaker who, in turn, must normally know that the hearer knows he has these preoccupations.

Mutual knowledge of this kind, i.e. knowledge which is shared and known to be shared, was first identified in these terms by Lewis (1969) and Schiffer (1972), although the problems involved had been hinted at more or less explicitly in a number of earlier works, most notably Grice's seminal paper *Meaning* (Grice, 1957). Schiffer's definition of mutual knowledge (quoted by Johnson-Laird (p. 40) and, under the heading "mutual belief" by Clark and Carlson (p. 3)) has been widely attacked because it contains what Schiffer himself (1972, p. 32) calls a "perfectly harmless" infinite regress. To establish mutual knowledge between A and B of proposition P, A has to know P, and know that B knows P, and that B knows that A knows P, and so on *ad infinitum*.

Clark and Carlson devote the first part of their paper to the defence of a quasi-Schifferian position in which mutual belief is inferred on the basis of a *finite* induction schema. Their position is a refinement of an earlier paper by Clark and Marshall (1981) which was widely cited but imperfectly appreciated during the colloquium. The body of Clark and Carlson's paper, however, is a detailed proposal for the modification of speech-act theory to take account of the special problems posed by "hearers": i.e. how people interpret utterances which are not directed exclusively to them, but to a group of which they may form a part. Both Clark and Carlson's defence of mutual knowledge and their suggested innovation that all speech acts addressed to one or more interlocutors are performed by a new kind of "informative" illocutionary act, proved controversial (cf. Sperber's and Johnson-Laird's comments and Clark and Carlson's rejoinder). The underlying cause of this hostile reception is hinted at in Sperber's remark (p. 46) that speech act theory itself should perhaps be "abandoned". The reason for suggesting this radical alternative becomes clear in Sperber and Wilson's own paper.

Speech-act theory was intended as a (partial) semantic theory (cf. Searle, 1969) but with the clarification in the demarcation of semantics and pragmatics which has taken place over the last few years, it is clear that speech-act theory is better viewed as a (partial) theory of pragmatics which is parasitic on some antecedent, truth-conditional, semantic theory. That is, speech-act theory is crucially concerned with language use, or performance, rather than with the knowledge of language *per se*. Sperber and Wilson have their own pragmatic theory in which neither speech acts nor mutual knowledge have any role to play at all. The core of that theory is presented in the present book. Their paper can be divided into two parts: one an attempt to demolish the validity of the notion of mutual knowledge (or mutual belief) as a viable part of a theory of communication; the other an attempt to provide a reasoned alternative to such a theory on the basis of a refined notion of Gricean *relevance*. It is indeed noteworthy that both speech-act theory and Sperber and Wilson's relevance theory are both in part the intellectual offspring of Grice (respectively of Grice 1957 and Grice 1967), for they are now radically opposed in their choice of theoretical primes. Sperber and Wilson argue that the central and most crucial part of any pragmatic theory, and one which renders the speech-act apparatus exploited by Clark and Carlson and others redundant, is a standard of *maximal relevance*. Virtually everything else, including Grice's (1975) remaining maxims, can be done away with.

No one is likely to quarrel with the informal claim that we interpret utterances so as to maximize their relevance. Claims of this sort are plentiful in the literature of several disciplines, most notably Artificial Intelligence as Wilks rather acidly observes (p. 113). Sperber and Wilson, however, are the first to spell out in detail how the idea of maximal relevance might be made explicit within a general theory that integrates linguistic, logical and encyclopaedic knowledge simultaneously. This paper represents a radical departure from earlier positions and it is not surprising that the definition of relevance in their unified theory is vigorously attacked in a lengthy critique by Gazdar and Good which also provides a partial defence of the use of mutual knowledge. It is unlikely that Sperber and Wilson's rejoinder to this attack will be the end of the debate.

It has already been observed that the issues debated at the colloquium straddle the domains of semantics and pragmatics, with developments in the latter field allowing new insights into utterance interpretation in particular and the theory of communication in general. It is in fact typical of much recent work that syntactic and semantic accounts have given way to pragmatic ones. The next paper, by Brody, takes up explicitly the problem of when a particular linguistic phenomenon should be handled pragmatically and when grammatically (specifically syntactically). The examples he takes are of "circular readings": i.e. constructions in which the antecedent of some pronominal anaphor contains that anaphor as a proper sub-part of it. The standard explanation (due to Higginbotham and May, 1979a) for the unacceptable status of such examples is that they are grammatically well formed, but are ruled out by a pragmatic principle: i.e. their deviance is a function of performance constraints not of syntactic (competence) violations. Brody argues to the contrary that a *general* account of the phenomenon, rather than *ad hoc* stipulation that certain strings are unacceptable, necessitates the postulation of a grammatical constraint (a–c dependency) in place of the pragmatic one. This grammatical constraint is furthermore to be derived as a prediction from a more abstract general principle of language (specifically, that all anaphoric pronouns which have a linguistic antecedent are expanded into a copy of that antecedent) in a way analogous to the deduction of specific effects from general theories in physics (e.g. the deflection of light rays by a gravitational field is a prediction of the theory of relativity). In this case, the detailed effects that follow from the general linguistic principles look superficially forbiddingly complex.

However, it is significant that linguistics is now beginning to be in a position where explanatory principles of some depth can be adduced in the way they can in the hard sciences. It is worth bearing this point in mind while reading the disputes between Brody and his two rapporteurs, Kempson and Brown, as the debate can be interpreted on three levels. First, there is the issue of the range of examples which are to be treated as manifestations of the same phenomenon: e.g. should the examples of crossing interpretations *without* circular dependencies, raised by Brown, be included? This issue can only be usefully settled when we proceed to the second level: that of adjudicating between proposed analyses of the phenomena in terms of specific constraints, either syntactic or pragmatic. It is here that most of the discussion takes place: Kempson argues strongly that a modified version of Higginbotham and May's pragmatic solution is to be preferred over Brody's grammatical solution. Brody's response, however, is to proceed to the third level: the pragmatic solution is not impossible but it is *ad hoc*, whereas his grammatical solution follows naturally from more abstract general principles, and is therefore to be preferred on explanatory grounds. The complexity of this section of the proceedings is then a direct reflection of the explanatory depth of the principles discussed. Moreover, it is salutary that, parallel to the explicit attacks on mutual knowledge by Sperber and Wilson and Johnson-Laird, this paper makes an implicit attack on mutual knowledge by demonstrating that the preferred solution to an apparently pragmatic problem involving the determination of deictic reference and hence indirectly mutual knowledge, is after all grammatical.

A considerable proportion of the literature devoted to mutual knowledge has emanated from laboratories of Artificial Intelligence, even though the researchers concerned and their colleagues in philosophy, psychology and linguistics, are often in a state of mutual ignorance or misunderstanding with respect to each other's work (cf. the exchange between Wilks and Sperber and Wilson). A partial palliative for this state of affairs is provided by Joshi, who discusses the parallels and contrasts between man–machine interaction and man–man interaction. Specifically he deals with co-operative behaviour which involves reconciling disparities in the mutual beliefs of the interlocutors by postulating a modification to Grice's (1975) maxim of quality. This suggestion is contested by both the rapporteurs. On the basis of an extended economic metaphor, Sampson impugns the validity of Grice's co-operative principle, hence of the maxims in general and, *a fortiori*, of Joshi's suggested amendment. Maclaran attempts to undercut Joshi's position by arguing that humans simply avoid the kind of problem he raises rather than solving it. They do this, she claims, by actively exploiting the notion of relevance already introduced and defended *in extenso* by Sperber and Wilson.

It will by now be obvious that the discussion of mutual knowledge in particular and of pragmatics in general has made repeated reference to the work of Grice. It is therefore fitting that the final paper in the colloquium should have been given by Grice. It is particularly appropriate in that he has returned in this paper to topics which he first broached in his papers of 1957 and 1968: the contrasts between natural and non-natural meaning on the one hand and speaker's meaning *vs.* text meaning on the other. In his final "mystery package", he also addresses the problem of the infinite regresses which played a major role throughout the colloquium. He uses it, however, to argue for a new interpretation of speaker's meaning incorporating the notion of *value*: an epistemological correlate of the linguistic idealization of "perfect competence"; and embellishes the discussion with an account of one of the ordinary language markers of value, the use of the word *deem*. Grice's paper is both rich and elusive, and it is clear that the rapporteurs' reactions to it (both Isard and Cormack concentrate on the derivation of non-natural meaning from natural meaning) will be but the first of many exegetic attempts.

The papers that follow are not easy to assimilate, covering as they do a spectrum embracing the major part of the philosophy of language, a large proportion of cognitive psychology, the top end of linguistics and most of artificial intelligence. Moreover, it is generally the case that one has to work very hard if one wants *explanations* rather than mere descriptions. In this book can be found incidental explanations for such diverse phenomena as the gullibility of the consultants of oracles, the closing time of small shops, and the pecking patterns of pigeons. In addition to this gilt on the gingerbread are a number of major contributions to pragmatic theory from a set of widely different theoretical perspectives. Some old problems remain and new problems have been defined, but much light has been shed and much misunderstanding dispelled: perhaps even sufficient to belie the epigraph.

Contents

Contributors v

Preface vii

Introduction xi

1. Speech Acts and Hearers' Beliefs
   H. H. Clark and *T. B. Carlson* 1
       Co-ordination of Actions
       Collective Directives
       Informatives
       Other Collective Requests
       The Informative Analysis
       Conclusions

       Comments on Clark and Carlson's Paper
       Y. Wilks 38

       Mutual Ignorance: Comments on Clark and Carlson's Paper
       P. N. Johnson-Laird 40

       Comments on Clark and Carlson's Paper
       D. Sperber 46

       Critics' Beliefs about Hearers' Beliefs: A Rejoinder
       H. H. Clark and *T. B. Carlson* 52

2. Mutual Knowledge and Relevance in Theories of Comprehension
   D. Sperber and *D. Wilson* 61
       Introduction
       Some Questions for the Mutual Knowledge Framework
       An Alternative Framework
       Conclusion

       On a Notion of Relevance
       G. Gazdar and *D. Good* 88

       Reply to Gazdar and Good
       D. Sperber and *D. Wilson* 101

Comments on Sperber and Wilson's Paper
T. Moore 111

Comments on Sperber and Wilson's Paper
Y. Wilks 113

Reply to Wilks
D. Sperber and *D. Wilson* 118

The Relevance of Common Ground
H. H. Clark 124

Reply to Clark
D. Sperber and *D. Wilson* 128

3. On Circular Readings
   M. Brody 133
        I. Introduction
       II. The Inadequacy of the Pragmatic Solution
      III. Referential Chains and Asymmetry
       IV. Anaphoric Expansion
        V. Some Consequences

   Comments on Brody's Paper
   K. Brown 148

   Reply to Brown
   M. Brody 156

   Problems of Co-reference and Logical Form
   R. Kempson 159
        I. Preliminaries
       II. On the Deviance of Circular Readings
      III. VP Anaphora
       IV. Problems with the Leftness Constraint
        V. No Circular Readings?

   Reply to Kempson
   M. Brody 175

4. Mutual Beliefs in Question–Answer Systems
   A. K. Joshi 181
       Introduction
       Mutual Beliefs and Co-operation
       Surplus Information
       Conclusion

   The Economics of Conversation
   G. Sampson 200

Comments on Joshi's Paper
R. Maclaran   211

A Brief Reply to some of the Remarks by Sampson and Maclaran
A. K. Joshi   219

5. Meaning Revisited
P. Grice   223
   Language, Thought and Reality
   Natural and Non-natural Meaning
   The Mystery Package

Comments on Grice's Paper
S. D. Isard   246

Comments on Grice's Paper
A. Cormack   251

References and Citation Index   258

Index   265

Chapter 1
Speech Acts and Hearers' Beliefs

Herbert H. Clark and Thomas B. Carlson

For communication to be successful, speakers must share certain knowledge, beliefs, and assumptions with the people they are talking to. Take this request:

(1) *Patricia to Eric:* Please sit down.

According to Lewis (1969), the conventions of language must be "common knowledge" between Patricia and Eric (for example, the conventions that *sit* can be used to denote sitting, *sit down* to denote sitting down, and so on). According to Schiffer (1972), what Patricia means in uttering (1) relies on her and Eric "mutually knowing or believing" that the words *Please sit down* plus other contextual information constitute good evidence that she is requesting him to sit down. Common or mutual knowledge or beliefs between speakers and addressees have also been claimed to play critical roles in assertions (Stalnaker, 1978), indirect speech acts (Clark, 1979; Cohen and Perrault, 1979), novel coinages (Clark and Clark, 1979), reference (Clark and Marshall, 1981; Nunberg, 1979) and presuppositions (Karttunen and Peters, 1975).

However, what about shared beliefs *among* hearers? Virtually all discussions of speech acts have been limited to what we will call *canonical speech acts*. In (1), there is a single speaker (Patricia) addressing a single hearer (Eric) who is fully known to the speaker, and there are no other relevant hearers. Canonical speech acts are speech acts, like (1), made by speakers to single namable addressees. In these, the question of beliefs shared by hearers doesn't even arise. But take (2):

(2) *Irving, to Pat* and *Mike:* Please shake hands.

Shaking hands is a joint act. For Irving to expect Pat and Mike to be able to carry it out, he must intend each of them to recognize not only what he asked of *him* but also what he has asked of the other. If they are told separately and have no guarantee the other has been told, they should realize they cannot carry out that joint act without further negotiation. Here, shared beliefs *among* the addressees appears crucial.

In this paper, we examine some common uses of language in which shared beliefs *among* hearers is critical. This is valuable in part because so little is known about speech situations with more than one hearer. Our ultimate goal, however, is to examine speech act theory in general. We argue that our findings require a rather fundamental addition to traditional theories of speech acts.

CO-ORDINATION OF ACTION

Our argument rests on an analysis of what we will call *joint acts*. A joint act is an act by two or more people who must, in general, intentionally co-ordinate their separate actions in order to succeed. Shaking hands is an everyday example, and so are rowing a boat, speaking and listening, driving down a highway, signalling in Morse code, walking in a crowd of people, meeting, and dancing (see Schelling, 1960; Lewis, 1969). What is required for joint acts to succeed? To this question, Lewis (1969) has offered an important answer. We will illustrate his solution, and expand on it, with one of the most intricate of joint acts, the playing of duets.

The Violin Duet

One evening Itzhak Perlman and Pinchas Zuckerman get together to play violin duets. Perlman suggests they play Bartok's "Duet Number 38, Rumanian Whirling Dance". Zuckerman agrees, and they prepare their music and violins. To start them off, Perlman lifts his violin slightly and brings it down with the gesture of a conductor, and at that moment they begin their first notes. From then on, they play according to the score, adjusting to each other auditorily and visually as they go.

The co-ordination required for this duet is indescribably complex. Perlman and Zuckerman must co-ordinate: the tuning of their violins to the same pitch; the edition of the music they are playing from; whether they both begin with a down-bow or an up-bow; the point in Perlman's gesture to take as the beginning; where in the music to begin; the tempo that "allegro" implies; whether or not they are to play at the tempo as marked; whether the piece is to be conducted by Perlman or Zuckerman; how loud "forte" is; how quickly to crescendo near the end; and so on. The list is so long and intricate it is a wonder Perlman and Zuckerman ever manage to bring it off.

The joint act of initiating the first note is complicated enough. Imagine that Perlman has been practising his gesture to start the first note, and now he wants the gesture to be taken for real. When he gestures this time, he must believe that Zuckerman will take the gesture for real (and not just practice), since Zuckerman won't otherwise play the first note, and their joint act will fail. However, he recognizes that Zuckerman will also not play if Zuckerman believes that Perlman believes himself to be still practising, since in that case *Perlman* won't play. Perlman must believe that Zuckerman believes that he, Perlman, is taking the gesture for real. This, however, is still not enough. What if Zuckerman believes that he, Perlman, believes Zuckerman still thinks he is practising? Zuckerman won't play in that case either, since he wouldn't expect Perlman to play. That is, Perlman must believe that Zuckerman believes that he, Perlman, believes that Zuckerman believes that this time he is gesturing for real. It is easy to see that *in principle* Perlman should continue this reasoning *ad infinitum*, and Lewis (1969) has provided the proof.[1]

To co-ordinate their first note, therefore, Perlman and Zuckerman require what Schiffer (1972) has called *mutual belief* of the proposition p that Perlman's gesture is for real this time. Let us call Perlman and Zuckerman A and B. Schiffer's definition for mutual belief is this:

A and B mutually believe that $p =$ def.

(1) A believes that p.

(1′) B believes that p.

(2) A believes that B believes that p.

(2′) B believes that A believes that p.

(3) A believes that B believes that A believes that p.

(3′) B believes that A believes that B believes that p.

et cetera *ad infinitum*.

This definition, with *know* in place of *believe*, is equivalent to what Lewis would call A and B's *common knowledge* of the proposition p.[2] To be more precise, however, we must talk about Perlman's and Zuckerman's states of mind separately, since they are separate people with separable beliefs. As for Perlman, what he must assure himself of, technically speaking, is that he and Zuckerman mutually believe that p. That is, the crucial condition is this: *A believes that A and B mutually believe that p*. The corresponding condition holds for Zuckerman.

The necessity for mutual belief doesn't stop at Perlman's gesturing the start of the first note. Perlman and Zuckerman must also mutually believe that they are both going to play the first note of Bartok's "Duet 38", that they are both going to down-bow, that they are both going to play mezzo forte, that they are both going to play in the key as written and not in some transposed key, and so on. Perlman and Zuckerman, of course, could happen to manage these things together by accident, but then they wouldn't be performing a *joint* act. A joint act is one that the parties engage in, *intending* to do it by design and not by accident. As professionals, Perlman and Zuckerman would never leave these elements to chance. Lewis's conclusion is that all genuine joint acts must be based, in principle, on mutual knowledge or beliefs.

Inferring Mutual Belief

Many people have objected to the concept of mutual knowledge or belief because of its infinity of conditions. Although "full" mutual knowledge or belief may be required for joint acts in the ideal, the argument goes, it cannot be attained in practice. A person couldn't possibly deal with the infinite number of knowledge or belief statements that are involved. Bach and Harnish (1979, p. 309), for example, say this about Lewis's and Schiffer's definitions of mutual knowledge as applied to language use:

> Their definitions are not limited to three levels of belief (as Bach and Harnish's definition is) but go on indefinitely. Higher-level beliefs are in principle possible, and indeed among spies or deceptive intimates there could be divergence at the first three levels, but we think such higher-level beliefs are not possible for a whole community or large group.

Harder and Kock (1976, p. 62) offer a similar argument:

> There is no logical limit to the number of levels that may be necessary to account for a given speech event. But there are psychological limits, just as, e.g., there are psychological limits on the capacity of the human brain for the embedding transformation (cf. Chomsky 1965, chapter 1). Probably not even the most subtle mind ever makes replicative assumptions in speech events involving more levels than, say, six.

These objections, however, are groundless, for they rest on two false assumptions. The first is the assumption that mutual beliefs must be represented in any model of the mind as an infinite series of belief statements. This assumption is unnecessary. Mutual beliefs can be represented as mental primitives of the form *A and B mutually believe that p* along with the inference rule: *If A and B mutually believe that p, then: (a) A and B believe that p and believe that (a)*. With the primitive and the inference rule, a person can truly be said to believe that A and B mutually believe that *p*. It is just that his capacity for applying the inference rule and remembering the output is limited to just a few iterations. The second false assumption is that mutual beliefs can only be inferred from infinitely many pieces of evidence, one piece per belief statement. As both Lewis and Schiffer have demonstrated, all one needs is a single piece of evidence, as long as it is of the right kind.

Consider Perlman and Zuckerman once again. Perlman, to make sure his next gesture will be taken as the beginning of the first note, says to Zuckerman, "On my next gesture, let us start", and Zuckerman replies, "Right". In this way, Perlman and Zuckerman have explicitly agreed that the next gesture will be for real. This agreement can serve as the *grounds* for their mutual belief the next gesture will be for real. It works this way:

(1) A and B have reason to believe that the agreement holds.
(2) This agreement indicates to A and B each that A and B each have reason to believe the agreement holds.
(3) The agreement indicates to A and B each that the next gesture will be for real.

Lewis has proven that these three conditions, along with some side assumptions about each other's rationality, are all Perlman and Zuckerman need in order to *inductively infer* the mutual belief that Perlman's next gesture is for real. Any grounds G that satisfies these three conditions, where G is inserted in place of "the agreement," is sufficient to allow for the inductive inference of that mutual belief.

Let us call this schema the *mutual belief induction schema* (see Clark and Marshall, 1981). Notice that it produces the proposition that A and B mutually believe that *p*, just the mental primitive we wanted. If Perlman or Zuckerman had to work out the logic of the schema each time, they might be forced to produce a set of iterated beliefs and to see that they can be iterated to infinity. But since they know the schema itself, all they need to do is find a grounds that satisfies conditions (1),

(2), and (3), apply the schema, and *infer* mutual belief. The infinite character of mutual belief is never at issue.[3]

Another objection sometimes raised to mutual beliefs is that they are too exacting, too precise.[4] No one would ever infer truly mutual beliefs in practice, since no one could ever be *certain* that each of the infinitely many individual belief statements held. Instead, so the objection continues, people actually make do with something less than mutual beliefs. They rely on some sort of "shared" beliefs that vary from strong to shaky.

This objection is also groundless. It is based on the false assumption that mutual beliefs cannot vary in strength. Imagine that Perlman notices as the evening wears on that Zuckerman is becoming uncharacteristically absent-minded. When they explicitly agree to begin this time, Perlman isn't completely certain that Zuckerman will remember the agreement. For condition (1) in the induction schema, Perlman has reason to believe the agreement holds, but not very *good* reason. His grounds are weaker than earlier in the evening, and his belief that they mutually believe that the next gesture is for real is correspondingly weaker. That is, mutual beliefs range from weak to strong in line with the grounds on which they are based. The stronger the grounds, the stronger the mutual beliefs.

Grounds for Mutual Beliefs

Based on just this sort of argument, Clark and Marshall (1981) proposed that people ordinarily rely on certain *co-presence heuristics* for inferring mutual beliefs. At the heart of these heuristics is the idea that people seek out special kinds of evidence, apply the mutual belief induction schema, and infer mutual beliefs. The evidence, they argued, is of three basic kinds (generally in combination): physical co-presence, linguistic co-presence, and community membership.

With physical co-presence, what is sought is evidence of the "triple co-presence" of A, B, and the object of the mutual knowledge. Imagine that A and B are sitting across the table from each other staring at a candle between them and at each other beyond the candle. Each is aware simultaneously of the candle and of each other attending to the candle. This is an example *par excellence* of the triple co-presence of A, B and the candle. All A and B need do is assume that the other is attending to the candle and to his opposite simultaneously, or roughly so, and that the other is rational. Then they can each inductively infer mutual belief in the presence of the candle. Other instances of physical co-presence lead to weaker mutual beliefs, but the logic is essentially the same.

With linguistic co-presence, what is sought is the triple co-presence of A, B and the linguistic positing of the object of mutual belief. Imagine that A tells B, "I bought a candle today". Each is aware that A posited the existence of a candle by this linguistic means, and each is aware that the other was attending to the speech act. This is what is meant by "linguistic co-presence". With the right auxiliary assumptions, A and B can each use this evidence to inductively infer mutual belief in the existence of that candle.

Physical and linguistic co-presence are themselves submerged in a sea of mutual beliefs based on community membership. At the most general level, once A and B have evidence that they mutually believe they are adult humans, they can assume as mutual beliefs everything that adult humans are assumed to know or believe. This includes such generic things as that dogs are animals, objects fall because of gravity, certain causes lead to certain effects, and trees have leaves. It also includes such particular things as that the earth is round, the sun appears periodically, and the stars shine at night in the sky. Once it is mutually recognized by A and B that they are also both residents of the US, both residents of California, and both professors at Stanford University, they can assume a host of other mutual beliefs as well, such things as Hoover Tower is on the Stanford campus, the Stanford Bookstore is beside the Post Office, and Sacramento is the capital of California. This source of mutual beliefs is often used in combination with physical or linguistic co-presence to infer still other mutual beliefs: like the belief that the candle that A just mentioned in conversation has a wick, even though A didn't mention that wick.[5]

These three grounds for mutual knowledge are readily apparent in Perlman's and Zuckerman's co-ordination of their duet. First, they rely on physical co-presence. They use visual and auditory contact to co-ordinate their first notes, the moment by moment tempo, the successive choices of up-bow and down-bow, the intensity, the end of fermatas, and so on. Secondly, they rely on linguistic co-presence: with their spoken agreements about what piece to play, how loud to play, how certain passages should be phrased, who is to lead, and so on. And thirdly, they rely on their common membership in the community of expert violinists, whose musical training gives them common beliefs about musical notation, the manner in which violins are to be played, and all the other conventions and practices violinists know. Duet playing would be impossible without all three sources for mutual beliefs.

The Quintet

Later in the evening, Jacqueline DuPré, cello, Zubin Mehta, double bass, and Daniel Barenboim, piano, arrive and join Perlman and Zuckerman in playing quintets. They decide on Schubert's *Piano Quintet, Opus 114*, which as it happens, starts with all five members playing the first chord simultaneously. As first violin, Perlman leads them off, after a few practice trials, with the gesture of his violin. Once again, there is the problem of co-ordination. What beliefs do the five of them have to have in order for Perlman's gesture to be taken this time for real?

When it was just the two of them, Perlman and Zuckerman needed the mutual belief that Perlman's gesture this time was for real. Notice that mutual beliefs are defined for two people, and only two people; so how should it be extended to five? One possibility is that each of the five must have mutual beliefs with each of the others: Perlman and Zuckerman must mutually believe that the gesture is for real this time; Perlman and DuPré must mutually believe it; Zuckerman and Mehta must mutually believe it; and so on. This, however, isn't enough. What if Perlman thought that Zuckerman and DuPré didn't mutually believe it? Despite their mutual beliefs with him, Perlman should believe that they might not play the first note, since they weren't sure about each other. If they didn't play, of course, the first note wouldn't come off jointly. For genuine co-ordination, Perlman must believe that Zuckerman and DuPré also mutually believe that the gesture is for real.

With this sort of reasoning, it is easy to show that Perlman, Zuckerman, DuPré, Mehta, and Barenboim, need what Lewis (1969) defined as *common knowledge* or *belief*:

The members of a group G commonly believe that $p =_{def}$.

(1) The members of G believe that p.

(2) The members of G believe that the members of G believe that p.

(3) The members of G believe that the members of G believe that the members of G believe that p.

et cetera *ad infinitum*.

McCarthy (1979) has called the same notion *joint belief*, which is the source for our term joint act. Common beliefs are not just the conjunction of the mutual beliefs of pairs within a group. They encompass mutual beliefs about mutual beliefs and a good deal more.[6]

There are two points of contact between mutual and common beliefs. First, mutual beliefs are a special case of common beliefs in which the group G has only two members. We can often dispense with the term "mutual belief" and speak only about common belief (or joint belief). Secondly, all the arguments brought out earlier about the nature and source of mutual beliefs carry through, with the appropriate alterations, to common beliefs. Like mutual beliefs, common beliefs can be treated as mental primitives, and as having associated with them a rule enabling a person to infer (1), (2), (3) and so on as long as he has the time and mental capacity to do so. Also, common beliefs are beliefs that people ordinarily infer on the basis of physical co-presence, linguistic co-presence or community membership, and these inferences are made by means of a common belief induction schema.

Adjustable Joint Acts

Most aspects of ensemble playing are complex joint acts that require the utmost precision. Professionals like Perlman and Zuckerman leave little to chance. They *know*, as they would put it, what the others are doing at all times (the co-ordination becomes second-nature) and the skill is in getting their fingers to do what they tell them to do.

Not all joint acts work this way. When Jill meets Jack, she might begin to extend her hand; when Jack realizes this, he begins to extend his hand; and the two of them adjust to each other's movements until they grasp hands in a joint handshake. Hand shaking is what we will call an *adjustable joint act*. It can be accomplished gradually, by approximation, with the participants adjusting to each other in arriving at its completion. Playing the first chord of a violin duet *could* of course be accomplished as an adjustable joint act, but it would sound like a couple of neighbourhood cats picking a fight.

Even adjustable joint acts require common beliefs for their co-ordination. When Jill begins to extend her hand to Jack, she is confident that he will use her gesture as one grounds for the mutual belief that she expects them to shake hands. He is also expected to consult their common belief that (1) they are meeting; (2) in this culture, people meeting often shake hands; (3) her gesture could be the start of a handshake; (4) the handshake to be co-ordinated is the standard one; and so on. If any one of these grounds is missing, then the joint act will go awry. Jack might think that they have not yet been introduced, making a handshake inappropriate; or that in this culture, women never offer their hands first; or that she is reaching for something behind him; or that she is going to shake hands in the non-standard way as many Americans do by grasping the base of his thumb.

Most joint acts are adjustable in one respect or another. In ensemble playing, the players adjust to the momentary intensity, pitch and tempo of their playing. Other joint acts have an even larger component of mutual adjustment. For clarity in the arguments that follow, we will avoid the adjustable aspects of joint acts, since the role that beliefs play in them is so much more complicated. Nevertheless, the arguments we will offer apply to them too insofar as common beliefs play a role in their accomplishment.

COLLECTIVE DIRECTIVES

Virtually all types of speech acts may be addressed to more than one hearer at a time. Yet, as we stated earlier, most theories of speech acts (we will call these the *standard* theories) are equipped to handle only canonical speech acts in which there is but one addressee.

Consider Searle's (1969, 1975) analysis of directives, which includes requests, commands, questions and pleas. These can be characterized, he argues, by certain conditions for their felicitous performance: their "felicity conditions". According to the "propositional content condition", for example, if an utterance is to count as a directive, the speaker must predicate a certain future act of the hearer (or more properly, the addressee). By the "essential condition", the utterance must count as an attempt to get the addressee to perform this act in accordance with the speaker's intentions.

When there is one addressee, Searle's characterization of directives seems adequate, as in (3):

(3) *Ann, to Bob:* Please bring a bottle of Glenlivet.

In uttering (3), Ann predicates of Bob the act of bringing a bottle of malt whisky, and she intends her words to count as an attempt to get Bob to do so. Problems arise when there is more than one addressee, as in (4):

(4) *Ann, to Bob and Ellen:* Please bring a bottle of Glenlivet.

Ann may have one of two distinct intentions in uttering (4). She may intend (a) that Bob and Ellen are to arrange to bring one bottle together, or (b) that each of them is to bring a bottle separately. That is, the act she is predicating is to be carried out by Bob and Ellen either (a) collectively, with one joint act of bringing, or (b) distributively, with two acts of bringing, each separate and distinct. Let us call these the *collective* and *distributive* readings, respectively.

Our claim is that standard speech act theories are incapable of accounting for the collective reading of directives. Under a collective reading, the addressees are to carry out a joint act, and for this to happen, they must commonly believe what illocutionary acts are being performed towards *all* of them. It is this last step that the standard theories cannot accommodate.

Individual Recognition

In the middle of the evening, for amusement, Perlman joins up with Isaac Stern, who has also dropped by, to play some piano pieces, with Perlman playing the right hand and Stern playing the left. Mehta offers to conduct them in "Study 119, Dance in 3/4 Time" from Bela Bartok's *Mikrokosmos,* a piece that starts with both hands playing simultaneously. Mehta practises saying *One, two, three, play* several times and finally starts them for real with the utterance in (5):

(5) *Mehta, to Perlman and Stern:* Play.

When the piece turns out to be too difficult, Perlman suggests that he play it by himself. Once again, Mehta practises his start and then utters (6), intending it to be taken for real:

(6) *Mehta, to Perlman:* Play.

With (5) and (6), we have a simple contrast. In both instances, Mehta is requesting a single act to be performed, the playing of the first chord in "Study 119". It is just that in (5) the act is a joint act performed by two people, whereas in (6) it is an individual act performed by one person. To a listener, the two acts should sound the same.

Standard speech act theories are designed to account for (6). By Searle's essential condition, Mehta's utterance counts as an attempt to get Perlman to play the first note. What about (5)? The obvious way to extend Searle's essential condition is like this: Mehta's utterance counts as an attempt to get Perlman *and* Stern to play the first note. But this statement is incomplete, for it doesn't say how Perlman and Stern are to *recognize* what they are to do.

The hearer's recognition of the speaker's intentions is an essential ingredient in all definitions of speaker's meaning (Grice, 1957, 1968; Schiffer, 1972) and illocutionary acts (Searle, 1969; Bach and Harnish, 1979). As Searle puts it, "The speaker S intends to produce an illocutionary effect IE in the hearer H by means of getting H to recognize S's intention to produce IE" (p. 47). In (6), Mehta is trying to get Perlman to recognize his intention to get Perlman to play the first note.

In (5), however, there are *two* recognizers. Mehta cannot intend Perlman and Stern *as a pair* to recognize what he wants them to do. They would have to be a Siamese twin called Perlman-and-Stern with a single mind if they were to perform such a single act of recognition. Rather, Perlman and Stern live separate mental lives, and each must recognize Mehta's intentions for himself. This assumption is no more than the commonplace idea that recognizing something is a mental act that each person must perform on his own; no one can perform it for him. We will call this the *individual recognition assumption*.

An adequate characterization of illocutionary acts, therefore, must explicate how the speaker intends *each individual hearer* to recognize his intentions. Like Mehta's request in (5), "complex" illocutionary acts must be representable, at some level of analysis, in terms of what we will call *elementary illocutionary acts*. An elementary illocutionary act is one that is intended to be recognized by one and only one hearer. The request in (6) is already an elementary illocutionary act in that it is directed at Perlman alone. In the notation we will use, what Mehta means would be represented as in (7):

(7) *Mehta, to Perlman:* 'I request of you that you play.'

To distinguish representations from utterances, we will enclose representations in single quotation marks as in (7).

Elementary illocutionary acts have two important properties, as illustrated by (7). The first is the *single-target criterion*. As the definition requires, each elementary illocutionary act must be directed at a single individual (in (7), Perlman) since recognition is an act performed only by single individuals. The second criterion, which applies only to directives, is the *target-as-agent criterion*. The act Mehta requests of Perlman must be one in which the target hearer, Perlman, is the sole agent. Mehta cannot ask Perlman to do something Stern is to do. All he could ask of Perlman is that Perlman *get* Stern to do somthing, which is not the same thing. This criterion follows directly from Searle's propositional content condition, which requires that the requested act be predicated of the target hearer.

To see how this analysis might work, let us consider the distributive request in (8):

(8) *Mehta, to Perlman and Stern:* Please sit down.

On the pattern of (7), we might try to represent (8) as (9):

(9) *Mehta, to Perlman and Stern:* 'I request of the two of you that the two of you sit down.'

But (9) fails both of our criteria for elementary requests. First, it has two addressees. To remedy this, we might represent (8) as a conjunction of (10) and (10').

(10) *Mehta, to Perlman:* 'I request of you that you and Stern sit down.'

(10') *Mehta, to Stern:* 'I request of you that you and Perlman sit down.'

But (10) and (10') fail the target-as-agent criterion. Since Mehta cannot request of Perlman that Stern sit down, he also cannot request of Perlman that he *and* Stern sit down.[7] To remedy this, we might turn to the representation in (11) and (11'):

(11) *Mehta, to Perlman:* 'I request of you that you sit down.'

(11') *Mehta, to Stern:* 'I request of you that you sit down.'

By our criteria, both of these are legitimate elementary requests. Furthermore, together they capture the intuition that the distributive request in (8) is really a conjunction of elementary requests to Perlman and Stern separately. Mehta is asking each of them individually to sit down.

The point of the representation in (11) and (11') is this: It separates what Perlman is intended to recognize from what Stern is intended to recognize. We can then evaluate whether Perlman, who is privy only to (11), has all the information he needs in order to recognize what Mehta intended him to recognize, and whether the same goes for Stern, who is privy only to (11'). We require the representation of Mehta's complex illocutionary act to be one that decomposes in such a way that it spells out Mehta's two sets of intentions to recognize separately.

Collective Requests

The problem we want to solve is how to represent (5), Mehta's request of Perlman and Stern that they jointly play the first chord of Bartok's "Study 119". Mehta must obviously get both men to take part. He might do this on the pattern of (11) and (11') as in (12) and (12'):

(12) *Mehta, to Perlman:* 'I request of you that you play E, your first note.'

(12′) *Mehta, to Stern:* 'I request of you that you play E sharp, your first note.'

Perlman and Stern would then play their first notes, and the piece would be off.

But with (12) and (12′), has Mehta asked Perlman and Stern to carry out a joint act? No. All he has done is ask each of them to carry out an individual act. The form of (12) and (12′) is indistinguishable from the form of (11) and (11′), which are individual requests to Perlman and Stern to sit down. The problem is to distinguish between these two cases: the distributive request in (8) to sit down and the collective request in (5) to play the first chord.

Something is missing in (12) and (12′). Recall that Mehta has been practising his start and now intends it for real. When Mehta then says *play*, Perlman may himself believe that Mehta is starting them off for real, but he has no idea whether Stern believes this. If Stern doesn't, Stern won't expect to play, and the joint act won't come off. By (12), Perlman believes only that Mehta is requesting *him* to play E. If he is to take part in a joint act, he must also believe that Mehta is simultaneously requesting Stern to play E sharp. Stern, of course, would reason in the same way from (12′). The representation suggested by this reasoning is the following:

(13)   a. *Mehta, to Perlman:* 'I request of you that you play E.'
       b. *Mehta, to Perlman:* 'I e-inform you of (13′a).'

(13′)   a. *Mehta, to Stern:* 'I request of you that you play E sharp.'
       b. *Mehta, to Stern:* 'I e-inform you of (13a).'

We will call the illocutionary acts in (13b) and (13′b) *elementary informatives* or *e-informatives*. They are called *informatives* in that they serve to inform certain hearers about other speech acts being performed. They are termed *elementary* for reasons we have already given.

With (13) and (13′), Perlman and Stern are better off than before, but they still shouldn't expect to be able to carry out a joint act. Take Perlman. He recognizes that he is being requested to play E and that Stern is being requested to play E sharp. But he should reason further, "Stern knows that *he* has been requested to play E sharp, but he may not know that *I* have been requested to play E at the same time. If he doesn't know about Mehta's request to me, he won't necessarily play, since he doesn't believe we are going to play jointly. For a joint act to come off, Mehta must inform me that he is informing Stern about his re-

quest for me to play E." Stern would reason in an analogous way. So we
need to add to (13) and (13′) these two illocutionary acts:

(13)   c.   *Mehta, to Perlman:* 'I e-inform you that I am e-informing
Stern of (13a).'

(13′)   c.   *Mehta, to Stern:* 'I e-inform you that I am e-informing Perlman of (13′a).'

The patch-up in (13c) and (13′c), however, won't succeed either.
The logic here is the same as for the violin duets. What is needed is an
infinite set of such e-informatives. For Perlman and Stern truly to expect to carry out the joint act of playing the first chord, they must commonly believe that they both expect to play their first notes. Mehta
must *jointly* inform the two of them of what he is requesting each of them
to do. This might be represented as in (14) and (14′):

(14)   a.   *Mehta, to Perlman:* 'I request of you that you play E.'

b.   *Mehta, to Perlman:* 'I j-inform you and Stern of (14a).'

c.   *Mehta, to Perlman:* 'I j-inform you and Stern of (14′a).'

(14′)   a.   *Mehta, to Stern:* 'I request of you that you play E sharp.'

b.   *Mehta, to Stern:* 'I j-inform you and Perlman of (14′a).'

c.   *Mehta, to Stern:* 'I j-inform you and Perlman of (14a).'

What we mean here by *j-informative*, or *joint informative*, is the obvious extension of e-informatives to common or joint beliefs. It can be defined as
follows:

S j-informs a group of hearers G that p = $_{def.}$

S e-informs each hearer in G that he intends it to be a common belief in G and S that p, where p is that S is performing a particular
addressee-directed illocutionary act.

Despite appearances, j-informatives are legitimate by the single-target
criterion. In (14b), "I j-inform you and Stern" is really a shorthand for
"I e-inform you that I intend it to be a common belief in you, Stern, and
me". We will use the shorthand for convenience.

As representations of what Perlman and Stern need, (14) and (14′)
fare pretty well. Perlman recognizes that he is being requested to play
his first note, E. He also recognizes that he and Stern mutually believe
that they are both being requested to play their first notes. He appears
to have all the information from Mehta that he needs for him and Stern
to co-ordinate their playing of the first notes successfully. The same
seems to go for Stern. But even (14) and (14′) don't capture the essence
of the collective request in (5). To see this, we must look more closely at
distributive requests.

Distributive Requests

Imagine that Mehta asks Perlman and Stern each to think of their favourite pieces of music and then he says:

(15) *Mehta, to Perlman and Stern:* Imagine the first note.

Let us assume that imagining a note cannot be done as a joint act, and so it is clear to Perlman and Stern that they are to act separately. Let us further suppose that Mehta and Perlman commonly believe that Perlman's favourite piece is Beethoven's *First*, which starts on E, and that Mehta and Stern commonly believe that Stern's favourite piece is Bach's *Brandenburg Concerto Number 1*, which starts on E sharp, or F. So Perlman recognizes that he is being requested to imagine E, and Stern that he is being requested to imagine E sharp, but neither knows what the other is being requested to imagine. In this situation, Perlman and Stern needn't know anything about the request to the other; they could be in separate recording chambers unaware that Mehta was even speaking to the other. The representation looks like this:

(16) a. *Mehta, to Perlman:* 'I request of you that you imagine E.'
       b. *Mehta, to Perlman:* 'I e-inform you of (16′a).'

(16′) a. *Mehta, to Stern;* 'I request of you that you imagine E sharp.'
       b. *Mehta, to Stern:* 'I e-inform you of (16a).'

Perlman knows all he needs to know in order to do as requested, and so does Stern. Conclusion: unlike collective requests, distributive requests do not require that the several addressees be jointly informed about what each of them has been requested to do.

At first, (16) and (16′) look unnecessarily complex. When Mehta requests Perlman to imagine E, he is of course informing him that he is making that request (Schiffer, 1972). It seems unnecessary to mention the e-informative in (16b).[8] However, it *is* necessary to include the e-informative if we are to distinguish the situation just described (let us call it Situation A) from the following two situations.

Situation B. To Situation A, let us add that all three men commonly believe that Perlman's favourite piece is Beethoven's *First*, and so Mehta is informing Perlman and Stern jointly, with all the right illocutionary intentions, of his request to Perlman to imagine E. In contrast, Perlman doesn't know what Stern's favourite piece is. The representation in (16) and (16′), therefore, needs to be changed as follows:[9]

(17) a. *Mehta, to Perlman:* 'I request of you that you imagine E.'
       b. *Mehta, to Perlman:* 'I j-inform you and Stern of (17a).'

(17′) a. *Mehta, to Stern:* 'I request of you that you imagine E sharp.'

b. *Mehta, to Stern:* 'I e-inform you of (17′a).'

c. *Mehta, to Stern:* 'I j-inform you and Perlman of (17a).'

Notice that for Perlman, the only thing that distinguishes Situation A from Situation B is the change in the informative. The informatives are therefore needed to distinguish Mehta's speech acts in the two situations: they are necessary parts of both representations.

Situation C. To Situation B, let us now add the common belief among all three that Stern's favourite piece is Bach's *First Brandenburg Concerto.* The representation turns out as follows:

(18) a. *Mehta, to Perlman:* 'I request of you that you imagine E.'

b. *Mehta, to Perlman:* 'I j-inform you and Stern of (18a).'

c. *Mehta, to Perlman:* 'I j-inform you and Stern of (18′a).'

(18′) a. *Mehta, to Stern:* 'I request of you that you imagine E sharp.'

b. *Mehta, to Sterm:* 'I j-inform you and Perlman of (18′a).'

c. *Mehta, to Stern:* 'I j-inform you and Perlman of (18a).'

In this situation, Perlman and Stern are each being jointly informed of what the other is being requested to do, even though they are to imagine their notes separately and not jointly.

With Situation C, we can begin to see what is wrong with the analysis of collective requests in (14) and (14′). Note that the content of (18) and (18′), which represents Mehta's distributive request, is identical (except for the verb *imagine* instead of *play*) to the content of (14) and (14′), which was intended to represent Mehta's collective request. That is, the two representations fail to distinguish collective from distributive requests.

The fault lies in the representation for the collective requests. When Mehta utters *Play* in (5), he is *not* requesting Perlman and Stern to play E and E sharp individually yet simultaneously. If he were, he would be doing nothing different from asking them to *imagine* the two notes individually yet simultaneously, which is not a joint act. Rather, what he is doing is requesting of the *pair* of them that the *pair* of them play the chord consisting of E and E sharp. This difference, though subtle, is critical. Mehta could make a collective request as in (5) without knowing who is to play what note. He could even make such a request while believing that only one of them was to play, but he didn't know which. All that Mehta need be requesting is for the first chord to be played by the pair of them, however they jointly work out how that is to be done.[10]

Simply put, when Mehta makes a truly collective request of Perlman and Stern, he isn't making elementary requests of each of them separately. His only request is of Perlman-and-Stern as a pair. Now it could be argued that Mehta is, nevertheless, making elementary requests that look something like this: *I request of you, Perlman, that you take part in the joint act in which you and Stern play the first chord.* Elementary requests such as this one, however, cannot account for other collective requests we will take up. Indeed, with the right analysis, they are superfluous in the representation of Mehta's collective request of Perlman and Stern.

Once we eliminate elementary requests from the analysis of collective requests, we have a new and more difficult problem: How can a speaker make a collective request of a pair of people without making elementary requests of each one separately? Before we can offer a solution, we must take a closer look at informatives.

INFORMATIVES

Informatives, we claimed earlier, are a type of illocutionary act that the speaker directs at certain hearers. But are they speech acts at all? Perhaps the speaker isn't directing anything at these hearers. When Mehta simultaneously asks Perlman and Stern to imagine their notes, he considers Perlman and Stern each to be merely overhearers, or eavesdroppers, of the request he is making to the other man, and that is how they become jointly informed. To show that informatives really *are* illocutionary acts, we will consider several possibilities.

The first possibility can be illustrated with (12) and (12′), which are repeated here:

(12) *Mehta, to Perlman:* 'I request of you that you play E.'

(12′) *Mehta, to Stern:* 'I request of you that you play E sharp.'

Let us assume that Perlman and Stern are each fully aware of what is being uttered to the other. Take Perlman's perspective. He recognizes that he has been requested to play E. As an eavesdropper, an overhearer, he also happens to hear that the word *play* has also been directed at Stern. Since he also sees that Stern is overhearing what is uttered to him, he can infer, by the common belief induction schema, that they commonly believe the words Mehta has directed at each of them. Can Perlman now be assured that the joint act of playing the first chord can take place?

No. The reasons are inherent to overhearing. In the general case, speakers do not design their utterances so as to guarantee that over-hearers will be able to recognize what they mean. They design their utterances so as to guarantee recognition only by specific hearers, generally only the addressees. When you overhear a man on a bus say to a woman, "Let's try your house this week", you may surmise or conjec-ture that he is proposing an assignation at her house that week, but you realize that you can't know for sure. The man may be suggesting her house for the next meeting of Alcoholics Anonymous, or as the next target for their fumigating business. You realize this because you recog-nize that the man didn't design his utterance in such a way that you, an overhearer, *should* be able to understand what he meant. Thus, if Perlman is merely overhearing Mehta's words to Stern, he could guess that Mehta is making request (12′), but he couldn't know for sure.

However, one type of overhearer *is* intended to be listening in, which leads us to a second possibility. Let us suppose that Perlman believes that Mehta intended him to overhear his words to Stern, and that Mehta intended Perlman to overhear his words to Stern. Perlman could then, with the right assumptions, infer the common belief of Mehta's *in-tentions* that these words were addressed to both men. This is surely enough to guarantee the joint act of playing the first chord, isn't it?

The answer, however, is again no. Intended overhearers are only somewhat better off than other overhearers. Suppose the man on the bus knew you were listening in and deliberately chose the words "Let's try your house this week" for your benefit. Did he want you to come to the right conclusion in conjecturing that they were having an affair? Did he want to deceive you into thinking that they were having an affair? Or did he merely want to be obscure so that you wouldn't come to *any* coherent conjecture? You still have no *solid* reason to assume that any of these interpretations is the intended one. What you are missing is an essential ingredient for the recognition of a speaker's meaning: the speaker's intention that you recognize his intentions. This is what Grice (1968) has called *m-intention*, and Bach and Harnish (1979) have called *R-intention*, for "reflexive" intention. For you to be sure that the man on the bus believes you have everything you need to know to recognize what he meant, you must believe that he not merely intended, but *m-in-tended*, that you come to that interpretation.

Informatives, therefore, are a type of illocutionary act. Like illocu-tionary acts, they are performed by uttering sentences. Like illocutionary acts, they are directed by speakers at particular hearers. Most of all, like illocutionary acts, they require m-intentions and not some simpler form of intentions. They fit Grice's definition of speaker's meaning and Searle's definition of illocutionary act.

The Firing Squad

In the study of illocutionary acts, one can often sharpen an analytical point by looking at acts that are part of institutional procedures like marriages, christenings and sentencings, as Austin (1962) did. With these, the consequences of breaking one or another requirement are particularly obvious. In this spirit, consider an execution by firing squad in which the commander orders two rifleman, George and Harry, to fire their rifles at a prisoner. Now in the society under consideration, the law requires that one of the riflemen, selected at random without anyone's knowledge, be given a live bullet and the other be given a blank. This way it can be said of each rifleman that it isn't certain whether or not he fired the bullet that killed the prisoner and, therefore, he cannot be held personally responsible for the prisoner's death. Every execution must follow this rule if it is to be considered legal.

What happens when the commander says "Fire!"? George should reason this way: "The commander has ordered us to fire. But that order is not legitimate (indeed, the law forbids me to fire) unless he has ordered us both to fire. Otherwise, I could be held personally liable for the prisoner's death. I must be certain, or as certain as I can be, that Harry is intended to fire too. But before Harry will fire he must assure himself that I am intended to fire, so I must assure myself that Harry has assured himself that I am intended to fire too." And so on. That is, each of the riflemen must mutually believe that the commander has genuinely ordered the two of them jointly to fire now. The commander must j-inform both addressees before his collective order is effectuated.

In this example, it is clear that the j-informatives must be illocutionary acts. The law requires that the commander instruct *both* riflemen to fire at the same time. He must therefore intend both riflemen to recognize his *intentions* that they both fire, since otherwise they are not legally bound, or even allowed, to carry out his order. That is, he must intend them each to recognize that they are both to fire in part by means of their recognition of his intention that they are both to fire. The command would be illegitimate without these m-intentions. Therefore, the j-informatives to George and Harry are illocutionary acts.

Participants and Informatives

Hearers who are targets of informatives ought to be distinguished from mere overhearers, who aren't targets of any illocutionary acts. These hearers we will call *participants*. We can then state the first of three basic hypotheses we wish to defend (see Clark and Carlson, 1980):

> *The participant hypothesis:* Certain illocutionary acts are directed at hearers in their role as addressees, and others are directed at hearers in their role as participants.

The first class will be called *addressee-directed illocutionary acts,* and the second, *participant-directed illocutionary acts.*

A good deal of evidence has already been provided for the participant hypothesis. Consider the analysis of (5) as provided in (14) and (14'), repeated here:

(14) a. *Mehta, to Perlman:* 'I request of you that you play E.'
   b. *Mehta, to Perlman:* 'I j-inform you and Stern of (14a).'
   c. *Mehta, to Perlman:* 'I j-inform you and Stern of (14'a).'

(14') a. *Mehta, to Stern:* 'I request of you that you play E sharp.'
   b. *Mehta, to Stern:* 'I j-inform you and Perlman of (14'a).'
   c. *Mehta, to Stern:* 'I j-inform you and Perlman of (14a).'

In traditional terminology, the addressees of requests are the requestees. Perlman plays this role in (14a) and Stern plays this role in (14'a). However, the roles they play in (14b), (14c), (14'b) and (14'c) are very different: they are no longer requestees, but "informees". It is the role of "informee" (an ugly term) that we are calling participant. The participant hypothesis merely says that the roles of addressee and participant are distinct. A hearer can be the target of an illocutionary.act in his role as addressee and, simultaneously, the target of a distinct illocutionary act in his role as participant. There is one class of illocutionary acts directed at hearers in their roles as addressees (such acts as requests, promises, assertions and apologies) and there is another class directed at hearers in their roles as participants, such as the acts we have called informatives. Still other hearers are in the role of overhearers. They aren't targets of any illocutionary acts since the speaker has no m-intentions towards them.

The second of our three hypotheses is this:

The informative hypothesis: The fundamental kind of participant-directed illocutionary act is one in which the speaker informs the participants of the addressee-directed illocutionary acts he is performing.

That is, the fundamental illocutionary act directed at participants is the informative. So far, we have only argued that informatives are necessary for collective requests. We will leave the claim that they are fundamental to be demonstrated elsewhere (Clark and Carlson, 1980).

The most far-reaching of our three hypotheses is this:

The informative first hypothesis: All addressee-directed illocutionary acts are performed by means of informatives.

Collective requests provide important evidence that at least *some* addressee-directed illocutionary acts are performed by means of informatives. The argument that *all* such acts are so performed we will leave until later.

Collective Requests Reconsidered

Let us return to Mehta's request in (5) that Perlman and Stern jointly play the first chord of Bartok's "Study 119". In arriving at (14) and (14′), we argued that Mehta's request couldn't be complete without Mehta's j-informatives to the two of them. These informatives, then, are at least a *necessary* condition for the performing of collective requests.

However, the problem with (14) and (14′) is that in (5), Mehta isn't asking Perlman to play E and Stern to play E sharp. He is asking the pair of them to play the chord consisting of E and E sharp. He is making not two requests, one of each musician, but a single request of the pair of them, just as if he were asking Perlman alone to play the chord, as in (6). The problem is how to direct a request at Perlman-and-Stern even though Perlman-and-Stern isn't a single individual capable of recognizing Mehta's intentions in a single act of recognition.

The solution we propose is for Mehta to make the collective request via his informatives. In this analysis, (5) has two levels. It is represented at the level of *elementary* illocutionary acts as the conjunction of (19) and (19′):

(19) *Mehta, to Perlman:* 'I j-inform you and Stern that I am requesting of you-and-Stern that you-and-Stern play the first chord.'

(19′) *Mehta, to Stern:* 'I j-inform you and Perlman that I am request-

ing of you-and-Perlman that you-and-Perlman play the first
chord.'
Mehta directs these informatives at Perlman and Stern individually.
But by doing so, he m-intends Perlman and Stern to recognize jointly
that they as a pair are to play the first chord. By performing the j-informatives, Mehta is, so to speak, turning Perlman and Stern into a
joint recognizer as far as his request is concerned. He is thereby, at the
level of addressee-directed illocutionary acts, also performing (20):

(20) *Mehta, to Perlman-and-Stern:* 'I request of you that you play the
first chord.'

That is, Mehta performs the request in (20) *by means of* the informatives
in (19) and (19').

Mehta's request in (20) can be thought of as requiring a single act of
recognition, thereby satisfying Grice's and Searle's requirements for
illocutionary acts and speaker's meanings. What is special about this
act of recognition is that it is itself a type of joint act. It takes Perlman's
and Stern's joint act of recognition of Mehta's m-intentions to co-
ordinate successfully the joint act of playing the first chord.

The analysis in (19), (19') and (20) has just the properties we want.
First, it satisfies the individual recognition assumption. At the level of
elementary illocutionary acts, Perlman and Stern are each to recognize
Mehta's m-intentions towards them. Secondly, what is being requested
is the *single* joint act of playing the chord, not *two* individual but simul-
taneous acts of Perlman playing E and Stern playing E sharp. Mehta is
making only a single request. And thirdly, the target of the request,
namely the pair Perlman-and-Stern, is also the agent who is to do the
requested act: to play the first chord.

We will call this sort of analysis the *informative analysis*. If all it
accounted for were collective requests like the one in (5), it would be of
little use. But it accounts for much more. It makes sense of a network of
facts about illocutionary acts when there are two or more participants.
It also handles canonical illocutionary acts, those acts that are directed
at single namable addressees. To illustrate its power, we turn next to
other requests that involve two or more participants.

OTHER COLLECTIVE REQUESTS

So far, we have taken up requests with two or more addressees who could have been referred to by name: Mehta could have said *Itzhak and Pinchas, play*. There are two broad classes of illocutionary acts in which the addressees cannot be referred to by name. In the first, the addressees are designated by indefinite references, such as *someone* or *anyone*. In the second class, they are designated by attributive noun phrases, such as *the person who wins* or *whoever leaves last*. Neither class, we will argue, can be handled by standard speech act theories.

Indefinite Addressees

Consider the requests in (21) and (22):

    (21) *David, to Ann, Bonnie and Carol:* Someone, please open the door.
    (22) *David, to Ann, Bonnie and Carol:* Anyone wanting to eat, come with me.

These two requests are non-canonical in that they are addressed to indefinite someone's and anyone's, not to single definite people. The reason they cannot be handled by standard speech act theories is obvious. By Searle's essential condition, (21) should be an attempt by David to get the "hearer" to open the door. Yet there are three hearers, and David doesn't have these intentions toward all of them, or even toward any particular one of them. Likewise, (22) should be an attempt by David to get the "hearer" to go with him. However, it is really David's attempt to get any one or more of the three hearers who wants to eat to go with him.

There is an important contrast between (21) and (22). In (21), David wants one of the three women to open the door, but doesn't specify which one it should be. He leaves it up to Ann, Bonnie and Carol *as a collective* to decide. In (22), David wants any of the three women who wants to eat to go with him. This time he leaves it to each *individual* woman whether or not she is to do the requested act. He doesn't intend them to make a collective decision as in (21).

Although (21) and (22) look very different from Mehta's collective and distributive requests, they work by similar principles. In uttering *Play*, Mehta intended Perlman and Stern to co-ordinate with each other in realizing a result: playing the first chord. Both men were to take part. With *Someone, please open the door*, David similarly intends Ann, Bonnie and Carol to co-ordinate with each other in realizing a result: opening the door. But in this result, only one person is to take part. The way the three women might co-ordinate with each other can take many forms.

This contrasts with (22) in which the three women don't have to co-ordinate at all. Without stretching the terms too much, we seem justified in calling (21) and (22) collective and distributive requests, respectively.

There is a clear division in (21) between the two roles that the hearers play. On the one hand, David is speaking to all three women, Ann, Bonnie and Carol. On the other, he is requesting only one of the three (he doesn't care which) to open the door. The set of hearers he is speaking to (Set 1) doesn't coincide with the set of hearers who are being requested to open the door (Set 2). For Mehta's request in (5), these two sets happen to coincide.

There are two arguments for calling Set 2 the "addressees" and Set 1 "participants". First, for all other illocutionary acts, it is the persons specified by the vocative who are considered to be the addressees. In (22), the vocative specifies some one woman and not all three women, and so by this criterion, the addressee is that indefinable someone, Set 2. Secondly, in Searle's characterization of canonical requests, the addressee (whom he labels "the hearer") is the person who is to do the requested act. In (21), the act of opening the door is predicated of only some one of the three women. By this criterion, the addressee is again the indefinitely specified person who is to open the door: the requestee or Set 2. The hearers in Set 1, the "addressees" of the informatives, are better called by another term, namely participants.

Now to the analysis of (21). Since it is a collective request, we might try to divide it up into individual requests and informatives, much as we tried to do in (14) and (14'). Let us consider (21) from just one of the women's point of view: Ann's. The analogue to (14) would be (23):

(23) a. *David, to Ann:* 'I request of one of you that that person open the door.'

     b. *David, to Ann:* 'I j-inform you, Bonnie, and Carol that I am requesting of one of any of you that that person open the door.'

The request in (23a), however, is illegitimate as an elementary request. David isn't making his request of Ann in particular. The only act he is performing toward her in particular is one that *makes it known that* he is requesting some one or other of them to open the door. This is captured in (23b). The question in (23a) must be expunged. The problem here is similar to the one in Mehta's *Play*. The request being made simply cannot be made directly of any single hearer.

The problem is resolved in the informative analysis. Suppose that in uttering (21), David is performing the illocutionary act in (24):

(24) *David, to Ann:* 'I j-inform you, Bonnie, and Carol that I am requesting of any one of you that that person open the door.'

He is simultaneously performing the corresponding j-informatives towards Bonnie and Carol too. By means of these informatives, David is also making a request of some one of the three women: a person of their joint choosing. This might be represented as in (25):

(25) *David, to the person jointly selected by Ann, Bonnie and Carol:* 'I request of you that you open the door.'

David is performing the request in (25) *by means of* the informative in (24). This, therefore, is further evidence for the informative-first hypothesis.

Attributive Addressees

Consider the requests in (26) and (27):

(26) *Ruth, to Tom, Dick and Harry:* The last two of you to leave, please move the piano back into the corner.

(27) *Ruth, to Tom, Dick and Harry:* The last two of you to leave, please go to Room 100.

In both utterances, the addressees (the hearers designated in the vocative to carry out the requested acts) are specified by what Donnellan (1966) has called the attributive use of the definite description. With the phrase *the last two of you to leave*, there aren't two particular people that Ruth intends to designate (say, Tom and Dick) who will in fact be the last two of the three to leave. There might be no way she could know who she is designating, since the three are to leave in the future. Rather, she intends to designate the two people, whoever they turn out to be, who are the last two to leave.

The contrast between (26) and (27) is the by now familiar contrast between collective and distributive readings. In (26), the last two people to leave must carry out the joint act (let us assume) of moving the piano back to the corner. Like other collective requests, this will require Ruth to perform certain joint informatives. In (27), on the other hand, the last two people to leave are each to carry out separate acts (let us assume), and the request is distributive. All Ruth need do is inform each of the two people separately.

Compared to our earlier examples, the collective request in (26) is complicated. As in Mehta's *Play*, the requested act in (26) is a joint act.

But as in David's *Someone, please open the door,* any two of the three participants could turn out to be the addressees. This suggests that (26) ought to be analysed like (21). From Tom's point of view, the analysis would go as follows:

(28) *Ruth, to Tom:* 'I j-inform you, Dick and Harry that I am requesting that the last two of you to leave to move the piano back to the corner.'

By performing this informative, Ruth is also performing the request in (29):

(29) *Ruth, to the two people who turn out in fact to be the last two of the three to leave:* 'I request you to move the piano back to the corner.'

As in (21), the request in (29) can only be accomplished by means of the informative in (28) since Ruth's request is not being made of Tom in particular.

The request in (29) is itself collective. It is a request that Ruth cannot make without jointly informing the two addressees, whoever they turn out to be, of what she is requesting. With (28), however, Ruth will already have jointly informed every pair of them, since she has jointly informed all three of them. So the informative in (28) accomplishes all that Ruth needs. It not only makes the request in (29) but also legitimates it as a collective request.

Virtually the same analysis is required for the distributive request in (27). The only difference is that the informatives to Tom, Dick and Harry need not be joint. From Tom's point of view, (27) consists of an e-informative as follows:

(30) *Ruth, to Tom:* 'I e-inform you (*or* j-inform you, Dick, and Harry) that I am requesting the last two of you to leave to go to Room 100.'

Ruth thereby also performs (31):

(31) *Ruth, to the two people who turn out in fact to be the last two of the three to leave:* 'I request each of you to go to Room 100.'

Ruth cannot perform (31) directly since she cannot know who will in fact be the last two to leave. She can only perform (31) by performing (30). This is further evidence in favor of the informative-first hypothesis.

THE INFORMATIVE ANALYSIS

The informative analysis, if it is correct, should also be able to handle the types of requests we have not yet mentioned. It should make sense, too, of such illocutionary acts as promises, assertions, apologies and christenings, whether canonical or not. The claim is that the informative analysis handles all these cases. Here we can only outline the argument in favor of that claim.

The informative analysis divides speech situations up into two parts. First, the speaker *informs* each of the designated participants he has designated that he is performing certain illocutionary acts towards the addressees. And second, he *thereby* performs the illocutionary acts towards those addressees. The informatives are the means by which the addressee-directed illocutionary acts are performed. It is worthwhile reviewing the six major cases of requests we have taken up so far.

Requests

Case 1: Collective requests with namable addressees. When Mehta says to Perlman and Stern *Play*, he cannot request each one directly that the pair of them play. All he can do towards each person individually is inform that person that he is requesting the pair of them to play. He makes the request itself by informing each one that he intends them to believe that they are to play. The informative is not merely a prerequisite for the request. It is the means by which the request is made.

Case 2: Collective requests with indefinite addressees. When David says to Ann, Bonnie and Carol *Someone, please open the door*, he cannot request of each woman individually that someone open the door. Who that someone is is under the joint control of all three women. All David can do is inform each one that he intends them to commonly believe that he is making that request. Since he intends them to recognize the request that logically follows, he thereby makes that request too.

Case 3: Collective request with attributive addressees. When Ruth says to Tom, Dick and Harry *The last two of you to leave, please move the piano back to the corner*, she too cannot make this request of any one individual. It is the circumstances that will determine who this request is being made of. All she can do is inform each man that she intends them to commonly believe that she is making such a request. That will be sufficient for her request to become operative. Collective requests, therefore, offer direct support for the informative analysis. They must be made indirectly, by means of j-informatives.

Case 4: Distributive requests with namable addressees. Let us return to Mehta's request in (15):

(15) *Mehta, to Perlman and Stern:* Imagine the first note.

Recall the three situations in which (15) was uttered:

> *Situation A.* Perlman and Stern each hold a common belief with Mehta about what his own favorite piece is, but they do not know about each other's favorite piece.
>
> *Situation B.* All three men hold a common belief about what Perlman's favorite piece is, but only Mehta and Stern hold a common belief about what Stern's favorite is.
>
> *Situation C.* All three hold common beliefs about Perlman's and Stern's favorite pieces.

Imagining a note, we assumed, was something that Perlman and Stern couldn't do jointly, and so in all three situations, Mehta's request was distributive. Nevertheless, since he was informing Perlman and Stern of different things in the three situations, we needed to bring in informatives in order to distinguish the speech acts Mehta was performing in the three situations. The conclusion was this: Informatives are just as necessary in representing distributive requests as in representing collective requests.

In the informative analysis, however, the informatives are not merely necessary parts of these situations. They are the means by which Mehta makes his requests, even though the requests are distributive. The alternative to this analysis, which we might call the *adjunct model*, makes the weaker assumption that Mehta's informatives are necessary "adjuncts" to his requests but nothing more. They are not the means by which he performs those requests. Which model is better?

The two models can be contrasted in this way. Imagine that Mehta had uttered (32) in the same three situations:

(32) *Mehta, to Perlman and Stern:* Hum the first note.

Let us assume that Perlman and Stern can hum in two ways: (a) individually to themselves, where what the other does is irrelevant; and (b) jointly out loud, where co-ordination is as necessary as ever. Imagine further that Mehta intended, m-intended even, that Perlman and Stern were to hum jointly out loud if all the conditions were right for them to do so jointly, as in Situation C, but that they were to hum to themselves individually if not all the conditions were right, as in Situation B. So by uttering (32) in Situation B, Mehta was making a distributive request, and by uttering it in Situation C, he was making a collective request.

In this example, Mehta's only means for signalling whether his request was distributive or collective was via his informatives. They were the only parts of what he meant that Perlman and Stern could recognize as changing from Situation B to Situation C. They were the only parts he needed in order to transform his request from distributive to collective. The informatives, then, weren't merely necessary adjuncts to the request being made. They were the means by which the request was intended to be recognized. Such an example favors the informative analysis by Occam's razor. The analysis, already required for collective requests, accounts for why informatives are not only necessary but the means for making requests such as Mehta's in Situations B and C. It is therefore superfluous to posit a second, weaker, adjunct model, since it would serve no additional purpose.

Case 5: Distributive requests with indefinite addressees. Imagine David saying to Ann, Bonnie and Carol *Anyone, tell me what answer you got.* In one context, he could intend a collective reading, and in another, a distributive reading, where the change from collective to distributive is signalled only by a change in informatives. If so, the arguments made in Case 4 apply to Case 5, giving further evidence for the informative analysis.

Case 6: Distributive requests with attributive addressees. Since Ruth's utterance *The last two of you to leave, please go to Room 100,* could also be changed from a collective to a distributive reading with a change in context, the arguments in Case 4 and Case 5 apply here too. However, an even more fundamental case can be made for the informative analysis whenever the addressees are designated attributively, and this is taken up in Case 7.

Case 7: Singular requests with an attributive addressee. Imagine that Ruth says to Tom, Dick and Harry *The last one of you to leave, please go to Room 100.* Now there is no distributive-collective ambiguity since there is only one addressee. Here, however, it is easy to see that Ruth can only make her request by informing each of the three men of that request either separately or jointly. Ruth can't request of *Tom*, for example, that the last one to leave is to go to Room 100, for he may not be the last to leave. All she can do is *inform* Tom of what she is requesting. If he turns out to be the last one to leave, he will perforce be the addressee. If he isn't the last to leave, the request has still been made, but not of him. So the informative analysis makes the right prediction here too. Ruth can only make her request by means of her informatives to Tom, Dick and Harry.

There can also be mixtures of these seven cases. For a complex example, consider (33):

(33) *Minister, to church gathering:* Those of you here with a spouse, give him or her a hug.

There are many addressees, who are designated attributively, and so we are in Case 5 or Case 6. But (33) is a mixture of the two cases. Each couple is to carry out the joint act of hugging. At the same time, each couple is to do its act separately from the other couples. The request is collective within couples, and distributive across couples. Complicated cases like this aren't difficult to find.

Canonical Requests

What about canonical requests: those with a single namable addressee? In standard speech–act theories, these are performed "directly", without the aid of other illocutionary acts. For example, (34) might be analysed as (35) and nothing more:

(34) *Eve, to Cain:* Bring me a cup of tea.

(35) *Eve, to Cain:* 'I order you to bring me a cup of tea.'

By the informative analysis, canonical orders are like all other addressee-directed illocutionary acts: They are performed by means of informatives. So (34) is analysed as in (36):

(36) a. *Eve, to Cain (as participant):* 'I inform you that I am ordering you to bring me a cup of tea.'

b. *Eve, to Cain (as addressee):* 'I order you to bring me a cup of tea.'

In uttering (34), Eve performs (36a), and in doing so, she simultaneously performs (36b). Her order is "indirect" to this extent: It is performed by means of her informative. How can we justify this extra step for such simple orders?

One line of argument makes reference again to common beliefs among the hearers. Consider (37), a minor variant of (34):

(37) *Eve, to Cain, in front of Abel:* Bring me a cup of tea.

Let us suppose that Eve intends Abel to be a participant and not just an overhearer. By the standard theories, (37) would still be analysed as in (35); Cain is still the single, namable addressee. The presence of other participants makes no difference. But in (37), Eve is j-informing both Cain *and* Abel of her order to Cain. That is, she truly means two distinct things in uttering (37):

(38) a. *Eve, to Cain and Abel (as participants):* 'I j-inform you that I am ordering Cain to bring me a cup of tea.'
     b. *Eve, to Cain (as addressee):* 'I order you to bring me a cup of tea.'

By the informative analysis, (34) and (37) receive distinct representations, as they should. Furthermore, the difference between them is located in Eve's informatives, where it belongs. For this distinction to be made, canonical requests must at least be accompanied by informatives.

But the informative analysis claims something stronger. Not only are Eve's orders in (34) and (37) accompanied by informatives, they are performed *by means of* those informatives. Imagine that Eve is in the next room, and yet the three commonly believe that Cain is the one obliged to bring the tea whenever Eve orders it. Suppose that Eve then utters (37). She is still issuing the command in (38b), and she is still informing Cain and Abel of that order, represented in (38a). Cain has all the information he needs to recognize that she is ordering him and not Abel, and so does Abel. Her utterance is just as good as if she had said *Cain, bring me a cup of tea,* using a conventional vocative to designate her addressee. In these circumstances, however, the only way she can order Cain to bring her a cup of tea (38b) is by means of her j-informative (38a).

The reasons are as follows. Since Eve is "speaking to" both Cain and Abel, they must each come to recognize that she is addressing Cain and not Abel. They can't infer this from Eve's gestures or eye gaze, since they cannot see her. They can't infer this from her vocatives, since she isn't using any. Their only route is via Eve's informatives. She is jointly informing them that she is ordering the one of them who is obliged to bring her tea to bring her a cup of tea. Since all three commonly believe that Cain is the one who is obliged to bring her tea, both Cain and Abel can recognize that the addressee of the request is Cain and not Abel. Once Cain recognizes this, he can also recognize that Eve is thereby ordering him to bring her a cup of tea. Once Abel recognizes this, he has nothing more to do, since she has not issued any order to him. In terms of logical priority, the first step in computing what Eve meant must be the same for both Cain and Abel. It is only once they recognize what order she is informing them of that Cain sees that he is supposed to bring Eve a cup of tea.[11]

The scenario just described can be viewed differently. When Eve utters *Bring me a cup of tea* in this situation, what she is effectively uttering is *The one of you who is obliged to bring me tea, bring me a cup of tea*, an order with an attributive addressee. This is our Case 7, which we have already argued requires an informative analysis. So even though Eve doesn't utter an attributive vocative, she is designating the addressee in an equivalent way. Let us call this process *designating the addressee by attribution*.

This scenario is just one end of a continuum of scenarios in which addressees are designated in some part by attribution. Virtually every request, we would argue, uses this sort of designation along with such other addressee-designating devices as hand gestures and eye gazes. At the other end of this continuum are the requests in which the addressee is designated by name only, as in *Cain, bring me a cup of tea*. Even this can be viewed as designating the addressee by attribution. What Eve means in using the vocative *Cain* is "the one of you named Cain". Eve couldn't use this vocative if she thought the two participants would be confused about which one was named Cain. Thus, for every case in which there is more than one participant, even requests with single namable addressees must be performed by means of informatives.

Let us return to the contrast between (34) and (37). The orders to Cain in these two utterances are exactly the same. The only difference is in who is being informed of those orders: Cain alone, or Cain and Abel jointly. It would be unparsimonious to claim that Eve is performing those two orders in radically different ways: that she is performing the order in (34) "directly", with the informative merely "accompanying" that order, but that she is performing the order in (37) *via* her informative. By Occam's razor, canonical orders too must be performed by means of informatives.

Conclusion: All requests and their kin (orders, questions, prohibitions, authorizations, recommendations, and the like) are performed by means of informatives.

Beyond Requests

For all other addressee-directed illocutionary acts (Searle's (1975) commissives, expressives, declarations, and representatives) the arguments are virtually the same as with requests. There are, however, notable differences in the requirements for common beliefs among the hearers.

Most other types of addressee-directed illocutionary acts can be either distributive or collective. One can promise, apologize to, or fire a group of people either individually or collectively. For the collective acts, however, it doesn't seem necessary to jointly inform all the members of the group. Sam can promise something to Connie and Irene collectively without informing them jointly that he is doing so. One exception perhaps is the marriage act in which the minister or priest says *I now pronounce you husband and wife*. Here it seems that groom and bride must be jointly informed.

What is the status of the informative-first hypothesis with these other illocutionary acts? Although the arguments based on the collective-distributive distinction in requests don't apply to the other acts, the remaining arguments do. Whenever the addressees are designated indefinitely, attributively, or "by attribution", the other illocutionary acts are subject to the same arguments as requests. These arguments show that all such illocutionary acts lie outside the accounts of standard speech act theories, but are properly handled by the informative analysis.

CONCLUSIONS

Since Austin's (1962) *How to do Things with Words*, there have been many attempts to account for what speakers can do with words. Philosophers such as Grice (1957), Searle (1969), and Bach and Harnish (1979) have focussed on the speaker's intentions in using words and on the hearer's recognition of those intentions. The progress they and others have made on Austin's question has been immense. Yet the only illocutionary acts they have analysed are the canonical ones, those directed at single namable addressees. This oversight has been costly. When there is more than one hearer, these hearers can play several different roles (addressee, participant, and overhearer) and the intentions that the speaker holds toward hearers in each role are different. Standard speech act theories tell us nothing about these differences.

What the standard theories lack, we have argued, is a layer of illocutionary acts that lies just below the standard illocutionary acts: assertions, requests, promises and their kin. The new illocutionary acts, called informatives, are directed at hearers in their roles as participants. They are the direct means, and by hypothesis the only means, by which the speaker can perform assertions, requests, promises and their kin. Without this new layer, it is impossible to account for what speakers do with their words when there is more than one addressee, or participant. For speech-act theories to be complete, they need to add this new layer of informatives.

Our route to this conclusion has taken us through rather foreign territory for most language scientists: the co-ordination of actions. Joint acts, such as playing the first chord of a duet, dancing in a *corps de ballet*, or even shaking hands, make heavy demands on the people taking part in them. For the individual agents to bring off these acts jointly, they must share certain beliefs, and in a rather special way. They must have common or joint beliefs. So if a speaker is to request such an act, he must intend all the individual agents, his addressees, to come to the common or joint beliefs that are needed for the joint acts to come off. To achieve this, he needs informatives.

The general lesson is that speech acts cannot be fully understood without considering the hearers as well as the speakers. Speech acts are directed at real people, whose abilities to recognize put limits on what speakers can do with their utterances. In taking up collective speech acts, we have touched on just one issue in which the hearer is especially important. There are doubtless many more.

ACKNOWLEDGEMENTS

The work reported here was supported in part by Grant MH-20021 from the National Institute of Mental Health. We wish to thank Eve V. Clark, Gregory Murphy, Ivan Sag, Amos Tversky and the participants of the Colloquium on Mutual Knowledge for their suggestions and comments on various points in this paper.

NOTES

1. For communication among computers, Yemini and Cohen (1979) and Cohen and Yemini (1979) have provided similar proofs, apparently discovered independently. We wish to thank Amos Tversky for bringing this work to our attention.

2. In this paper, we will skirt the issue of whether we should be using mutual beliefs or mutual knowledge. Schiffer speaks of "mutual knowledge or beliefs". For simplicity, we will use beliefs.

3. At the Colloquium, Grice took a similar stand about the infinite character of m-intentions in the definition of speaker's meaning. As he put it, when the evidence is right, people simply "deem" a speaker's intentions to be of the right kind. They do not need to traverse an infinite series of intentions to find out. See Grice's own discussion in this volume.

4. This objection was raised by Johnson-Laird both in his comments at the Colloquium and in his written discussion.

5. It is this belief that enables one to settle on the intended referent of *the wick* in *I bought an expensive candle, but the wick wouldn't light*.

6. Schiffer (p. 131) also considered mutual knowledge or beliefs within a group, but his formulation is not equivalent to Lewis's common knowledge or beliefs. For one thing, his definition allows for a proposition to be mutually believed within a group without it being mutually believed between two members of the group. Bach and Harnish (1979) give a similar definition, but without the infinite iterations of either Lewis or Schiffer.

7. If Jerry were to ask Richard, with Ruth not present, *Won't you and Ruth come to dinner tonight?*, we would not consider Jerry to be requesting of Richard that Ruth come to dinner, but that Richard bring it about that he and Ruth come.

8. Notice that the e-informative in (16b) is merely a j-informative in which the group G consists of only one person. It could equally well have been called a j-informative.

9. Even this representation isn't complete, since it doesn't include certain "partial informatives", as proposed by Clark and Carlson (1980). They are not needed for the point we are making here.

10. Kempson and Cormack (1981) have noted that for predicates like *destroy, finish*, and *write*, which they call "agent-accomplishment predicates", the agents need only contribute to the accomplishment of the actions. For the assertion *Pat and Mike destroyed six flower beds*, Pat, for example, may have destroyed none, one, or all six flower beds; all he needs to have done is contribute in some way to the total destruction. So when Irving makes a joint request of Pat and Mike to destroy six flower beds, he isn't making *specifiable* requests to Pat and Mike separately. All he is specifying is what they are to accomplish jointly. We are indebted to Ruth Kempson for bringing this point to our attention.

11. Imagine that Abel is the supplier of coffee, so he must be concerned whether she is ordering tea or coffee.

Chapter 1

Comments and Replies

Comments on Clark and Carlson's paper

Yorick Wilks

These brief remarks address Clark and Carlson (CC)'s analysis of speech acts. There is no space here for a just treatment of CC on Speech Acts, which would have to begin with a careful comparison of their approach with that of Schiffer to the same topic (Schiffer, 1972, pp. 131 ff.; CC footnote his treatment of the same issue in terms of mutual knowledge at p. 36 fn 6.).

In general, I remain to be convinced that collectives require radical changes to Speech Act theory as CC claim. It seems to me that establishing the appropriate Speech Act "reading" of an utterance, in terms of commonsense heuristics, is always a tricky matter, too quickly glossed over by most theorists. But, however it is done in fact, and CC do not suggest anything fresh for that task, once the "collective reading" has been established (by methods not different from those for normal, non-collective, speech-act utterances for a standard hearer), we must assume some mutual planning techniques for achieving an agreed goal: techniques that may always fail, in practice. Any handshake may, in the event, be fumbled.

So far, so commonsensical. Where CC add more to this, they seem to me to risk serious error. Their treatment of informatives could be a return to the destructive iterations of Speech Acts in Ross's "performative hypothesis" (1970). So, for example, at (15) (p. 16), Mehta requests Perlman (and Stern) to imagine the first note. For CC's analysis, the request of Mehta to Perlman (15) also requires an informative of Mehta to Perlman.

(15′) I j-inform you that I am requesting of you to imagine the first note. It seems to me highly questionable that the request is necessarily accompanied by an inform; in particular because an inform may then itself require an inform to establish it as a Speech Act. This is, of course, exactly the damning point that Fraser (1971) made against Ross's analysis. If CC's machinery does really require informs for its requests, I am unhopeful about its prognosis.

In discussion, Clark defended the need for informatives with examples such as "Don't you need to change your nappy?" said to a one-year-old child, with the intention that the utterance be overheard, and acted upon, by its mother. Clearly in such an example, the real addressee cannot be the apparent one, but it seems to me that such utterances can be readily assimilated to the sorts of inference Searle calls "Indirect Speech Acts", just by slightly changing the conditions for being a request. In no way does it follow that a shift of, or uncertainty in, the addressee requires extra (and perhaps an infinity of extra) acts of informing.

---

1. Wilks' comments were originally in two parts: the first addressed to CC's construal of mutual knowledge, the second to their extension of Speech Act theory. In part as a result of these and other criticisms, CC made significant changes to the final version of their paper, thereby undercutting the first part of Wilks' criticism. Specifically, they changed the emphasis of their discussion from mutual knowledge to mutual belief, and introduced the examples of the violin duet and quintet in place of a less elegant alternative which Wilks had attacked as confusing. Accordingly, only the second part of Wilks' comments are given here. (ed.)

Mutual Ignorance:
Comments on Clark and Carlson's Paper

P. N. Johnson-Laird

Clark and Carlson have delivered a provocative paper, and whether they are right or wrong, they deserve credit for forcing us to consider the role of mutual knowledge in communication, and for examining how the innocent bystander may be "roped in" to participate in discourse. I suspect that Clark and Carlson are on the side of the angels, but as a discussant, I have heretically to side with the powers of darkness. Hence, I intend to champion ignorance (mutual ignorance, if you like) and its importance to communication.

According to Schiffer (1972), two people, A and B, *mutually know that p* has the following analysis:

A knows that p
B knows that p
A knows that B knows that p
B knows that A knows that p
A knows that B knows that A knows that p
and . . . so on,

ad infinitum, or at least until semantic satiation or existential nausea set in. (Incidentally, are we to assume that if A knows that p, then A knows that A knows that p? This is a question that has certainly exercised philosophers, see Hintikka, 1962.) Clark and Carlson argue that mutual knowledge is a necessary condition for the correct communication of meaning, e.g. what a speaker means in saying, "Please sit down", relies on the mutual knowledge that the verb, "sit" denotes the act of sitting. In an earlier paper, Clark and Marshall (1981) argued that it is an essential ingredient in definite reference. As a champion of ignorance, I am not entirely convinced by either of these two claims. In commenting on the earlier paper, I proposed the following counter-example:

How did you enjoy the movie that you don't know that I know you saw?

The definite description is intended to violate mutual knowledge, and even if it succeeds in so doing, it can nevertheless refer satisfactorily to a particular entity. Alan Garnham and I used a related example to show that Donnellan's (1966) analysis of attributively used descriptions is slightly flawed (Johnson-Laird and Garnham, 1980).

The major difficulty with mutual knowledge as a psychological entity is its infinite character. Clark and Carlson get round this problem by claiming that there is a mental primitive:

A and B mutually know that p

associated with a recursive inference rule that yields the required infinite sequence of statements. They argue that certain evidence can establish that this primitive relation holds between entities: one can make an inductive inference that the relation holds. It is not entirely clear how the inference schema works, but the nature of the required evidence is clear: physical co-presence, e.g. you and I looking at the last cake on a plate and at each other, or linguistic co-presence, or cultural co-presence. But, where does the inference rule come from; how do children acquire it, and when? If it is innate, then how did it evolve? Moreover, if on a particular occasion, you only need to make some of the inferences in the chain, then surely on those occasions it is false to say that there is mutual knowledge. By assumption, there is a finite number of knowledge statements, but mutual knowledge requires you to generate the infinite set of assertions. But since you never need to generate all of them, mutual knowledge is never necessary!

The essence of my view is that mutual knowledge is not a prerequisite for successful communication. For example, I go up to the box-office in the theatre, and I ask:

Is there a ticket for tonight's performance of *Macbeth*?

The ticket vendor replies, "Yes", and sells me the ticket. I had no idea whether or not the ticket vendor knew that there was a performance of Macbeth tonight; I hoped that he did, but I didn't know. Similarly, in the case that I illustrated earlier, I may know that my addressee is ignorant and intend my description to hinge on that ignorance.

Let us suppose that my argument is correct, then the question arises as to what Clark and his colleagues have been analysing. The answer seems to be: a necessary condition for a guarantee of successful communication. No misunderstandings can arise if mutual knowledge has been established, but in its absence, one cannot be certain that a definite reference will succeed. In daily life, however, there is seldom such a guarantee, at least at the start of a conversation. Of course, if discourse is successful then it may put the participants into a position where they could begin to infer the long sequence of assertions corresponding to mutual knowledge. But if they start with completely mutual knowledge there might not be much point in communicating: they might be stating the obvious. As in the old drive–reduction theories of psychology, mutual ignorance is a drive that is a spur to conversation which in turn, reduces it; sometimes completely.

Clark and Carlson's distinctive contribution to the theory of speech acts is to consider what happens when a speaker calls for a joint action by the addressees, e.g. "Please shake hands". Their central claim is that there must be common knowledge betwen the participants, i.e. an infinite sequence of knowledge statements of the form: the members of the group know that p, the members of the group know that the members of the group know that p, and so on. . . . Common knowledge concerns what illocutionary acts the speaker is performing to all the addressees, and it is missing from the standard speech-act theories. Clark and Carlson argue that the addressees must separately recognize the speaker's intentions. Hence, a collective request (such as "Man the lifeboats" or "Women and children first") must decompose into elementary requests to be carried out by individuals, and the joint nature of the enterprise must be conveyed somehow. This condition leads in no time to the infinite sequence of assertions required for common knowledge. Hence, according to Clark and Carlson, the correct analysis of my request, "shake hands", to my son and daughter is that to my son I am (a) making a request that he shake hands with my daughter, and (b) making an assertion to the effect that I am jointly informing both him and my daughter that I am requesting them to shake hands. Without this joint informative, my son may be in doubt about the co-ordination and may refuse to offer his hand. With respect to the request, my son is an addressee; with respect to the informative, he is a participant. Clark and Carlson go on to argue that it is the informative that does the real work, and they generalize this argument to the claim that all addressee-directed illocutionary acts are performed by means of informatives.

I want to try to block this argument at its source and to argue that it is not the case that the correct analysis of my request, "Shake hands", demands a jointly-informative assertion. Clark and Carlson at one point[1] say that without it, "the request must fail," that it is a necessary condition for making collective requests. This claim seems manifestly false. Let me try to explain why.

Suppose my intention is that my son and daughter should shake hands, and that I realize this intention by saying to both of them: "Shake hands". But, as a champion of mutual ignorance, it so happens that I have no intention to jointly inform them of my request. My performance is seriously defective according to Clark and Carlson's analysis, but I claim that it might well happen and that it won't make any difference.

Clark and Carlson may retort: The fact that you are not aware of such an intention is irrelevant, it could be unconscious. Or, more likely, they will say: Your addressee will nevertheless infer that you are uttering a joint informative. But, supposing my son merely infers that he should try to shake hands with my daughter, and my daughter merely infers that she should try to shake hands with my son. There is still every chance that they will succeed in the joint action even though the joint-informative has not entered anyone's mind.

In a sense, the ingenuity of the theory counts against it: speakers are not generally aware of having such complex intentions as Clark and Carlson ascribe to them. They certainly do not express them explicitly. Likewise, hearers are not generally aware of having inferred that the speaker has such complex intentions. If speakers and hearers *were* aware of such intentions, it would be *no* credit to Clark and Carlson for having dreamed up their theory. Suppose, nevertheless, that Clark and Carlson are correct: the speaker is not aware of the complex intention; nothing he says expresses it overtly; the hearer is not aware of having inferred it. Yet the intentions do exist, perhaps unconsciously. There remain two questions that appear unanswerable:

(1) How do children develop the ability to have such intentions and to infer that others have them from what they say?

(2) How would anyone know that a speaker had omitted to have the appropriate intention?

Once again, what Clark and Carlson have done is to analyse a necessary condition for guaranteed success in the communication of a request for joint action. If this thesis is correct, then you may wonder why it is that speakers do not more often aim to fulfil this necessary condition. The answer is simple: the real problem with requests is not so much in getting people to understand them, but in getting them to obey them, especially if you are dealing with my son and daughter. Getting the perlocutionary force over is more important than successfully communicating the illocutionary act: in the case of my son and daughter I have been known to get them in separate rooms and to invite them to shake hands with the other as a "spontaneous" gesture of goodwill, i.e. I deliberately violate common knowledge so that there is no loss of face.

There are other sources of mutual ignorance that can destroy the guarantee of success. One of them concerns a problem that is not touched on by Clark and Carlson: the identification of the addressee. If a simple request is to succeed, then obviously its addressee must grasp that he or she *is* the addressee. Hence, in order to guarantee its successful communication, it is necessary to fulfil conditions that enable the addressee to identify him/her-self. One of my favourite dialogues goes like this:

A: You bloody fool!
B: Are you speaking to me?
A: No.
B: Then why did you just say "no" to me?
A: I didn't.

A speaker may have a definite addressee in mind; or a speaker may merely have in mind an addressee that matches a particular description attributively (e.g. the person on the other end of the phone); or a speaker may not have any addressee in mind as in an involuntary cry for help. There are sufficient conditions for picking out certain sorts of addressee: use of a proper name, etc.; but much of the time speakers rely on social conventions. If I march up to someone, stare fixedly into his eyes from a distance of six inches and say, "You bloody fool!", the chances are that I will not succeed in claiming that I was talking to someone else. In general, there are unlikely to be a set of necessary and sufficient conditions for the identification of addressees, and speakers do fail from time to time. In the absence of such conditions, which are even more basic than those that guarantee the successful communication of a particular speech act, it is perhaps not too surprising that speakers seldom live up to the high ideals of mutual knowledge.

In closing, I note that Deirdre Wilson and Dan Sperber (this volume) are similarly sceptical about mutual knowledge. As a psychologist, I cannot resist drawing your attention to the role of national characteristics in this debate. Americans are open, friendly extraverts, and they tend to believe in the importance of mutual knowledge. We Europeans are closed, formal, introverted, and we tend to doubt whether we ever have mutual knowledge.

NOTE

1. This claim is only implicit, not explicit, in the final version of C & C's paper. (ed.)

Comments on Clark and Carlson's Paper

Dan Sperber

By taking into account certain interesting cases of speech acts aimed at more than one hearer, Clark and Carlson have shown that "speech act theory" as developed in Searle (1969, 1975) needs to be revised. (There may, of course, be other grounds for thinking that speech-act theory should be radically revised, or even abandoned, but that is not the issue here.) The revision they propose is a fundamental expansion of the theory: they argue that all the usual addressee-directed speech acts are performed by means of speech acts of another type: "participant-directed informatives" (cf. p. 21). I want to argue that a more modest revision of speech act theory, namely a redefinition of the propositional content of requests, is enough to accommodate their evidence.

Searle's proposed condition on the propositional content of a request is that it must describe "a future act of the hearer". Even leaving aside for the moment the fact that there can be more than one hearer, this seems too narrow. It does not adequately describe the propositional content of many literal and direct requests.

(1) Be cool.

(2) Trust him.

The propositions expressed by (1) and (2) describe states of the requestee rather than acts. The request as a whole implicates that the requestee should bring about this state in himself.

(3) Don't move.

(4) Don't be sad.

The propositions expressed by (3) and (4) describe the *absence* of a certain act or state.

(5) Those toys are to be back in the cupboard by the time I return.

(6) Waiter, I'll have a glass of brandy, please!

The propositions expressed by (5) and (6) describe a state of affairs or event that the requestee may help bring about. The request as a whole may implicate a description of the behaviour (putting the toys back in the cupboard, bringing the glass of brandy) which would make the proposition true.

(7) Stay at home if it rains.

(8) Please James, if it rains, the drinks are to be served in the library.

Two analyses can be proposed for (7) and (8), and for other requests of the form *if p then q*:

(9) If *p* then (I request *q*).

(10) I request (if *p* then *q*).

The analysis in (9) implies that unless it happens to rain at some time after the utterance, (7) and (8) are not requests, but then what kinds of speech acts are they? Moreover, if (9) were correct, then on the same pattern, the proper analysis of (11) should be (12), which obviously it is not:

(11) Stay at home only if it rains.

(12) If not *p* then not (I request *q*).

The analysis given in (10) does not run into such objections, and in any case seems intuitively more acceptable. However, if this analysis is correct, the propositional content of these requests is a complex conditional which may contain or implicate, but does not itself constitute, a description of an act by the hearer.

Cases such as (1)–(8) suggest that Searle's characterization of a request should be modified. It might be modified in the following way: the propositional content of a request is any proposition; however, a request (as opposed to a mere wish) is an explicit attempt to get the requestee to behave in such a way that the proposition will be true.

Other standardly cited properties of requests (for example, that they concern the future, or that they either describe or implicate a description of some behaviour by the requestee) follow, I would argue, from this definition of a request together with a general pragmatic principle of relevance (see the contribution to this volume by Sperber and Wilson and the references therein).

This revision of the notion of a request eliminates what Clark and Carlson call the "target-as-agent criterion" (p. 12): that is, the idea that the addressee of a request has to be the agent of a requested action, an idea which follows from Searle's over-restrictive definition.

Now Clark and Carlson's proposed revision of speech act theory is, to a great extent, an elaborate method of salvaging the target-as-agent criterion in the face of their own strong counter-evidence. What they do not explain is why this criterion should have been maintained in the first place; especially since, as we have just seen in the case of (1)–(8), there are already independent reasons for thinking that it should be eliminated.

Let me show how the revised notion of a request provides a more economical way of accounting for Clark and Carlson's evidence (and is indeed corroborated by it) by going over some of their examples.

(13) *Ruth to Tom, Dick and Harry:* The last one of you to leave, please go to room 100. (Case 7, p. 30)

Clark and Carlson argue that since compliance with (13) calls for only one agent (i.e. whoever is the last one to leave), there is only one requestee. Yet the utterance is directed at Tom, Dick and Harry. Clark and Carlson propose to say, then, that Tom, Dick and Harry are all three informed of the request as "participants", while only the last of them to leave is the addressee of the request.

With the revised definition of requests, we can more simply say that all three are addressees of the request: they are all requested to behave in such a way that the proposition expressed by the request will be true. For this to happen, the last one to leave has to go to room 100; but also, each of them has to remember the request until he knows whether he will be the last to leave: a fact which Clark and Carlson would find it hard to explain without making further assumptions about what is requested (!) of "participants".

(14) *David to Ann, Bonnie and Carol:* Someone please open the door. (=CC (21))

According to Clark and Carlson, (14) calls for co-ordination among the three "participants" in order to determine who the requestee, i.e. the one addressed by the indefinite "someone", will be. This is questionable. Suppose that only Carol had actually heard the request, and that the circumstances did not allow for repetition or repair; after a while she would have to open the door, and she would not be able to invoke lack of co-ordination as an excuse for failure to do this.

In my analysis, all three hearers are requested to behave so that *someone opens the door* will be true. They might choose to co-ordinate, but they do not have to. For each of them, this request means that she is to open the door if the others will not. Such requests create a growing pressure on all the addressees, a pressure which often grows faster for one, e.g. for the one nearest the door. But if this one does not yield, then the next one must, and so on.

(15) *Irving to Pat and Mike:* Please shake hands. (=CC (2))

This is Clark and Carlson's central example. It differs from (13) and
(14) in two respects. Both hearers have to act and, unquestionably, they
have to co-ordinate. Clark and Carlson's argument is nevertheless
based on the claim that the target of Irving's utterance and the agent of
the requested action are not, despite appearances, identical. Only individuals, here Pat and Mike, can be intended to comprehend utterances.
On the other hand, Clark and Carlson argue, a handshake is not the
sum of two individual actions: it is the single action of a collective agent,
here Pat-and-Mike. Given the target-as-agent criterion, the requestee
has to be Pat-and-Mike; but then the request can only be conveyed to
its collective addressee by means of informatives directed at the two individual "participants" Pat and Mike.

From my point of view, whatever the nature of a handshake, there is
no problem in identifying Pat and Mike as the two requestees. They are
requested to behave in such a way that the proposition expressed by
(15) (whether it should be represented as *Pat and Mike shake hands* or as
Pat-and-Mike shakes hands) will be true.

In other words, I am saying that the distinction between requests for
collective actions and requests for unco-ordinated individual actions
does not belong to speech act theory (any more than, say, the distinction between moral and immoral requests). In all cases, individual
requestees are requested to make a certain proposition true, whether
the proposition describes collective actions, or individual actions, or no
actions at all.

From the study of requests such as (15), Clark and Carlson derive
another quite different argument in favour of participant-directed informatives. When Irving asks Pat and Mike to shake hands, he thereby
provides them with all the information they need to co-ordinate their
action: they jointly know that they have been requested to shake hands
and, normally, they need no further information in order to comply.
Clark and Carlson's example is rather exceptional in this respect. If the
request had been "Please shake hands sometime tomorrow", or "Please
write a joint article", quite a bit of explicit co-ordination would have
been left to the requestees to achieve. But even so, it is true that when
two people have been requested in each other's presence to perform
some joint act, they can normally dispense with at least the initial step
of co-ordination, i.e. with agreeing to act jointly.

Clark and Carlson argue that this joint information received by the requestees is, and *has to be*, conveyed through the distinct speech acts they call "informatives". That is, the transmission of this information has to be intentional, and even m-intentional in Grice's sense: the requestees get the information by recognizing the speaker's m-intentions. I want to argue, on the contrary, that this joint information is derived from the fact that the request is made while both requestees are in each other's presence: that is, it is inferred from the immediate context of the utterance. It may then, although it does not always, lead to inferences about the speaker's intentions and m-intentions.

Now it might seem impossible to find evidence that would directly choose between these two views. One cannot make a request without intending the requestee to be informed of the request, and intuition will not tell us whether this has to be a distinct m-intention rather than a non-distinct ordinary intention (or, at least, I expect that intuition will tell different stories to Clark and Carlson on the one hand and to me on the other).

Part of the difficulty comes from the fact that all ordinary intentions can on occasion become m-intentions, though they do not have to. For instance, when I m-intend to say something, I cannot but also intend to make my voice heard, although this is usually not a distinct m-intention of mine. Now if I know that somebody believes that I am mute and I say to him *You are mistaken about me*, I intend him to hear my voice, to realize that I intended him to hear my voice, to realize that I intended him to realize this, and so on. In short, I m-intend him to hear my voice. I am not, however, performing some new type of speech act, and Occam's razor would not permit the claim that a specific speech act of making one's voice heard occurs every time one speaks. I am just, as usual, m-intending the hearer to establish the contextual relevance of my utterance, and in particular to use those elements of the context that are part of our mutual knowledge and contribute decisively to relevance. By the very fact of my speaking, it has become part of the mutually known context that I have made my voice heard. In this odd case, this fact does make the content of my utterance particularly relevant; that is why the hearer can take for granted that I not only intended but also m-intended him to hear my voice. Similarly, making a request in a way that provides necessary information for complying with the request can generally be taken to be m-intentional. But Clark and Carlson's point is stronger: it *has to* be m-intentional and it does constitute a distinct and ever present type of speech act. What direct evidence could bear on such a claim?

Here again, Clark and Carlson's idea of using speech acts aimed at several hearers proves fruitful: however, it suggests evidence which goes against their position:

FIRST CASE: Irving is an experimental psycholinguist and Pat and Mike are two subjects who have not met before. Irving has instructed his assistant to tell Pat that Mike is stone deaf and to tell Mike that Pat is stone deaf. Pat and Mike are then taken to a room where Irving tells them *Please shake hands*. Given the experimental situation he has himself set up, Irving knows that Pat and Mike cannot, on hearing him, assume joint knowledge of the request. Therefore Irving does not intend (let alone m-intend) to establish such joint knowledge. Indeed, no such joint knowledge gets established, just as Clark and Carlson would predict. I would make the same prediction, although it is based not on Irving's m-intentions but on the context created by the assistant's warnings. My guess is that Pat and Mike might well shake hands, but then I also guess that Clark and Carlson could explain this, one way or another.

SECOND CASE: Irving's assistant forgets to misinform Pat and Mike. Irving, who is not aware of this, still has no intention to establish joint knowledge. Joint knowledge gets established all the same (and hands are probably shaken forthwith). In this case, Clark and Carlson would have to claim that Pat and Mike got their joint knowledge from a mistaken perception of Irving's intentions. I would say that, if they had a mistaken perception of Irving's intentions, it is rather as a result of having correctly inferred joint knowledge from the context, and mistakenly assumed that Irving shared that context.

THIRD CASE: Irving's assistant mischievously tells Pat and Mike together that he was supposed to tell each separately that the other is stone deaf. Irving, who is unaware of this, still has no intention to establish joint knowledge between Pat and Mike. Pat and Mike know that Irving lacks such an intention. Yet, when they are told *Please shake hands*, they acquire joint knowledge of the request and have no good excuse for not complying. I would say that Pat and Mike made the proper contextual inference, in spite of their knowing that Irving did not intend them to.

What should Clark and Carlson say?

Critics' Beliefs about Hearers' Beliefs: A Rejoinder to Johnson-Laird, Sperber and Wilks

Herbert H. Clark and Thomas B. Carlson

"If a man will begin with certainties", wrote Sir Francis Bacon, "he shall end in doubts; but if he will be content to begin with doubts, he shall end in certainties". Johnson-Laird, Sperber and Wilks have expressed certain doubts about our proposals to emend speech-act theory. Rightly so. When we first considered these proposals, we too were sceptical. It has taken a good deal of fresh evidence to change our minds. We trust that when our critics have examined this evidence, their doubts too will be allayed. In this rejoinder, we take up only a few of these doubts, and these only briefly. The remainder we leave to another day.

SPERBER ON REQUESTS

There are many facts about requests, we argued, that cannot be handled by standard speech-act theories, but that can be handled by the informative analysis. In an ingenious suggestion, Sperber argues that the troublesome facts *can* be handled by the standard theories with a revised definition of request. According to Searle (1969), a request is an attempt to get the hearer to do some future act. In Sperber's revision, a request is an attempt to get the hearer to make it the case that some proposition be true. Consider (1):

(1) *Ruth, to Tom, Dick and Harry:* The last one of you to leave, please go to room 100.

In Searle's account, Ruth would be requesting all three hearers to go to room 100, which is clearly incorrect. In Sperber's account, she is trying to get the three hearers to make it be true that the last one to leave goes to room 100. This seems possibly right. Sperber's solution, however, has been considered before and rejected decisively (e.g. see Rescher, 1964, pp. 38–41). The main problem is that it misanalyses conditional requests. But even as an analysis of other requests, it has defects.

First, it mislabels addressees. We brought up examples like (1) to show that not all hearers who are m-intended to understand are addressees: that is, requestees. If Tom were actually the last one to leave, he would be the requestee, and not Dick or Harry. About (1), Sperber says, "With the revised definition of requests, we more simply say that all three [hearers: Tom, Dick and Harry] are addressees of the request: They are all requested to behave in such a way that the proposition expressed by the request will come true."

Sperber's proposal runs into difficulties with these variations on (1):

(2) *Ruth, to Tom, Dick and Harry:* The last one of you to leave—and we all know that will be you, Tom—please go to room 100.

(3) *Ruth, to Tom, Dick and Harry:* Tom, and I don't mean you Dick or you Harry, please go to room 100.

(4) *Ruth, to Tom, in front of Dick and Harry:* Tom, please go to room 100.

In (2) through (4) as in (1), all three hearers are m-intended to understand what Ruth meant. Apparently, Sperber would therefore label all three hearers as addressees. We say "apparently", since the remaining criterion he offers for addressees is otherwise circular: "A request (as opposed to a mere wish) is an explicit attempt to get the *requestee* to behave in such a way that the proposition will be true [our emphasis]". But are all three hearers in (2) through (4) addressees? The informants we have consulted say no. Tom is an addressee; Dick and Harry are not. So while the informative analysis labels these hearers correctly, Sperber's analysis does not.

The fatal defect in Sperber's analysis is that it leads to a misanalysis of other illocutionary acts. Let us change (1) from a request into an apology, offer, firing, or assertion, as in (5):

(5) *Ruth, to Tom, Dick and Harry:* The last one of you to leave last night, I apologize for not having shown you out.

To be consistent, Sperber would have to say that Ruth was apologizing to all three hearers. Yet the informants we have consulted insist that she is apologizing only to the last person to leave, whoever that may have been. So Sperber's analysis of requests doesn't extend to apologies, offers, firings and other non-requests. The informative analysis does, and with the correct predictions.

Sperber uses his revised analysis to claim that "the distinction between requests for collective actions and requests for unco-ordinated individual actions does not belong to speech-act theory (any more than, say, the distinction between moral and immoral requests". Once his revised analysis is overturned, so is this additional claim. This claim seems unjustified in any case. Take *Bring a bottle of wine*. If Irving says this simultaneously to Pat and Mike who are unaware of each other in sound-proof booths, he is making two requests, expecting two bottles of wine. If he says this to Pat and Mike in each other's presence, he can make a single collective request, expecting only one bottle of wine. The contrast between using an utterance to make two requests and one is surely a matter for speech-act theory. Even if Sperber's revised analysis were correct, this contrast wouldn't disappear.

SPEAKER'S INTENTIONS

Speech-act theory, the subject of our paper, is a theory about the speaker's intentions, not about the hearer's successful recognition of those intentions and subsequent behavior, usually called hearer uptake. Irving may make a perfect request of Pat to sit down. Nevertheless, Pat may not recognize it because he mishears, fails to attend, or is misled by a third party. Or Pat may recognize the request correctly but refuse to comply. Despite the importance of hearer uptake, the subject of speech act theory is the speaker's intentions.

Many of Johnson-Laird's and Sperber's objections are based on a confusion of speaker's intentions and hearer's uptake. Once this confusion is eliminated, the objections evaporate.

Take Johnson-Laird's attempts to get his son and daughter to shake hands. As he demonstrated, he could achieve this result in several ways. He could ask his son to get his daughter to shake hands, or ask his daughter to get his son to shake hands, or do both, separately, without their mutual awareness. He could even say to them both, together, *Each of you, shake the other's hand*. In each case, the perlocutionary effect might look the same. The two of them would shake hands.

All of Johnson-Laird's requests, however, are individual or distributive requests. None of them is a collective request. To make a collective request, Johnson-Laird would have to ask his son and daughter, *as a pair*, to initiate the joint act of shaking hands, which is still another way of achieving the same hearer uptake. Our arguments for the informative analysis are based on the analysis of collective requests, so Johnson-Laird's examples, as interesting as they are, are irrelevant.

Next take Sperber's three cases of Irving trying to get Pat and Mike to shake hands. Recall that Irving asks his assistant to tell Pat that Mike is stone deaf and, separately, to tell Mike that Pat is stone deaf. In all three cases, Irving believes that his assistant has carried out his wishes. Irving then says to Pat and Mike in each other's presence *Please shake hands*. Irving's intentions are clearly *not* to make a collective request, regardless of how Pat and Mike interpret him. He intends Pat and Mike each to try to get the other to shake hands: two individual requests. This is just as the informative analysis predicts.

Sperber, however, takes Pat's and Mike's mistaken uptake of Irving's requests as counter-evidence to the analysis. Recall that in Case 1, the assistant does as he is told, in Case 2 he forgets to tell Pat and Mike what he is supposed to tell them, and in Case 3 he mischievously tells them both what Irving wanted him to tell each one. In Case 2, then, Pat and Mike would misunderstand Irving. However, they would do so not because Irving's intentions were wrong, but because Irving's beliefs abut the situation (what he took to be their common ground) were wrong. Pat's and Mike's actual uptake is irrelevant to the analysis of Irving's intentions.

The informative analysis, nevertheless, specifies certain prerequisites for the hearer's successful recognition of the speaker's intentions, and Sperber's three cases offer excellent examples of how this works. In Case 1, Irving's, and Pat's and Mike's, beliefs about their common ground are identical, hence Pat and Mike can recognize Irving's intentions correctly, and they do. In Case 2, Pat's and Mike's beliefs about their common ground with Irving are mistaken, and should lead them to take Irving as making a *collective* request. This is what happens. In Case 3, Pat and Mike realize that although *they* believe they are hearing Irving's utterance jointly, *Irving* believes that they believe that they aren't. They see that their mutual beliefs are *not* part of the common ground for the three of them, as would be required for Irving to be making a collective request. As a result, Pat and Mike correctly understand that Irving is making two individual requests, but that he is doing so by deception. In all three cases, then, the informative analysis correctly predicts how Pat and Mike should interpret Irving.

What Johnson-Laird does say about speaker's intentions is that he finds them implausible because he has no conscious awareness of them. Consciousness, however, is not a necessary condition for intentions. Johnson-Laird has assumed as much in his own models of understanding and reasoning.

Consider Johnson-Laird and Wason's (1970) model for how people reason in the so-called "four-card problem". These people aim, plan, or *intend* to solve it, and in so doing, they deliberately, or *intentionally*, carry out certain mental operations. Johnson-Laird and Wason's model of reasoning is, in effect, a representation of these intentions and intentional acts, as well as other things. In it, the solver is said to "retrieve 'truth table'"; "place antecedent and consequent on LIST of items to be examined"; "remove from LIST"; and so on. Johnson-Laird and Wason offer no evidence that these operations are conscious, nor should they. The evidence they do offer is that these intentions and intentional acts account for people's intuitions about how they solve the four-card problem. The evidence that we (and Grice, Searle, and others) have offered for the speaker's intentions is analogous: these intentions are needed to account for people's intuitions about how they ask questions, make requests, and offer apologies. Consciousness is no more important here than in Johnson-Laird and Wason's model for the four-card problem.

MUTUAL BELIEFS

We and many others have argued that mutual knowledge, mutual beliefs, and mutual suppositions (what we have called common ground) play an important role in language use. Johnson-Laird questions this argument. But his questions arise from a misunderstanding of that argument. "The essence of my view", Johnson-Laird says, "is that mutual knowledge is not a prerequisite for successful communication". Our arguments, and Clark and Marshall's, however, have not been about mutual knowledge alone, but about mutual knowledge, beliefs *and* suppositions. Once this is understood, Johnson-Laird's counterexamples lose their force.

Consider what Johnson-Laird says about this utterance:

(6) *Johnson-Laird, to ticket-vendor at box office:* Is there a ticket for tonight's performance of Macbeth?

"I had no idea whether or not the ticket vendor knew that there was a performance of Macbeth tonight; I hoped that he did, but I didn't know." Of course. But Johnson-Laird did take it as mutually *supposed* that there was a performance of Macbeth that night, say from the fact that it was advertized next to the ticket window. Most uses of language are founded on mutual beliefs or mutual suppositions, which are not nearly as demanding as mutual knowledge.

Next consider Johnson-Laird's comment about this example:

(7) How did you enjoy the movie that you don't know that I know you saw?

"The definite description is intended to violate mutual knowledge, and even if it succeeds in so doing, it can nevertheless refer satisfactorily to a particular entity." This is taken to be counter-evidence to a proposal by Clark and Marshall (1981) about the role of common ground in definite reference. It isn't. In that proposal, the speaker's and listener's common ground is not required to include the referent itself, as Johnson-Laird assumes, but only the *means* to infer that referent uniquely. For this, the listener is often required to draw "bridging inferences". In (7), he might think, "Ah, you found out about that other movie I went to". These inferences, and the theory behind them, are discussed in a paper (Clark, 1977a) that appears in a book edited by Johnson-Laird and Wason.

But does Johnson-Laird truly believe, as he claims, that "mutual knowledge is not a prerequisite for successful communication"? Imagine that he and his wife didn't mutually know what *dog*, or *run*, or *I*, or any other standard English word meant. It is doubtful that they could successfully communicate with these words. Surely, the two of them mutually know the core of the English language. Barring mutual knowledge of sign language or French or Turkish, they couldn't communicate without that mutual knowledge. Once Johnson-Laird asks "Mutual knowledge, beliefs, or assumption of what?" he will see that he couldn't get along without them.

MISREADINGS AND MISUNDERSTANDINGS

Johnson-Laird thinks we believe, as he says, that "mutual knowledge requires you to generate the infinite set of assertions" in the definition of mutual knowledge. He is misreading Clark and Marshall (1981). The central point of that paper, a point we repeat, is that mutual knowledge does *not* require you to generate the infinite set of assertions. Once this premise is corrected, the several arguments Johnson-Laird bases on it explode.

Sperber is seriously in error about m-intentions. Grice (1968), in introducing the term, defined it this way:

> 'U intends to produce in A effect E by means of A's recognition of that intention' will be abbreviated to 'U *M-intends* to produce in A effect E'. (p. 58, Grice's emphasis)

That is, an m-intention is a speaker's intention to produce an effect in the hearer *by means* of the hearer's recognition of that intention. This is the same definition that is used by Searle, Schiffer, Bach and Harnish, and us. Compare this to what Sperber says:

> Now if I know that somebody believes that I am mute and I say to him *You are mistaken about me*, I intend him to hear my voice, to realize that I intended him to realize this, and so on. In short, I m-intended him to hear my voice.

This characterization of m-intention is incorrect. Sperber does not intend to get his interlocutor to hear his voice by means of the other's recognition of that intention. Nor could he have done so. Whether or not his interlocutor hears Sperber's voice is independent of his *recognition* of Sperber's intention to produce that effect. Sperber bases several arguments on this mistaken notion. Once the notion is corrected, the arguments vanish.

Wilks argues that the informative analysis is subject to the same criticisms that have been used against Ross's performative analysis. The argument doesn't stand up to close scrutiny. The assumption fatal to Ross's analysis was that performative verbs are part of the syntax and semantics of sentences. His analysis comes alive again once the work done by performative verbs is accomplished in the pragmatics (see Gazdar, 1979). Speech-act theories, ours included, are theories of pragmatics *par excellence*. They are immune to Wilks' criticism.

Finally, Wilks takes up our example of the mother who says to a one-year-old "Don't you need to have your diapers changed?" and thereby requests the father to change the diapers. Wilks states, without further argument, that "it seems to me that such utterances can be readily assimilated to the sorts of inference Searle calls "indirect speech acts", just by slightly changing the conditions for being a request". In Searle's theory, however, an indirect speech act can only be made by means of a direct speech act addressed *to the same hearer*. In this utterance, the mother's only direct speech act is directed at the child; there is *no* direct speech act directed at the father. Wilks would have to devise a change in the "conditions for being a request" that would lead to the necessary repairs. We don't believe he can. Indeed, it was evidence like this that led us to argue that these cases can only be handled by the introduction of informatives (Clark and Carlson, 1980).

Chapter 2
Mutual Knowledge and Relevance in Theories of Comprehension[1]

Dan Sperber and Deirdre Wilson

I. INTRODUCTION

The main aim of pragmatic theory is to explain how successful communication is possible, and in particular, how utterances are understood. Understanding an utterance involves recovering the proposition it expresses and drawing certain inferences based on this proposition as premise. The difficulty lies in explaining not how some arbitrary proposition is discovered and some random inferences drawn, but how the intended content and intended implications are recovered: that is, how comprehension is achieved.

Comprehension is a function of the context: that much is uncontroversial. But what does the context consist of? How does the hearer exploit it in discovering the intended content and implications of an utterance? Various answers to these questions have been proposed, but all of them are tentative at best.

It is compatible with much of the current literature to envisage three distinct mechanisms: one to determine the context involved in the comprehension of an utterance, a second to determine the content on the basis of the context and of the linguistic properties of the utterance, and a third to draw the intended inferences on the basis of the content and the context.

As regards the context, some recent work suggests that it is restricted to the mutual knowledge, beliefs and suppositions of speaker and hearer, where mutual knowledge is knowledge that is not only shared, but known to be shared, and known to be known to be shared, and so on. On this approach, the identification of mutual knowledge is a major factor in every aspect of comprehension, and one of the most urgent goals of pragmatic theory is to explain how it is achieved.

We would like to develop three main arguments against this approach. First, the identification of mutual knowledge presents problems which, contrary to the predictions of the mutual knowledge framework, do not give rise to corresponding problems of comprehension. Secondly, mutual knowledge is not a sufficient condition for belonging to the context: a proposition may be mutually known without being part of the context. Thirdly, it is not a necessary condition either: a proposition may belong to the context without being mutually known.

We shall then suggest an alternative approach. We shall argue that there is a single principle which simultaneously determines context, content and intended inferences, with no appeal to mutual knowledge.[2] The fact that some knowledge is considered mutual is generally a result of comprehension rather than a precondition for it. Hence mistakes in comprehension are much more likely to cause a wrong assessment of mutual knowledge than the other way around.

II. SOME QUESTIONS FOR THE MUTUAL KNOWLEDGE FRAMEWORK

A. Do Problems in Identifying Mutual Knowledge Cause Problems in Comprehension?

In order to understand an utterance, the hearer has to bring to bear certain items of background information not specifically mentioned in the utterance. For instance, in order to understand the utterance "I didn't", the hearer must be able to identify some activity, not specified in the utterance, which he can take the speaker to be saying he did not engage in. The context, as generally understood, is the background information that can be brought to bear on comprehension.

What is the extent of the context intrinsically involved in the comprehension process? (For the contrast between "intrinsic" and "incidental" context, see Clark and Carlson, forthcoming.) The weakest hypothesis would be that all the information the hearer possesses can be brought to bear on comprehension: that is, that the context is co-extensive with the hearer's memory. However, a more restrictive hypothesis is generally favoured. It is argued, for instance by Clark and Carlson (forthcoming) that the intrinsic context can be straightforwardly identified with the mutual knowledge, beliefs and assumptions of speaker and hearer: that is, with what has been referred to elsewhere in the literature as their common ground (Stalnaker 1974; Karttunen and Peters 1975). There are formal arguments for this identification of context with mutual knowledge or common ground. We shall discuss them later. But to begin with, there are problems with the identification of mutual knowledge itself.

The concept of mutual knowledge was first introduced as part of the philosophical analysis of speaker-meaning, utterance-meaning, convention and other meaning-related concepts (Schiffer 1972, 30–42; Lewis 1969, 52–60). For those interested in constructing an empirical pragmatic theory, the question is not whether these analyses are philosophically adequate, but whether they have any psychological correlates. Here an immediate problem arises. If mutual knowledge is to play a role in the real-time production and comprehension of utterances, it must be very easily identifiable: there must be some straightforward method by which a speaker and hearer who both know a given proposition can discover that they mutually know it. But at first sight, it is hard to see how such a method could exist.

Mutual knowledge is knowledge of an infinite set of propositions. By the usual definitions, a speaker S and an addressee A mutually know a proposition P if and only if:

(1) S knows that P.
(2) A knows that P.
(3) S knows (2).
(4) A knows (1).
(5) S knows (4).
(6) A knows (3).
    . . . and so on *ad infinitum*.

How does A discover that he has the requisite mutual knowledge for understanding an utterance? Assuming that he cannot compute an infinite set of propositions in a finite amount of time, and that the possession of mutual knowledge is not self-evident (since one can be mistaken about it), the problem is to find a finite procedure for distinguishing mutual knowledge from knowledge that is not mutual.

Clark and Marshall (1981) argue that mutual knowledge can be identified by a finite inductive procedure. They argue that from the psychological point of view, mutual knowledge must be a simple, un-analysable concept, whose logical consequences do not have to be computed in order to establish its applicability. Instead, its applicability is established by invoking more or less adequate inductive evidence (see also Lewis 1969, 52–58; Schiffer 1972, 33–36). Clark and Marshall classify this evidence according to its possible sources: physical co-presence, linguistic co-presence and community membership.

Physical co-presence provides the strongest evidence for mutual knowledge. It involves the presence of two people, S and A, at an event which gives them direct empirical evidence for a certain proposition, and for the fact that both of them have this evidence. For example, if S and A are facing each other across a table with a bowl of fruit between them, then with certain minimal assumptions about rationality and powers of observation, both would be justified in concluding that they had mutual knowledge of (7):

(7) There is a bowl of fruit on the table between S and A.

This piece of mutual knowledge could be stored in memory as such, or reconstructed at a later date given mutual knowledge of its retrievability.

Linguistic co-presence involves the co-presence of S, A and an utterance which expresses or implies a certain proposition. For example, if S and A are standing together waiting for a train to Oxford when the station-announcer makes the announcement in (8), they could reasonably infer mutual knowledge of (8):

(8) The 6:00 train for Oxford will leave from platform 6.

Again, this could be stored at the time as a piece of mutual knowledge, or reconstructed later if it is mutually known to be retrievable.

Finally, if S and A establish that they belong to the same community or group, they can reasonably assume mutual knowledge of all propositions normally known by group members. For example, if it is established that they have both been exposed to a recent Heineken's advertizing campaign, they can assume mutual knowledge of (9):

(9) It has been claimed that Heineken's refreshes the parts other beers cannot reach.

The above remarks about storage and retrievability still apply.

Much of the literature on mutual knowledge explicitly assumes that all knowledge is evidenced. Clark and Marshall implicitly assume that all evidence for mutual knowledge is ultimately physical. In their terms, linguistic co-presence is simply physical co-presence at an acoustic (or visual) event, and community co-membership has to be established through events of physical or linguistic co-presence. Clearly, one might need quite lengthy chains of evidence to connect a particular item of mutual knowledge to the physical evidence which supports it, and in a largely inductive framework, each step in the chain may go well beyond the data. Moreover, even in the case of physical co-presence, which provides the strongest evidence for mutual knowledge, powerful systems of auxiliary assumptions may have to be used in establishing a conclusion. For example, although the presence of a visible object may be self-evident to any observant, sighted person, a considerable number of auxiliary assumptions would be needed to establish mutual knowledge of it under a particular description: as a cricket match, or the coronation of Queen Elizabeth II, or even a bowl of fruit.

Given these difficulties in the identification of mutual knowledge, if identification is a prerequisite to comprehension, an obvious empirical prediction follows. The problems that arise in assessing mutual knowledge should cause corresponding problems in comprehension. In particular, when the evidence required for mutual knowledge goes well beyond straight physical co-presence, there should always be some room for doubt in the hearer's mind about whether he has correctly understood. This is not borne out by introspective evidence. It seems much easier to understand an utterance than it does to assess mutual knowledge. Moreover, an utterance such as (10) does not seem harder to understand than (11), although the mutual knowledge involved is much harder to establish inductively:

(10) I dislike the eldest Brontë sister.

(11) I dislike that girl over there.

Of course, such unsystematic introspective evidence is not enough to settle the issue. But it should at least cast doubt on the identification of context with common ground, and make it desirable to look for an alternative framework.

B. Is Mutual Knowledge a Sufficient Condition for Belonging to the Context?

As we have said, using the context in comprehension involves retrieving specific items of information. For instance, if the speaker says:

(12) I am a moslem. I don't drink alcohol,
the hearer's task is to retrieve the background information in (13):

(13) Moslems are forbidden to drink alcohol.

Given (13), (12) can be understood as both stating a fact and explaining it. Without (13), (12) would seem to state two unrelated facts, and the speaker's intention would not be understood.

In order to retrieve propositions such as (13), that may have a bearing on comprehension, some search of the context has to take place. However, given the speed of actual comprehension and the size of the common ground shared by members of the same community, it is not really possible that every proposition in the common ground is parsed and checked for a possible role in the comprehension of every utterance. For instance, in the case of (12), although speaker and hearer may have much more mutual knowledge of Christianity than of Islam, it seems likely that the hearer will search only his knowledge about Islam. Some other criterion than just belonging to common ground must be used to determine the context actually searched, reducing it to a manageable size.

Apart from manageability, there is another reason for taking a much more restrictive view of the context actually searched. The role of context in comprehension that has probably been the most discussed is in the assignment of reference. In interpreting an utterance which contains the referring expression *the door*, the hearer has to search the context in order to identify the actual door being referred to. In many cases, speaker and hearer mutually know of the existence of more than one door. However, not all of these will be actively considered as possible referents. This again suggests that the actual context used in comprehension is much smaller than the common ground.

When Clark and Marshall and others equate the context with mutual knowledge or common ground, what they have in mind is not the context actually searched but a potential context of which the actual one is a small subset. That is to say, they might grant that belonging to mutual knowledge is not a sufficient condition for a proposition's being part of the actual context, but claim that it is a necessary condition and, furthermore, the only necessary condition. If this claim were correct, it would make sense to talk of mutual knowledge as providing a potential context, smaller than the subject's encyclopaedic memory and larger than the actual context. There is no evidence or argument in the literature to show that belonging to mutual knowledge is the only necessary condition, so that the case for identifying potential context with mutual knowledge is anyway incomplete. However, there are arguments to show that it is a necessary condition, and to these we now turn.

C. Is Mutual Knowledge a Necessary Condition for Belonging to the Context?

Given that it is, if not downright impossible, at least fairly cumbersome to establish mutual knowledge, and given that mutual knowledge is not sufficient for determining the context in which an utterance has to be understood, why bother to establish it at all? Clark and Marshall (1981), while acknowledging that "it is likely to complicate matters for some time to come", argue that "mutual knowledge is an issue we cannot avoid", because

> virtually every . . . aspect of meaning and reference . . . requires mutual knowledge, which also is at the very heart of the notion of linguistic convention and speaker meaning.

The argument for this admittedly expensive claim consists in showing that, as long as background knowledge is only shared to some degree but is not fully mutual, comprehension is not guaranteed. The argument bears a strong structural similarity to earlier philosophical arguments that mutual knowledge plays a necessary role in the analysis of speaker-meaning (see, for example, Schiffer 1972, pp. 30–42).

Clark and Marshall's version of this argument involves definite reference, and revolves around episodes such as the following:

> On Wednesday morning Ann and Bob read the early edition of the newspaper, and they discuss the fact that it says that *A Day at The Races* is showing that night at the Roxy. When the late edition arrives, Bob reads the movie section, notes that the film has been corrected to *Monkey Business*, and circles it with his red pen. Later, Ann picks up the late edition, notes the correction, and recognizes Bob's circle around it. She also realizes that Bob has no way of knowing that she has seen the late edition. Later that day Ann sees Bob and asks, "Have you ever seen the movie showing at the Roxy tonight?" (p. 5)

Here, Bob is likely to misunderstand Ann's reference to the movie showing at the Roxy, because although Ann knows that Bob knows that *Monkey Business* is the film showing, she doesn't know whether Bob knows that she knows it too. More elaborate episodes involve further degrees of sharedness, and since there is no intrinsic limit on this process of elaboration, it follows that full-scale *mutual* knowledge is necessary in order to be sure that reference will be properly understood.

We believe that the unnaturalness of these examples is not accidental, and that it should have warned psychologists against following the lead of the philosophers in this area. In real life, if any such unnaturally complex situation arose, either the hearer would ask for clarifiction, or as likely as not, misunderstanding *would* occur.

The very strength of the formal argument should cast doubt on its empirical relevance. Its proponents see language as governed by a set of conventions, grammars as constructed out of sets of conventions, and conventions themselves as analysable in terms of mutual knowledge (Schiffer 1972, pp. 118–160; Lewis 1969, pp. 60–68; Clark and Carlson forthcoming, pp. 22–23). One issue here is whether grammars are best seen as collections of conventions. We see no reason for thinking that they are, but we will not dispute it here (see Smith and Wilson, 1979, pp. 14–21). But what is true is that the mutual knowledge argument formally applies as much when it comes to determining what language has been used as it does to determining what context was intended.

If someone addresses me with an utterance that has all the appearances of being an utterance in my own native language, how can I know for sure that it is one? It could belong to some entirely different language and, by coincidence, sound exactly like an utterance of mine.[3] Less fantastically, it could belong to some language that has the same phonological structures but not the same meanings as mine: it could be some distant dialect, for example. To be sure that this is not happening, I have to know that the speaker knows my native language, and knows that I know it, and knows that I know that he knows it, and so on. Moreover, it is not just mutual knowledge of my native language that would be necessary, but also of the fact that this particular utterance was made in it.

On the other hand, it is patently obvious that much, if not all, of verbal communication takes place without these conditions being satisfied. For instance, an English speaker visiting a foreign country, who walks up to some passer-by and asks "Do you speak English?" would not do so if they had mutual knowledge of English, and cannot safely do so unless they have. In other words, the tourist takes a risk. In fact we all take risks, whenever we engage in verbal communication. At this moment, we are taking the risk of being misunderstood, you are taking the risk of misunderstanding us, and yet we proceed.

What this suggests is that the formal argument is irrelevant to actual comprehension. It leaves out a simple fact: we don't need to be *sure* that a remark is, say, in English, but only to have sufficient ground for assuming that it is. The fact that it could be an utterance in English is, in almost every case, sufficient reason for thinking that it is one. It is not just that we do not need to be sure: in fact, we *could not* be sure, since mutual knowledge itself cannot be established with absolute certainty.

Similarly, it is probably correct that we could not be sure of successful disambiguation, reference assignment, recovery of the intended inferences, and so on, without mutual knowledge of the context. But what this establishes is the trivial point that we cannot be sure, not the controversial point that mutual knowledge of the context is a necessary part of comprehension. It could still be, as Clark and associates might want to argue, that the strategy of comprehension consists in aiming at certainty and trying to get as close as possible to it. This would imply that the subject takes all feasible steps which would be necessary for achieving certainty, although they could not be sufficient. This, however, is an implausible strategy: it takes only cognitive benefits into account and ignores processing costs.

Going through all the problems involved in assessing mutual knowledge in order to be sure of understanding is like paying a heavy premium to an insurance company which cannot be trusted to cover the risk insured. It is generally not worth it. The only cases where a genuine effort is made to establish mutual knowledge of the meaning, reference and implications of texts are legal documents and treatises, where the risk involved in misunderstanding is so great that the cost of reducing it is acceptable. Even then, as lawyers well know, mutual knowledge is by no means always achieved.

The formal argument that mutual knowledge is a necessary condition for comprehension applies only to perfect comprehension, and not to the imperfect form which is felt to be quite sufficient in daily life. Once this is realized, it is easy to see the many counter-examples to the mutual knowledge approach. For instance:

Ann believes that Bob does not know which film is showing tonight at the Plaza. But to annoy him, she nevertheless asks: "Have you ever seen the film showing at the Plaza tonight?". It so happens that Bob knows that the film in question is *Wuthering Heights* and knows that Ann believes that he does not know it. He answers nevertheless "Yes, I have". She understands correctly that he has seen *Wuthering Heights*, and infers that she was wrong to believe that he did not know which film was showing at the Plaza. The lack of mutual knowledge leaves room for doubt: she cannot be sure that Bob is referring to *Wuthering Heights*, but she is led to think (correctly) that he is. As a *result*, but not a *condition*, of this act of comprehension, it is mutually assumed to be known what film is showing tonight.

Or:

Bill, while travelling in Southern Europe, offers a cigarette to a peasant whom he believes to be ignorant. The peasant answers "No thank you, I have read the latest statistics". Bill is surprised, but understands correctly that the peasant wants him to take as part of the context the fact that the latest statistics show that smoking is hazardous to one's health, and to infer from that context and the peasant's answer the reason why his offer of a cigarette is declined. (Of course, Bill cannot be sure that this is what the peasant meant.) As a result of this act of comprehension, the fact that smoking is hazardous becomes mutually assumed to be known.

As these two examples show, a proposition can be included in the context although it is not part of the common ground, and indeed although it is believed not to be shared at all. It can be used in establishing reference or intended inferences. As a result of its having been so used, and only then, it will be assumed to be mutually known. Hence, a model of comprehension need not have a device for establishing the common ground as one of its sub-parts: on the contrary, the model as a whole should constitute one of the elements of a theory of how the common ground is established.

III. AN ALTERNATIVE FRAMEWORK

A. Relevance

The following objection could be made to the arguments of the last section. In identifying the language in which a remark is made, mutual knowledge is, in practice, unnecessary for a simple reason. If an utterance sounds like a sentence of English, it is safe enough to assume that it is one, because there are in almost every case no real alternatives. So although mutual knowledge would be necessary for an absolute identification, a reasonable identification can be achieved without it. In understanding a given utterance, on the other hand, there *are* alternatives. Almost every sentence is semantically ambiguous; it contains referring expressions which range over a large, perhaps infinite, domain; from the logical point of view, it has an infinite set of contextual implications in each of an indefinite number of possible contexts. Even if infinites can be trimmed down to finite numbers, there is always, for any given utterance, a large range of interpretations compatible with its semantic, referential and inferential properties. Because of this, there has to be some mechanism, whether simple or complex, which singles out the intended interpretation. What little understanding we have of this mechanism at present seems to rest on the exploitation of knowledge that is not just shared but mutual. Unless some alternative framework is provided, criticism of the mutual knowledge framework might force one to amend it, but surely not to abandon it.

We believe that an alternative framework can be developed. The basic insight on which it rests was suggested by Grice (1967; see Grice 1975, 1978 for published parts). Comprehension, he argued, involves not only a particular utterance and a particular context, but also the presumption that the speaker has tried to conform to some general standards of verbal communication. This presumption is used as a guide to the intended interpretation. The question is whether this guide is good enough for comprehension to proceed without a prior assessment of mutual knowledge: this in turn depends on how constraining the standards governing verbal communication turn out to be.

The standards actually proposed by Grice (his now famous Co-operative Principle and maxims of conversation) are not constraining enough for these purposes. They fail for two reasons: first, they are far too vague: it has never been fully specified exactly what their content is, nor exactly how they are supposed to function. However, this defect could, at least in principle, be overcome. Secondly, and more seriously, Grice's model relaxes some crucial constraints on the comprehension process by allowing the literal meaning of figurative utterances to act as no more than a loose set of hints at the intended message, rather than being a necessary part of the message itself. As a result, the number of available interpretations for every utterance is increased in an uncontrollable way (see Sperber and Wilson, 1981; Wilson and Sperber, 1981, for further discussion of these points).

We would like to propose a constraint that will be much more restrictive than Grice's. We shall argue that speakers try, and hearers expect them to try, to meet a single general standard in producing an utterance: a standard of relevance. We have developed the argument more technically and in much greater detail elsewhere (see Sperber and Wilson, forthcoming). Here we shall give only a very informal presentation; perhaps not enough to demonstrate its validity, but enough, we hope, to show that it is possible to conceive of an alternative to the mutual knowledge framework.

Thinking in general, and verbal comprehension in particular, involves drawing inferences. If inferring in these cases consisted in applying the rules of standard logic to some set of premises, an infinite process would take place: an infinite set of inferences would be drawn, most of them of no psychological interest whatsoever. For instance, from two premises 'P' and 'Q', conclusions such as 'P and P', 'P and Q', 'Q and Q', 'P or P', 'P or Q', 'Q or Q', 'P and P and P and P and P or P and Q or Q or Q' can be derived. Clearly, when not doing exercises in formal logic, people do not waste their time deriving these trivial implications. Instead, they concentrate on non-trivial deductions, of which the following are examples:

(14) Slivovitz is an alcohol
      Omar is a moslem
      Moslems don't drink alcohol
      _____

      Omar does not drink slivovitz.

(15) The bank closes at five
      It is half past five
      _____

      The bank has closed.

An adequate model of inferential processes must likewise distinguish between the infinite set of trivial inferences and the finite set of non-trivial inferences which can be drawn from a finite set of premises, and draw only the latter. In Sperber and Wilson (forthcoming) we provide a characterization of such a model. Here we shall assume the problem solved. We assume, then, that it is possible to compare two sets of premises for the number of non-trivial implications they have. We shall maintain that this is a crucial factor in assessing the relevance of an utterance.

A new utterance in a given context makes it possible to draw inferences which would not be available if either the context or the utterance were missing. We shall call these *contextual implications*. A contextual implication of an utterance is a non-trivial logical implication derivable not from the content of the utterance alone, nor from the context alone, but only from context and content combined. As an illustration, consider the following (attested) exchange:

(16) a. Flag-seller: Would you like to buy a flag for the Royal National Lifeboat Institution?
b. Passer-by: No thanks, I always spend my holidays with my sister in Birmingham.

Not everyone finds the response in (16b) immediately comprehensible. In order to understand it fully, the hearer has to supply (at least) the premises in (17), and derive the conclusion in (18):

(17) a. Birmingham is inland.
b. The Royal National Lifeboat Institution is a charity.
c. Buying a flag is one way of subscribing to a charity.
d. Someone who spends his holidays inland has no need of the services of the Royal National Lifeboat Institution.
e. Someone who has no need of the services of a charity cannot be expected to subscribe to that charity.

(18) The speaker of (16b) cannot be expected to subscribe to the Royal National Lifeboat Institution.

In our terms, (18) is a contextual implication of (16b) in a context which contains (17). It follows from (16b) and (17) take together, but from neither (16) nor (17) in isolation from each other.

What is interesting about (16b) from our point of view is the intuitive connection it reveals between being able to derive the contextual implications of an utterance and being able to see its relevance. Those who fail to see the relevance of (16b) at first sight are precisely those who have failed to derive the contextual implication in (18), and anyone who sees this implication will concede the relevance of (16b). This suggests that having contextual implications in a given context is a necessary and sufficient condition for relevance, and can be used as the basis of a definition of relevance.

However, although we could use this definition to formulate a more explicit version of Grice's maxim of relevance, there would be little point in doing so. We are looking for a constraint powerful enough to select at most a single interpretation for any utterance in context. Clearly, the mere requirement that an utterance should have some contextual implications, have some degree of relevance, is not powerful enough to do this. We would like instead to investigate the possibility that relevance is not a simple binary concept, but a matter of degree; that one can assign degrees of relevance to possible interpretations, so that speakers and hearers might be conceived of as operating not by a standard of simple relevance, but by a standard of maximal relevance.

B. Degrees of Relevance

The idea of maximal relevance might be usefully approached by an analogy. Consider the measurement of productivity. A firm with output of any value, however small, will be productive to some degree. However, when it comes to measuring productivity, it is not the value of output alone that must be taken into account, but the ratio of output to the value of capital and labour input used in producing it. Of two firms which produce the same output, it will be the one with the smaller input that is the most productive; and of two firms with the same input, it will be the one with the greatest output that is the most productive.

Similar remarks apply to the measurement of relevance. An utterance with any contextual implications, however few, will be relevant to some degree. However, when it comes to comparing degrees of relevance, of different utterances in the same context or the same utterance in different contexts, the number of contextual implications derivable is not the sole factor to be taken into account. Degrees of relevance depend on a ratio of input to output, where output is number of contextual implications, and input is amount of processing needed to derive these contextual implications; by "amount of processing" we mean some function of time and degree of attention expended. Of two utterances that take the same amount of processing, it is the one with most contextual implications that will be the more relevant; and of two utterances which have the same number of contextual implications, it is the one which takes the least amount of processing that will be the more relevant.

To illustrate, compare utterances (19)–(21) in a context consisting of (22a–c):

   (19) Susan, who has thalassemia, is getting married to Bill.

   (20) Susan is getting married to Bill, who has thalassemia.

   (21) Susan, who has thalassemia, is getting married to Bill, and 1967 was a very good year for Bordeaux wine.

(22) a. People who are getting married should consult a doctor about possible hereditary risks to their children.

    b. Two people both of whom have thalassemia should be warned against having children.

    c. Susan has thalassemia.

In this context, both (19) and (20) carry the contextual implication that Susan and Bill should consult a doctor, but (20) also carries the implication that Susan and Bill should be warned against having children. The sentences in (19) and (20) are almost identical in linguistic and lexical structure. Suppose that processing involves identifying the proposition expressed by the utterance, computing its non-trivial implications, and matching each of these against the propositions in the context to see if further non-trivial implications can be derived. Then (19) and (20) should take roughly equal amounts of processing. In this context, since (20) yields more contextual implications than (19), with the same amount of processing, it should be more relevant than (19), and this seems intuitively correct. By contrast, (19) and (21) have the single contextual implication that Susan and Bill should consult a doctor. (21) is linguistically more complex than (19). On the above assumptions about processing, (21) will thus require more processing and be predicted as less relevant in the context; again, this prediction seems to be intuitively correct.

Given this characterization of relevance in terms of number of contextual implications and amount of processing involved in deriving them, we can spell out what, we suggest, is the single principle governing every aspect of comprehension, the *principle of relevance*:

> The speaker tries to express the proposition which is the most relevant one possible to the hearer.

In ordinary circumstances, the hearer assumes that the speaker has not only tried to be as relevant as possible, but has also succeeded. The hearer therefore selects, from all the propositions (i.e. combinations of sense and reference) that the utterance could express, the most relevant one, and assumes that it is the one intended by the speaker.

However, the claim that the principle of relevance governs comprehension in general and disambiguation in particular has little empirical import as long as the context used in comprehension is not specified, and it is to this that we now turn.

C. Choosing a Context: Simplified Version

Most pragmatic accounts assume that the context for the comprehension of a given utterance is fixed in advance, and undergoes no more than minor adjustments during the comprehension process: for example, by the addition of Gricean conversational implicatures (McCawley, 1979 is an interesting exception). We want to argue, on the contrary, that the search for the interpretation on which an utterance will be most relevant involves a search for the context which will make this interpretation possible. In other words, determination of the context is not a prerequisite to the comprehension process, but a part of it. It proceeds, we suggest, as follows.

There is, to begin with, an initial context which consists of the interpretation of the immediately preceding utterance in the conversation or in the text. The hearer attempts an interpretation in this context by looking at what contextual implicatioins can be derived in it. If these are lacking or not considered sufficient to satisfy the principle of relevance, the context can be expanded several times, in three different directions. The hearer can add to the context what he remembers of utterances further back in the conversation (or in previous exchanges with the same speaker). He can add encyclopaedic knowledge which is attached in his memory to the concepts present in the utterance or in the context: for instance, in the example (19)–(21) knowledge of thalassemia, of Susan and of marriage is present in the context (22). Or he can add to the context information about whatever he is attending to at the same time as the conversation is taking place: for example, information about a football match that speaker and hearer are watching together. The hearer does not have to worry at this stage whether the additions he is making to the context belong to the common ground or not.

Each expansion of the context creates new possibilities of deriving contextual implications. On the other hand, these extensions involve an ever-increasing cost in amount of processing and, in this respect, *diminish* relevance. As a result, if an utterance is not sufficiently relevant in the initial context or a minimally extended one, it is unlikely that its relevance will be increased by further extensions of the context, even though more contextual implications may be found.

The expectation that greater relevance can be achieved by expanding the context, and with it the hearer's readiness to process further, vary with the type of discourse. In ordinary conversation, the time spent on a given utterance is rarely more than the duration of the utterance itself, and the degree of attention remains relatively low. On the other hand, a believer reading a sacred text tends to take for granted that more time spent, greater attention given, will always lead to an increase in relevance.

Generally speaking, we would suggest that the amount of processing tends to remain roughly constant throughout a stretch of discourse. If this is true, one should expect cases of over- or under-processing to occur, and indeed they do. For instance, readers and writers of scholarly works will know that the point of a dense paragraph, suitable for a professional paper but appearing without warning in the middle of textbook prose, might be missed because of underprocessing, even by readers who would have no problem understanding it otherwise. Conversely, a paragraph in textbook style appearing in a technical paper will get overprocessed and be felt to be insufficiently relevant although, if the whole paper had been written in that style, no problem of relevance need have arisen.

Given the cost of expanding the context and the lack of flexibility in amount of processing, the search for an adequate context tends to remain within a predictable and generally narrow domain. In trying to maximize relevance, the speaker must adapt to this fact, and the hearer can assume that he has. Hence, as a direct result of the principle of relevance, the context is kept down to a manageable size. Restricting it to material from the common ground is unnecessary in this respect at least.

But of course the main argument for restricting context to the common ground has to do with ensuring comprehension. We shall now show that, in this respect too, the principle of relevance makes this restriction unnecessary.

In order to feel confident that his utterance will be adequately relevant to the hearer, the speaker must have grounds for thinking that the hearer has an easily accessible context in which a sufficient number of contextual implications can be derived. One good reason for believing this might be that the required context is part of the common ground; for instance it consists of the interpretation of the three immediately preceding utterances. But this is by no means the only possibility.

The speaker may have grounds for believing that the hearer has access to the required context, without even knowing what this context consists of. For instance, if someone walks up to you in the street and asks "What time is it?", you assume that the answer you give is relevant to him, that is, that it has a number of contextual implications, without knowing at all what they are and what the context may be.

To take another example, the speaker may know some football results, say, which the hearer does not yet know of, and may believe that the hearer is generally interested in football results. The speaker can then assume that the hearer has a rich enough, easily accessible background of information in the context of which the information being provided will yield many contextual implications. What exactly the context consists of, what these implications are, the speaker does not need to know in order to act in accordance with the principle of relevance.

In neither of these examples were the contextual implications drawn by the hearer specifically intended by the speaker. They were drawn not as part of comprehension proper, but as part of a broader type of processing. However, what our theory of relevance implies is that one of the speaker's intentions (and a crucial one) is that the hearer, by recognizing the speaker's intentions, should be made capable of going beyond them and of establishing the relevance of the utterance for himself. This general intention of being relevant gives the crucial guide to recovery of the meaning, references and inferences (if any) specifically intended by the speaker. A successful act of comprehension (which is what is aimed at by both speaker and hearer) is one which allows the hearer to go beyond comprehension proper.

The speaker thus intends the hearer to draw, or at least to be able to draw, a number of inferences from his utterance. But none of these inferences need be specifically intended. Those inferences which use as premises only the utterance and propositions from the common ground may be presumed to become common ground too, and to be so used in future exchanges. However, that makes them "authorized" rather than "intended" inferences. For example, given the utterance in (23), if (24) is common ground, then presumably the inference in (25) also becomes common ground; this is so even though in uttering (23), the speaker need not have specifically intended that the hearer should infer (25):

(23) Bob is in love with Ann.

(24) Ann is a nuclear physicist.

(25) Bob is in love with a nuclear physicist.

There are two kinds of case where the speaker must assume that a *specific* piece of information will be included in the hearer's context:

cases of definite reference on the one hand, and of intended inference on the other.

In cases of definite reference, the hearer must find in the context one referent for each referring expression. In order to do so, he may have to expand the context (McCawley 1979 develops a similar suggestion). Often enough, the linguistic form of the referring expression gives a clue to the direction in which the extension is to take place: anaphora suggests going back in discourse, proper names suggest a look in the encyclopaedia, and deictics suggest a look around (compare Clark and Marshall's parallel remark, 1981, 41–44). The hearer may then test the assumption that the referents found are the ones intended. If the resulting proposition turns out to be relevant as expected, the assumption will be upheld. Otherwise the context will have to be expanded so as to include other possible referents. When, either from the outset or as a result of expansions, the context contains several possible referents for one referring expression, the principle of relevance will determine the intended one. For example, if pointing at a group of five boys, one of whom is crying, the speaker says "He has just been scolded", the one crying will be selected as the referent of "he". More contextual implications can be derived about this boy than about the other boys by including in the context the fact that he is crying and general background knowledge about crying and scolding.

In cases of intended inference, relevance depends crucially on some specific contextual implication without which the other implications (or at least many of them) cannot be derived. Then, given the principle of relevance, the hearer must assume that the speaker has specifically intended him to draw that inference. For example, consider the following dialogue:

(26) Ann: Will you have a glass of brandy?
　　　Omar: You know I am a good moslem.

If Ann knows that brandy is alcohol and that good moslems do not drink alcohol, she can infer (27):

(27) Omar will not have a glass of brandy.

She can also infer that Omar intended her to draw that specific inference, without which his utterance would not be relevant.

It may happen both in the case of reference and in the case of intended inference, that the hearer can quite easily see what contextual premise would be needed to identify the referent or to draw the intended inference; however, this premise may happen not to be included in or entailed by what he knows. In such cases, the hearer is entitled to infer from the fact that the utterance has been made, together with the principle of relevance, that the speaker took for granted that the hearer would include this premise in the context for comprehension.

Consider, for example, the utterance in (28) and the contextual premise in (29), which is needed to establish the relevance of (28):

(28) I have read John's novel. The character of Eliza is so moving!

(29) There is a character called Eliza in John's novel.

If the hearer of (28), not having read John's novel, does not know (29), he is entitled to infer it on the basis of his presumption that the speaker of (28) has spoken relevantly. This provides the hearer with a referent for the proper name "Eliza".

Or consider the dialogue in (30) and the contextual premise (31):

(30) Ann: Did you like the book you were reading?

Bob: I don't much like science fiction.

(31) The book Bob was reading is a book of science fiction.

If Ann did not know (31), she can infer it from the fact that without it, Bob's answer would be irrelevant.

The fact that missing premises will be supplied in this way by the hearer can be exploited by the speaker with rhetorical intent. Suppose, for instance, that it was mutual knowledge between Bob and Ann that the book Bob was reading was Chomsky's *Syntactic Structures*. Then Bob's reply to Ann would suggest to her that Bob took for granted that she already believed, or would have no difficulty in accepting, that *Syntactic Structures* is science fiction.

With or without rhetorical intent, these missing premises correspond to Grice's conversational implicatures, and can be derived from the principle of relevance alone, without recourse to the other Gricean maxims.

D. Choosing a Context: Some Refinements

Up to now, we have been considering a simplified version of a model of comprehension based on a single principle of relevance. In this simplified version, the hearer assumes not only that the speaker has tried to make his utterance maximally relevant from the hearer's point of view, but that he has succeeded. In order to do this, the speaker must make some more or less specific assumptions about the contextual propositions that the hearer has access to or can infer. In the simplified model, the hearer assumes that the speaker's assumptions were correct. It seems to us that most of the time in real life, this would be enough to ensure successful comprehension.

People are fairly accurate in the assumptions they make about what others know. Also, in the case of speech, the speaker can make sure that his assumptions are correct by directly expressing any propositions that he is not sure the hearer would be able to add to the context by himself. Moreover, if the speaker has been significantly wrong in his assumptions, what is likely to happen is not that the hearer will understand something other than the intended propositions: it is rather that the hearer will fail to arrive at a plausible interpretation at all, and will, if he cares enough, ask for repair. It takes quite a coincidence for an utterance to have among its possible interpretations one which the speaker thought would be the most relevant, and a genuinely different one which *is* the most relevant for the hearer. As we noted above, the fact that some utterance closely corresponds to a sentence of English is strong evidence that it was intended as one. Similarly, though to a lesser extent, the fact that one interpretation of an utterance stands out by its greater relevance is strong evidence that it is the intended one.

Nevertheless, for an adequate model of comprehension, we need the principle of relevance as stated: the speaker *tries* to express the most relevant proposition; rather than a simplified version: the speaker expresses the most relevant proposition. Otherwise the model would predict a number of mistakes in comprehension that do not occur in any systematic way.

Take, first, the simple case where the proposition intended by the speaker is completely irrelevant because the hearer already holds this proposition to be true. For instance, the hearer already knew the football results that the speaker was trying to inform him of. In the simplified model, the hearer should fail to identify the intended proposition, and would probably believe that he has not understood. In fact, the full principle of relevance provides the criterion for comprehension: the intended interpretation is generally the only one that the speaker might have thought would be maximally relevant to the hearer, and hence is the only one compatible with the principle of relevance.

A more interesting case is when there is some proposition easily accessible to the hearer which could enormously increase the relevance of the utterance for him but which, being unknown to the speaker, could not possibly have been intended to play a role in the interpretation. In the simplified model, the hearer should choose the interpretation which maximizes relevance for him, and should thus misunderstand the speaker's intentions and the utterance itself.

However, the full principle of relevance provides a natural check on the conclusion that a certain background proposition was intended to be used. Suppose that to achieve a particular interpretation for an utterance a certain background premise would have to be used; and suppose that if this premise had been intended by the speaker, the fact that he had intended it to be used would be more relevant than the content of the utterance itself. This interpretation would automatically violate the principle of relevance because, by hypothesis, the proposition expressed by the utterance was not the most relevant proposition available to the speaker in the circumstances. Hence, this interpretation could not have been intended by a speaker attempting to observe the principle of relevance.

For example, imagine a student who, by breaking into the examiner's room at night, secretly knows that he has failed an exam. His professor, who has seen the results but is unaware of the break-in, says to him in casual conversation:

(32) Everyone who failed the exam will have his case considered at the next faculty meeting.

It is clear that by using the information in (33), the student can considerably increase the relevance of the utterance to him by deriving the contextual implication (34) rather than just (35):

(33) I have failed the exam.

(34) My case will be considered at the next faculty meeting.

(35) If I have failed the exam, my case will be considered at the next faculty meeting.

Indeed, he will certainly derive this implication. However, he will know that this could only be the *intended* interpretation if the professor had intended him to use (33) and derive the contextual implication (34). But if he *had* intended him to use it, he would have had to know that the student had secretly broken into the examiner's room, and the fact that he knew this would clearly be more relevant than (32) itself. The interpretation based on (33) could therefore not have been intended in these circumstances by a speaker observing the principle of relevance. Contrast this with the cases where speaker and hearer have already established (33) as part of their mutual knowledge and where, clearly, the speaker would intend the hearer to use (33) and derive (34).

Or take the case where an utterance has two interpretations, one with a normal degree of relevance and the other with considerably more than that. In the simplified model, the latter should be chosen. However, the full principle of relevance will (correctly) generally select the former. For instance, imagine two mothers chatting, and one saying to the other:

(36) My son has grown another foot.

This can mean either that her son has grown bigger or that he has grown an extra limb. The second interpretation is of course much more relevant. However, if this *were* the interpretation intended, then the principle of relevance would have been grossly violated. The speaker could indeed, if her son had become three-footed, produce a much more relevant utterance than a mere statement of the fact. She could elaborate in many ways while maintaining the level of relevance quite high, and not leave it to the hearer to work out all the crucial implications and raise all the questions that such an extraordinary fact would involve. Hence the full principle of relevance unquestionably selects the less dramatic and less relevant interpretations in such a case.

However, there are cases where the principle of relevance would not only fail to prevent mistakes, but would actually cause them to occur. If such mistakes do in fact occur, then the model of comprehension based on this principle is vindicated. We shall give two brief illustrations of these predicted mistakes.

We have argued that relevance is a function of the amount of processing and hence of the accessibility of the context required to derive contextual implications. Consider first the case of very touchy people who are easily hurt by the most innocent remark. Their behaviour and mistakes are easily predicted by the principle of relevance on the simple additional assumption that for them propositions about themselves and about what others may think of them constitute an inordinately rich and easily accessible potential context. It is an area which they are permanently attending to, and which therefore always provides a possible extension of the context. It will be appealed to and exploited whenever there is a chance. Such people will select the most relevant interpretation for them: that is, one whose main implications are about them. The checks that the principle of relevance provides in other cases are not likely to work here. Often, if the paranoid interpretation were correct, the speaker could, and hence should, have developed his remark and made it still more relevant. On the other hand, as the hearer will know, there are social considerations and rules which may have prevented the speaker from being too explicit in his criticism.

Similarly, it is almost impossible to convince people who see a sexual intention in every other utterance that they are wrong: they select the most relevant interpretation for them, and easily account for its under-exploitation on the part of the speaker by considerations of propriety. Notice that if greater attention were paid to mutual knowledge, such mistakes would occur less.

A second example of a type of mistake predicted by the principle of relevance is the interpretation of the diviner's words by the consultant. Anthropologists have puzzled about why so many people keep trusting and consulting diviners. They have given a partial explanation by showing how the diviner's words were generally vague and open to a variety of interpretations, rather than downright wrong. It still remains to be explained why people should seek vague information from a diviner. The principle of relevance predicts that the consultant will automatically find the most relevant interpretation, and take it to be the one intended. Even though the consultant may have his doubts about the particular diviner he is consulting and want to test him (as is often reported to happen), it is enough that he should consider that divination is possible for the checks normally provided by the principle of relevance not to work. The diviner might know everything; hence there are no constraints at all on the premises he may have intended the consultant to use. He may have intended premises to be used that will only be available to the consultant at some time in the future. There is also a standard style of delivery and a standard degree of elaboration in the diviner's discourse which are taken to be part of the divinatory procedure. Hence the underexploitation on the part of the diviner of the interpretation arrived at by the consultant is no check on this interpretation.

IV. CONCLUSION

To return to the issue of mutual knowledge, we would argue that the best evidence for mutual knowledge (although it is by no means watertight) is not physical co-presence but rather comprehension: while we may construct very different descriptions of the same physical stimulus, adequate comprehension implies near identity of interpretation between interlocutors. Thus, if I understand what you say and give you no reason to doubt that I have understood it, then the interpretation of your utterance and all the contextual premises which were crucially used in arriving at it, can be assumed to be mutually known to us.

It takes very odd cases, such as those surveyed in Schiffer and Clark and Marshall (cf. supra) for a mistake in the assessment of mutual knowledge to cause a mistake in comprehension. This is not surprising if, as we have been arguing, mutual knowledge is inferred from comprehension rather than the other way round. On the contrary, mistakes in comprehension almost automatically cause mistakes in the assessment of mutual knowledge. Trivially, I will take my mistaken interpretation of your utterance to be part of common knowledge from the moment I have formed it.

Less trivially, the consultant assumes that the most relevant interpretation of the diviner's words, and all the premises used in arriving at it, were part of the diviner's knowledge from the start, and are mutually known from the moment he "understands" them. If consultants behaved as the mutual knowledge theorist would have them behave, they should assess mutual knowledge first. According to the mutual knowledge model, when they have doubts about the diviner they are consulting, and decide to test him, they should be easily able to see the vagueness of the predictions made, and should lose faith in each diviner they put to the test. Since diviners and divination have fared rather well, it is arguable that we should instead give up those models of comprehension based on an identification of context with mutual knowledge.

NOTES

1. We would like to thank Neil Smith for much valued encouragement and advice during the writing of this paper.
2. In an interesting paper, Hobbs (1979) has argued that a single general principle of coherence is involved in every aspect of interpretation. Although our proposals differ in detail, their aims are clearly similar.
3. This possibility is in fact the basis of Stoppard's play *Dogg's Hamlet Cahoot's Macbeth*, ed.

Chapter 2

Comments and Replies

On a Notion of Relevance*
Comments on Sperber and Wilson's Paper

Gerald Gazdar and David Good

In their paper, Sperber and Wilson (S&W) sketch a framework which is intended to provide a basis for a theory of pragmatics. This framework crucially relies on a notion of relevance rather than one of mutual knowledge (MK), the latter being explicitly rejected as a defining characteristic of the context in which comprehension occurs. In what follows, we shall argue that their notion of relevance gives rise to a number of apparently intractable problems. We will begin by providing a formal reconstruction of their proposals in order to make explicit that which is, for the most part, only implicit in their paper. The central pivot of their framework is the following:

(1) *Principle of Relevance*

The speaker tries to express the proposition which is the most relevant one possible to the hearer.

For S&W, relevance (RELV) is, in effect, a function which takes a proposition (P) and a hearer as arguments and returns a number as value. For their purposes, however, hearers decompose into an immediate context (C) "which consists of the interpretation of the immediately preceding utterance in the conversation or in the text" (p. 76) and a memory (M). Actually, what we are calling M conflates the hearer's memory of what happened earlier in the discourse, information about whatever is being attended to at the same time as the conversation, and the hearer's encyclopaedic knowledge. S&W distinguish these three things, but the distinctions have no bearing on any of the argumentation that follows below. Thus relevance can be taken to be the function $RELV(P,C,M)$. The value of $RELV(P,C,M)$ is the "ratio of input to output, where output is number of contextual implications, and input is amount of processing needed to derive these contextual implications" (p. 74). We let $NTCI(P,C')$ be the set of non-trivial contextual implications derivable from a proposition P and an augmented context C'. Then the output mentioned above is the cardinality (CARD) of this set, i.e. $CARD(NTCI(P,C'))$. The input is the amount of processing needed to get to the augmented context C' given the immediate context C (where $C \subseteq C'$) and the memory M. Let us notate this as $PROC(C',C,M)$. For simplicity, and following S&W (p. 74), we shall simply ignore that component of processing cost that varies with the size of $CARD(NTCI(P,C'))$: nothing said below hinges on it, and inclusion of it would only make the equation that follows less transparent. We may now define S&W's notion of relevance as follows:

$$\textbf{(2)} \quad RELV(P,C,M) = \frac{CARD(NTCI(P,C'))}{PROC(C',C,M)}$$

And this in turn allows us to formulate their principle of relevance in a more precise manner:

(3) *Principle of Relevance*

The speaker of an utterance U which is open to interpretations P1, P2, . . . , Pn, intends to convey to a hearer $\langle C, M \rangle$ that proposition Pi, $1 \le i \le n$, which the speaker believes will ensure that $RELV(Pi,C,M) > RELV(Pj,C,M)$ for all $j \ne i$, $1 \le j \le n$.

Now let us turn to consider the question as to whether any of the above is meaningful or useful. To arrive at $NTCI(P,C')$ we need, crucially, a definition of non-trivial inference. S&W do not provide this, instead they refer us to a presently unavailable work of their own and remark that "here we shall assume the problem solved" (p. 72).

There are good reasons to be sceptical about this assumption. Consider the following non-trivial bit of reasoning:

(4) $(P \vee Q) \rightarrow R$
P

_____

R

This can be shown to be valid as follows:

(5) $(P \vee Q) \rightarrow R$
P
$P \vee Q$ [disjunction introduction]

_____

R   [modus ponens]

The crucial point to notice here is that in order to arrive at a non-trivial inference, we have employed a trivial inference rule, namely disjunction introduction. Exactly the same point could be made with examples involving the rule of conjunction introduction, which S&W also wish to expunge from their logic (see p. 72). Such examples impale S&W on the horns of a dilemma: if they continue to exclude disjunction introduction from their non-trivial inference logic then they may have no way of generating intuitively non-trivial inferences such as that in (4), whereas if they allow disjunction introduction (and conjunction introduction) back in, then they will generate all kinds of intuitively trivial inferences.[1]

Allowing either conjunction introduction or disjunction introduction back into the logic will also entail that infinitely many inferences can be drawn from any set of premises. But S&W have to assume that $NTCI(P,C')$ is of finite cardinality, otherwise a proposition that gives rise to an infinite set of non-trivial contextual inferences runs the risk of being infinitely relevant given the definition above. S&W recognize this (p. 72), and appear to be assuming that the finite cardinality of $NTCI(P,C')$ will follow from their definition of non-trivial inference, whatever that may be. If it does not, then they are in trouble. And if it does, then so much the worse for their definition of non-trivial inference. Intuitively, it is obvious that a finite set of premises may give rise to an infinite set of non-trivial inferences. Suppose you are given two premises, one an equation characterizing the set of integer squares, and the other which claims that all integer squares have some property Q. This enables you to make the following non-trivial inferences: $Q(1)$, $Q(4)$, $Q(9)$, $Q(16)$, ...

Let us make the counterfactual assumption that these problems can be overcome, and that we can arrive at finite cardinalities for all sets of non-trivial inferences. S&W write "we assume, then, that it is possible to compare two sets of premises for the *number* of non-trivial implications that they have. We shall maintain that this is a *crucial factor* in assessing the relevance of an utterance" (p. 72, our emphasis). Notice first that it makes no sense to compare the cardinality of sets of propositions until one has defined a notion of atomic proposition, otherwise all such sets could be reduced to cardinality one simply by conjunction of all their members. Secondly, a moment's reflection reveals that the cardinality of a set of inferences is a number which has no bearing on relevance. Consider the example in (6):

(6) George Best walked to the ball.

Now this sentence can be interpreted as denoting either a proposition about how George Best got to a formal party or dance, or a proposition about how he approached a spherical object used in sport. Let us suppose that, for a given hearer, who knows, among other things, that George Best is a party-going footballer, the first proposition leads to a NTCI set of cardinality 93 for one unit of processing and the second proposition leads to a set of cardinality 87 for one unit of processing. So what? These numbers obviously have nothing to do with the relative relevance of the two interpretations.[2]

When this point was made after the oral presentation of their paper, one author acknowledged it and claimed that they were only concerned with cases where one NTCI set was a subset of the other. But if this restriction is to be taken seriously, then it vitiates their entire programme. The proper superset relation replaces cardinality as the axis of comparison. Without cardinalities we have no way of formulating definition (2) to yield *degrees* of relevance. And the relation "more relevant than" can only be defined for the following very special cases:

(7) i.   Both NTCI sets are identical, but
　　　ii. one took more processing than the other.
(8) i.   One NTCI set is a proper subset of the other, and
　　　ii. the smaller set took no less processing than the larger one.

Correspondingly, the relation "exactly as relevant as" can only be defined for the following special case:

(9) i.   Both NTCI sets are identical, and
　　　ii. both required an identical amount of processing time.

Neither relevance relation can be defined for any of the following circumstances:

(10) i.   One NTCI set is a proper subset of the other, but
　　　ii. the larger set took more processing.
(11) The NTCI sets intersect but neither is a subset of the other.
(12) The NTCI sets are disjoint.

A relevance relation which fails to cover these cases hardly deserves the name.

It is quite clear that S&W intend their theory to provide a route to disambiguation via comparison of the relevance of the readings: "the principle of relevance governs comprehension in general and disambiguation in particular" (p. 75). But the typical cases of lexical ambiguity (as with *ball* in (6), above) or syntactic ambiguity (as in (13), below) will all give rise to the situations described in (11) and (12) above.

(13) We are visiting relatives.

And these situations cannot be catered for when the superset relation replaces cardinality as the axis of comparison. As far as we can see, there is no escape from this dilemma: the cardinality route leads nowhere, and the superset route leads to a definition of relative relevance that has nothing to say about most of the interesting cases (e.g. S&W's example (36)).

Actually it is by no means obvious that the revised analysis even works for the cases it covers. Consider the utterance of (14b) in the immediate context of the preceding utterance (14a):

(14) a. Kim bit Sandy.

b. Kim is a dog.

Utterance (14b) can denote either of the two propositions glossed in (15) in virtue of the ambiguity of *dog*:

(15) i. Kim is a member of the species *Canis*.

ii. Kim is a male member of the species *Canis*.

These two readings will give rise to the NTCI sets shown in (16i) and (16ii), respectively:

(16) i. {A member of the species *Canis* bit Sandy}

ii. {A member of the species *Canis* bit Sandy,
A male member of the species *Canis* bit Sandy}

The NTCI set (16i) is a proper subset of the NTCI set (16ii), from which fact it follows, given that condition (8ii) is met, that (15ii) is the interpretation that maximizes relevance and hence the one that the hearer should take to be the speaker's intended meaning. But, intuitively, this seems to be the wrong prediction in this instance. Of course, if condition (8ii) is not met then the revised analysis simply makes no prediction at all about this case.

Let us now leave the problems with the numerator in (2), and turn our attention to the denominator, namely $PROC(C',C,M)$. This, it will be recalled, stands for the amount of processing needed to expand the immediate context C, given memory M, to the augmented context C' from which non-trivial inferences will be derived (it is not excluded that $C' = C$, of course). Notice that the variable C' is not an argument of RELV in definition (2) and thus is free in the definiens. The consequence of this is that RELV will not provide some unique number as its value, but rather a number for every value of C'. Clearly this complicates the business of comparing the relevance of propositions. For example, there is no reason to believe that for every proposition P, immediate context C, and memory M, there will be some unique C' which provides for a maximum value for the definiens in (2). S&W seem to be aware that there is some kind of problem with C', and they suggest that "the amount of processing tends to remain roughly constant throughout a stretch of discourse" (p. 77). Let us take this suggestion seriously and assume that there is some discourse-dependent processing constant K. Then we can reformulate (2) as follows:

(17) $RELV(P,C,M) = CARD(NTCI(P,C'))/K$
where K is a constant and $PROC(C',C,M) = K$.

But this reformulation still does not guarantee the existence of some unique C' for given P, C, and M, which will maximize the numerical value of $CARD(NTCI(P,C'))/K$. Notice that even if we eliminate the context expansion component of their framework and assume that C' is always identical to C, thus leaving the marginal processing costs we earlier ignored, we still cannot be sure that $CARD(NTCI(P_i,C))/K$ (where $1 \leq i \leq n$) will have a unique maximum value for some P_i out of a set of possible interpretations $P1, P2, \ldots, Pn$. Thus their framework fails to achieve their goal of providing a mechanism "powerful enough to select at most a single interpretation for any utterance in context" (p. 73).

S&W represent themselves as proposing a real-time on-line model of utterance comprehension, and their conception of psychological process is one of functional simplicity supported by extensive processing power. The hearer generates a set of candidate readings,[3] and ascertains the value of RELV for each of these in C, the context provided by the interpretation of the prior utterance, and each successive expansion of that context. The reading/context pairing which produces the highest value for RELV is then offered to the next part of the system, which, *inter alia,* checks on whether the speaker could conceivably have had the knowledge that such an interpretation would presume.

Clearly, such a procedure would require prodigious processing resources. They correctly note that "there is always . . . a large range of interpretations compatible with [an utterance's] semantic, referential and inferential properties" (p. 71), and each of these must be assessed in C and its successive expansions. S&W recognize that this would require much work on the part of any system that implemented their model, but unfortunately, the cost of these operations is likely to be greater than even they believe. They propose that "the context can be expanded several times, in three different directions" (p. 76), with each direction being taken as unidimensional. Taking, for example, their (19), reproduced as (18) below, the context may be expanded in several different ways, a fact that they recognize, but the implications of which they do not draw.

(18) Susan, who has thalassemia, is getting married to Bill.

On the first expansion, the context may be augmented by adding a piece of the available information about Susan, Bill, thalassemia, or the act of getting married. Under each of these headings there will be a wealth of knowledge, and so the number of possible expansions will be extremely large, even at the first step. At the next expansion, the number of possibilities will be of the same order of magnitude, and so on. The end result of a series of expansions will be a set of possible contexts whose cardinality is equal to the sum of a geometric progression of truly awesome proportions.

S&W correctly note that the subset of the encyclopaedic knowledge which is classifiable as mutual knowledge would be too unwieldy as a context for utterance processing (p. 66), so they must accept that the larger set will also be unmanageable. In an attempt to limit this processing task, they claim that the context will only be expanded "if [the pragmatic implications] are lacking or not considered sufficient" (p. 76), and that for a particular type of discourse there will only be a certain amount of processing per utterance (p. 77).[4]

These two suggestions may be characterized as "if after n milliseconds $CARD(NTCI(P,C'))$ has not reached a certain value then expand the context", and "after n milliseconds assume that the candidate reading with the highest value for RELV is the intended reading". As heuristics, these would, in all probability, not be particularly useful. Restricting search time merely means that the candidate readings that are assessed first are more likely to be assigned a higher value for RELV, but there can be no guarantee that these are more likely to represent the intended interpretation. To optimize the operation of these procedures would require that the most likely reading/context pairing would be processed first. Such a tactic is not available though since it would require at least a partial solution to the problem of finding the context that their machinery was intended to solve.

Taking the interpretation of the immediately preceding utterance as the core of the context also induces certain problems. Consider (19), (20), (21) and (22);

(19) A1. Are you coming tonight?

B1. Can I bring someone with me?

A2. Sure.

B2. I'll be there.

From Schegloff (1972, 78)

(20) A1. And a good-looking girl comes up to you and asks you y'know,

B1. Gi(hh)rl asks you to-

C1. Well its happened a lotta times,

B2. Okay okay go ahead.

A2. So he says "no".

From Jefferson (1972, 322)

(21) A1. But if your grammar collapses NIC and ECP, then how do you deal with Italian pseudo-clefts?

B1. Here, try some of this sixty-seven Bordeaux.

A2. Thanks.

B2. Well, it's quite easy really. . . .

(22) Mother. I must say you've been looking a little plumper since you've been going out with that Williams boy.

Daughter. My I do like that dress you're wearing. Is it new?

In (19), B2 is relevant to A1 which is three utterances back in the conversation. In (20) a "side-sequence", B1–B2, intervenes and A2 relates more to A1 than B2 which precedes it. In (21), the meal time conversation of Government-binding theoreticians is interrupted to offer the wine, but clearly B2 relates to A1. (22) is an instance of the use of a *non sequitur* to avoid a difficult or embarrassing issue.[5] Ultimately S&W's context expansion policy will derive a context which includes the appropriate utterance, assuming the discourse processing constant doesn't induce a stop condition, but presumably at a great processing cost. However, unless some way is found to selectively eliminate redundant items from the augmented context, the value of RELV will be greatly diminished as PROC will be greatly increased. If the value of RELV is our only guide to the status of the associated context, which eliminations to make can only be decided by attempting the elimination of items singly, and in combination. This will clearly magnify the already onerous processing task. As it stands, their model must predict that (19)–(22) are cases where there will be many difficulties in comprehension. Typically, this does not seem to be the case.

Undoubtedly, these particular problems, which derive from the size of the processing task, could be overcome, by the addition of a few judiciously chosen heuristics.[6] It is hard though to imagine what useful heuristics they could propose that would not, as we have already suggested, smuggle into their theory an alternative definition of how the context is found, and thus how relevance is defined. The only permissible heuristics would be those which depended on the number of NTCI's derived and the amount of processing time required. The heuristics could not be sensitive to the content of the NTCI's without violating the whole spirit of S&W's enterprise, which is to define relevance quantitatively, rather than qualitatively.

Not only does S&W's theory seem implausible when we consider the hearer's task, it also has unpalatable consequences for our conception of the speaker. We have indicated the enormity of the processing load for the hearer, but that which would face the speaker would be even greater. Given the pursuit of maximum relevance, and working under the assumption that the hearer will assume this in processing the utterance, the speaker must attempt to replicate, more or less,[7] those computations that the hearer will undertake, to discover the figures that will be assigned to the possible interpretations, and thus which one will be taken as the intended one. But this only represents a part of that which the speaker has to do. The utterance actually produced is only one member of the larger set of things that could have been said. The speaker has a variety of options in the choice of lexical items, syntax and prosody, at the very least. The on-line availability of these options to the speaker is attested to by their appearance in certain kinds of speech error, see Meringer and Mayer (1895), and Fromkin (1973) for examples. Presumably, the relevance of each of these, and its possible interpretations, must be assessed. If, under their view, comprehension will take a long time, then production will take far longer.

One way out of this would be to claim that the speaker produces an utterance by a route which does not use knowledge of how the hearer would proceed, relying instead on a radically different mechanism. Not only would this manoeuvre produce a need to account for the apparent fit between a speaker's and a hearer's conception of relevance, it would also require the speaker to ignore the experience of being a hearer. As such, it has a certain *prima facie* implausibility.

As the reader will have realized by now, there is something very strange indeed about the role played by processing time in S&W's theory. It makes perfectly good sense to think of examining inferences *vs* processing time graphs in the abstract in order to find maxima. But it does not make any sense in a real-time on-line model: in order to compare processing times, one has to do processing. But if one has to do the processing in order to discover the best point at which to stop processing, then the information gained cannot be exploited to economize on that operation itself. If one is engaged in the kind of search of encyclopaedic memory that S&W invoke for context-expansion, one clearly cannot predict in advance at what point some gobbet of information will suddenly trigger a whole batch of non-trivial inferences. If one was in a position to predict this, then presumably the search itself would be unnecessary.

S&W's crucial dependence on the notion of processing cost for memory access deprives their framework of whatever empirical content it might otherwise have had. It is hardly controversial to observe that psychologists know much less about the organization of memory than logicians know about inference or linguists know about syntax. Claims to the effect that one class of propositions is easier to access than another are not, in general, open to empirical test at the present time. With this in mind, consider the following example:

(23) Sue has married Bill, who is a Mason.

Now, intuitively, this seems to be a relevant thing to say to person A who is known to be obsessed with Masonry but actually knows almost nothing about it. This person will not be able to derive many non-trivial contextual implications from the utterance of (23). However, intuitively, it will not be as relevant a thing to say to person B who knows all about Masonry but is completely disinterested in the topic. Such a person will, nevertheless, be in a position to derive numerous non-trivial contextual implications from the utterance of (23) (e.g. Bill belongs to a lodge, Bill has participated in such and such rites, etc.). When this example was raised after the oral presentation of S&W's paper, one author denied that it constituted a counter-example to their characterization of relevance on the grounds that person A, being obsessed with Masonry, would find his or her facts about the topic much easier to access from memory than person B, whose disinterest in the topic would make his or her many facts harder to access. Consequently, it was claimed, S&W's model would make the right predictions in this case since the ratio of implications to processing time would be higher for A than for B. But if this is a legitimate response to putative counter-examples, then their approach is unfalsifiable: as of now, we have no way of checking either the access times or the resulting cardinality to time ratios. S&W appear to have bought psychological reality at the cost of empirical vacuity.

The point where S&W began was the rejection of MK as a basis for context, and it is with this issue that we will conclude. They offer their framework as an alternative to that suggested by MK theorists such as Clark and Marshall (1981). In so doing, they have refrained from using the epistemological status (w.r.t. MK) of an item as a guide to the construction of the context. In expanding the context ". . . The hearer does not have to worry at this stage whether the additions he is making . . . belong to the common ground or not" (p. 76). But, given their framework of assumptions, it seems somewhat perverse not to make reference to the MK status of a proposition when engaged in the process of context expansion, thereby diminishing the processing load discussed above, especially since, as they implicitly acknowledge (see pp. 78, 82), such information has to be available at some subsequent point.

Paradoxically, we note that despite their protestations, S&W's theory crucially presupposes a kind of MK that has never been suggested before, namely the MK of relevance calculations. As we have seen, in order to achieve relevance, the speaker has to do addressee-perspective relevance calculations. And the addressee, in order to work out the intended meaning of an utterance, has to do speaker-perspective relevance calculations. But included in the latter are addressee-perspective relevance calculations, and included in those are speaker-perspective relevance calculations. And thus speaker and addressee must embark on a regress that is strikingly reminiscent of the MK regress, but somehow much less plausible.

NOTES

* We are grateful to Herb Clark and Rob van der Sandt for relevant conversations, and to Jon Cunningham, Pat Hayes, Phil Johnson-Laird, Ewan Klein and Aaron Sloman for their comments on the first draft of this paper. Since completing this paper, we

have discovered that many of the points we develop below have also been made independently by Stephen Levinson in unpublished work.

1. One might attempt to escape from this dilemma by stipulating that non-trivial inferences are those that employ the application of at least one non-trivial inference rule (e.g. modus ponens) in their derivation. But that will only work if one can find some way to rule out derivations that contain vacuous or redundant applications of non-trivial inference rules. And that, in turn, seems likely to get us into decidability problems given that the logic employs quantifiers.

2. As Phil Johnson-Laird has pointed out to us, such numbers do play a role in Bar-Hillel and Carnap's (1953) theory of semantic information. If S&W were attempting to reconstruct Grice's Maxim of Quantity ("Be informative!"), as opposed to his Maxim of Relevance ("Be relevant!"), then their use of cardinalities might deserve slightly more serious attention. However, it is worth noting that the Bar-Hillel and Carnap theory gets into considerable difficulties once one allows one's logic to contain quantifiers (see Hintikka (1973) for discussion of the issue).

3. Logically, generation of a set of candidate readings must precede S&W's assessment procedure, and there is thus an issue about how this set is arrived at. Clearly it must be done by a relatively simple mechanism since if it included relevance-based procedures for restricting the set, then it would be undertaking part of the task that S&W assign to the rest of their machinery. They do not address this problem, and we are given no grounds for believing that they have a solution to it.

4. They also claim that, in general, since extensions of the context increase processing cost, "if an utterance is not sufficiently relevant in the initial context or a minimally extended one, it is unlikely that its relevance will be increased by further extensions of the context" (p. 76). This remark may be interpreted in two ways.

Clearly, the probability of a particular expansion significantly increasing _or_ decreasing the achieved value of RELV will diminish with successive expansions. If we take dCARDi as the additional number of NTCI's derived from the i'th expansion, and dPROCi as the processing cost of that expansion, then the value of RELV(n) (i.e. the value of RELV for n expansions), taking the creation of the initial context as expansion number one, may be stated as in (i);

$$\text{(i) RELV}(n) = \frac{\sum\limits_{i=1}^{i=n} dCARDi}{\sum\limits_{i=1}^{i=n} dPROCi}$$

If after nine expansions, RELV equals 50 and the tenth expansion requires the same mean processing effort, but produces twice the mean number of NTCI's, RELV will increase to 55. However, if the same thing happens on the twentieth expansion, RELV will only increase to 52.5. As the number of expansions increases, more extreme values of dCARDi for given dPROCi will be needed to produce the same effect on RELV, and the more extreme the value, the less likely it is to occur. So we can see that on this interpretation of the remark quoted above, the reader of sacred texts who extracts more and more relevance the longer he or she peruses them (p. 77) provides a counter-example to their analysis. The longer one spends on a text, the less likely it is that a significant increase in RELV will result.

Alternatively, if we focus simply on the direction of a change and not its magnitude, they may be interpreted as proposing that the probability of obtaining a value for dCARDi/dPROCi greater than RELV, is less than the probability of dCARDi/dPROCi being equal to or smaller than RELV, in those instances where the initial value of RELV does not reach some critical level. If these probabilities are conditioned by the initial value of RELV, then (19)–(22) stand as counter-examples, because the key turns are not relevant in the context of the preceding utterance, and therefore will presumably generate low initial values of RELV. This problem aside, if the probability of dCARDi/dPROCi being less than or equal to RELV is greater than 0.5, and the procedure is to be guided by probabilities, then any expansion of the context would be more likely to decrease RELV, and would therefore not be initiated.

S&W could avoid this criticism of the second interpretation by claiming that these probabilities vary over time, such that it is only after n milliseconds that the probability of dCARDi/dPROCi being less than or equal to RELV rises above 0.5. However, since they offer no way of specifying either fixed or varying values of these probabilities, neither these claims nor their possible rejoinders are open to conceptual or empirical examination and we shall accordingly ignore them henceforth.

5. It is not clear from their paper as to how their model would handle a *non sequitur*. The daughter's reply is not relevant, and generates inferences consequent upon that fact. It is hard to see how their system for generating NTCI's could ever handle such cases. Notice that they cannot simply dismiss such everyday examples as "matters of performance, not competence", since S&W take pragmatics to be a theory of performance, rather than a theory of competence.

6. The form of an utterance will also guide the processing, but clearly this can only be of limited value to a system defined in terms of processing cost rather than content.

7. "More or less" because, as they rightly observe, comprehension can only be guaranteed by identical knowledge bases, and these would render communication redundant.

Reply to Gazdar and Good

Dan Sperber and Deirdre Wilson

Gazdar and Good raise a number of interesting questions about the formal adequacy, psychological significance and terminological appropriateness of our account of relevance. We would like to concentrate on these questions here, and ignore or deal only briefly with a number of further issues, in particular those raised by their rather inaccurate formalization of our proposals.[1]

I. Defining Contextual Implications

The notion of contextual implication is fundamental to our framework not only from the formal point of view, as part of our definition of relevance, but also from the psychological point of view. We define the contextual implications of a proposition by means of a non-standard deductive system whose output is a finite set of non-trivial implications which we take to correspond to the implications actually derivable by spontaneous human reasoning processes. Gazdar and Good question our approach on two grounds: first, that our system fails to yield certain intuitively valid non-trivial implications (see their examples (4) and (5)); second, that the set of intuitively valid non-trivial implications is in any case not finite but infinite (see p. 90).

As regards the first point, we share their intuition that premises (1a) and (1b), for example, yield the valid non-trivial conclusion (1c):

(1) a. If Susan is elected to Oxford or Cambridge, she'll have to sell her flat in London.
   b. Susan has been elected to Oxford.
   c. Susan will have to sell her flat in London.

Gazdar and Good believe that this conclusion must be derived by interposing a step of vel-introduction (1b′) between (1b) and (1c):

(1) b'. Susan has been elected to Oxford or Cambridge.

However, there is an alternative derivation which would be possible in our system and would involve no appeal to a rule of *vel*-introduction. This would involve converting (1a) to its logical equivalent (1a') and proceeding to (1a") by *and*-elimination:

(1) a'. If Susan has been elected to Oxford, she'll have to sell her flat in London, and if Susan has been elected to Cambridge, she'll have to sell her flat in London.

    a". If Susan has been elected to Oxford, she'll have to sell her flat in London.

Conclusion (1c) would then be reached by MPP from (1b) and (1a").

Both derivations are formally adequate; both would be possible in standard logical systems, and it is an empirical question which of them human beings would actually use in deriving (1c) from (1a) and (1b). In fact, the evidence favours our derivation rather than Gazdar and Good's. In our system, a hearer who has processed the information in (1a) and is given the information in (1b) can proceed directly to the conclusion (1c). In Gazdar and Good's derivation, a hearer who has processed the information in (1a) and is given the information in (1b) cannot proceed directly to (1c), but must pass via the disjunctive conclusion (1b'). The reader may check for himself that our derivation is intuitively correct. On this point at least, our system is not only formally adequate but more psychologically realistic than the standard alternative.[2]

Our deductive system is a highly restricted one: it not only lacks all concept-introduction rules, but is also unable to perform mathematical calculations. For example, given the premise (2a), someone using it would be unable to proceed directly to the conclusion (2b):

(2) a. John's child left and Mary's child left.

    b. At least two children left.[3]

On the appropriate occasion, of course, a hearer given the information in (2a) might use his mathematical abilities to supply the further premise (2a'), and thus be able to reach (2b):

(2) a'. If John's child left and Mary's child left, then at least two children left.

However, we draw a sharp distinction between the finite set of non-trivial implications of a given finite set of premises, and the indefinitely expandable set of implications obtainable by adding further premises such as (2a').

We thus reject Gazdar and Good's claim (p. 90) that an equation characterizing the integer squares, together with some further statement about the properties of squares, should have an infinite set of non-trivial implications in our sense. Since the implications of these statements cannot be drawn out without performing mathematical calculations, they will not be derivable by the automatic functioning of our deductive system. Nor is there any reason for thinking that they should be. When they *are* derived, it will be as a result of calculations which add further premises to the context on the appropriate occasion, subject to the same general constraints on context-expansion that apply in the interpretation of all utterances. No special problems should be raised. Note that a quite substantial issue is involved here. Human beings exhibit a variety of inferential abilities: arithmetical, geometrical, logico-semantic, and so on. Are these all governed by a single mechanism, say "general intelligence", or are there specialized "modules" corresponding to distinct abilities? Gazdar and Good seem to take the first alternative for granted, whereas we explicitly base our work in pragmatics on a modular approach. (For a general discussion of the issue, see Chomsky, 1980b.)

II. Contextual Implications and Relevance

One of the factors in assessments of relevance is numbers of contextual implications. We argue that other things being equal, the more contextual implications a proposition has, the more relevant it is. Gazdar and Good argue that this claim is useless as it stands, since there is nothing to prevent any set of contextual implications being reduced to a single member by conjoining its constituents into a single, complex proposition. In our system, in fact, since there is no rule of *and*-introduction, there *is* something to prevent any such conjoining operation taking place during utterance interpretation. But even if such an operation could take place, Gazdar and Good are wrong in thinking that it would reduce the set of contextual implications to one: it would merely add an extra member to the set. Contextual implications are defined by a deductive system which automatically generates the full set of non-trivial implications of a given set of premises. It is thus impossible (leaving aside some formal exceptions of no empirical import) for any set of contextual implications to contain a conjoined proposition but neither of its constituent conjuncts, or a logically complex proposition but none of its non-trivial implications. For this reason, two utterances, each of which expresses a single proposition, may nonetheless differ dramatically in their numbers of non-trivial logical implications, and these differences could not be eliminated by permitting conjoining operations to take place.

As regards the relation between relevance and contextual implications, Gazdar and Good claim that "a moment's reflection" reveals that numbers of contextual implications have "no bearing on relevance" (p. 90). The basis for this claim is their intuition that it would be hard to decide which of two propositions was the more relevant if one had 87 contextual implications and the other 93. We share that intuition. However, the argument they base on it is grossly fallacious, as can be seen by considering a parallel argument. The taste of sourness is standardly described as varying with the concentration of hydrogen ions in a substance. Gazdar and Good might point out that a difference of 5% in concentration is not always matched by consistent judgements of relative sourness, and hence argue that the concentration of hydrogen ions has no bearing on sourness. This goes to show that a moment's reflection is not always enough. Both sourness and relevance are psychological measures: they vary to a certain extent with subjects and circumstances and are not effective below a certain threshold.

However, although comparisons of relevance are not always straightforward, in some cases they are obvious and easy. It is these cases that are being exploited in conversation: they alone allow the speaker to make a reasonable estimate of the relevance a given interpretation of his utterance will have for the hearer. It is these cases that we want to characterize. We claim that other things being equal, a proposition with many contextual implications will be judged more relevant than a proposition with few or no contextual implications. On where the dividing line between many and few is drawn for particular individuals and occasions we have little of interest to say at the moment. Our claim is simply that when comparisons are easy, they reflect gross differences in numbers of contextual implications. Gazdar and Good have said nothing to challenge this.

Gazdar and Good also argue that certain types of ambiguity should present a problem for our approach. For example, the word *dog* has a general reading "canine" which subsumes a more specific reading "male canine" as a special case. The specific reading will thus share all the contextual implications of the general reading, and have more besides. To the extent that numbers of contextual implications determine degrees of relevance, then, the specific reading will always be more relevant. Yet as Gazdar and Good rightly point out, intuitively the weaker reading is the preferred interpretation.

It is important to notice that in our system the proposition with the most contextual implications is not always the one that satisfies the principle of relevance (see our discussion of example (36)). It is the principle of relevance that governs disambiguation. We predict that even a highly relevant interpretation will be discarded if a speaker who intended it could have made his utterance significantly *more* relevant by doing something to reduce his hearer's processing load. Given a proposition with a strong and a weak interpretation, there are thus three possible outcomes: first, only the weak reading satisfies the principle of relevance; second, only the strong interpretation satisfies the principle of relevance; and third, both interpretations satisfy the principle of relevance. In the last case, there will be equivocation, and we predict that the hearer will be unable to choose between the two readings. In the case of *dog*, being unable to choose between the two readings is equivalent to choosing the weaker reading "canine". The third outcome is by far the most usual, and it is the one Gazdar and Good must have in mind. Thus, contrary to what they claim, our principle of relevance matches their intuition.

III. Amount of Processing and Relevance

The second factor in assessments of relevance is the amount of processing required to obtain the contextual implications of the proposition whose relevance is being assessed. We claim that other things being equal, the smaller the amount of processing, the greater the relevance of the proposition. Gazdar and Good are seriously mistaken both about the nature of the processing involved and about the role it plays in our theory.

To obtain the contextual implications of a proposition in a context, two distinct types of processing are necessary. The first type, which Gazdar and Good entirely ignore, is inferential, and could be represented as the number of steps some automaton would have to go through in deriving the full set of contextual implications of the union of the proposition and the context. As our examples (19)–(21) were meant to show, this aspect of processing depends on two factors: the size of the context and the logical complexity of the proposition being processed; the larger the context, and the more complex the proposition, the greater the amount of processing required. This makes comparisons among propositions and among contexts easy in two types of case: where one proposition entails another, or one context includes another, and numbers of contextual implications remain roughly constant. It plays an important role in our theory of disambiguation and context-construction.

The second type of processing is non-inferential, and could be represented as the number of steps some automaton would have to go through in order to access the context itself. There is no reason to assume that processing speed is constant. We have suggested, on the contrary, that it may increase with the level of attention (p. 74). It is thus doubly wrong to assume, as Gazdar and Good do, that amount of processing depends solely on the time taken to access a certain context.[4]

As regards the role of processing in our theory, there is a more serious misunderstanding. Gazdar and Good take us to be proposing a "real-time on-line model of utterance comprehension" (p. 93), and the last half of their paper is based on this assumption. Thus, when we say we are looking for "a constraint powerful enough to select at most a single interpretation for any utterance in context" (p. 73), Gazdar and Good represent us as searching for a *mechanism* powerful enough to do this. There is a substantial difference between a constraint on interpretation and a mechanism for interpreting: our present interest is in the former, not the latter.

Consider disambiguation, for example. Many psycholinguists have done empirical work on the mechanisms used in disambiguation (see for example Foss and Jenkins 1973; for a more general account of language-processing mechanisms, see Marslen-Wilson and Tyler, 1980). However, few psycholinguists have been interested in the goal that the disambiguation mechanism is designed to achieve: in what property an interpretation must have to make it preferred. The disambiguation mechanism surely has a goal. Our argument is simply that the goal of the disambiguation process is to find an interpretation which obviously satisfies the principle of relevance. That is the property that the disambiguation mechanism, and more generally, the mechanisms used in language-processing, are designed to select.

We assume, as does everyone else working in the area, that perception involves its own mechanisms, short-cuts and heuristics, which are a matter for empirical study. When we say that the speaker's goal in producing an utterance is to be as relevant as possible, and that the hearer's goal is to interpret it as satisfying the principle of relevance, we are thus not claiming that either speaker or hearer has to do all the processing that would be necessary in order to *prove* that the principle of relevance has been satisfied. As we see it, what happens on line is that speakers and hearers estimate, guess or simply assume that a certain utterance, on a certain interpretation, will satisfy the principle of relevance. By our definition of relevance, this will involve making guesses, estimates or assumptions about the number of contextual implications derivable, and the amount of processing needed to derive them. Here, Gazdar and Good make the curious claim that "in order to compare processing times one has to do processing" (p. 97) which is rather like claiming that in order to compare the driving-times from London to Glasgow and London to Harpenden one actually has to do the driving. What such comparisons are based on, what mechanisms are needed to achieve them, is again a matter for empirical research. However, it seems undeniable that the mechanisms have a goal, and for the last ten years or so the goals of the interpretive process, and the general theory of communication of which they form a part, have been the central concern of pragmatic theory. We see our work as a contribution to this.

IV. Pragmatics and Relevance

Gazdar and Good are worried not only by the content of our concept of relevance, but also by its name. They say that if we had been attempting to give an account of Grice's maxim of informativeness, rather than his maxim of relevance, our proposals "might deserve slightly more serious attention" (p. 99). In fact, Grice himself believed that one of his two maxims of informativeness would be made redundant by an adequately formulated maxim of relevance (Grice, 1975, p. 46). We have tried to show elsewhere (Wilson and Sperber, 1981) that our principle of relevance makes not only the remaining maxim of informativeness but *all* Grice's maxims redundant. It is hard to see why this claim should detract from the interest of our proposals.

The intuitive justification for defining relevance in terms of contextual implications was given on p. 72–73 of our paper. Intuitively, the relevance of an utterance in a context depends on its connecting up with that context in some way. We simply specify the type of connection required so that relevance becomes a matter of connecting up with the context to yield contextual implications, and degrees of relevance depend on balancing numbers of contextual implications against the amount of processing needed to derive them. Gazdar and Good's only argument against this position (apart from their claim that "a moment's reflection" will show that it is wrong) is that relevance depends on the interests of hearers in a way we have not allowed for.

Consider the utterance in (3) (Gazdar and Good's (23)):

(3) Sue has married Bill, who is a Mason.

According to Gazdar and Good, (23) might be highly relevant to someone who was obsessed with Masonry but knew so little about it that the remark would have very few contextual implications for him. On the other hand, it might have little relevance to someone who was totally uninterested in Masonry but knew enough about it to be able to derive a considerable number of contextual implications. Relevance, then, must be a function of the hearer's interests as well as, or rather than, his knowledge.

There are a number of puzzling points about these hypothetical examples. Generally, there is a connection between being interested in a subject and knowing something about it. We are sure that Gazdar and Good react as we do to applicants for linguistics courses who claim to be fascinated by the subject but have actually taken no steps to find out anything about it. Moreover, someone obsessed with Masonry, even if he knew little about it, would have a rich stock of opinions, attitudes, suspicions and speculations about it, which he could bring to bear on the interpretation of examples such as (3); the idea that obsession should leave *no* mark on someone's memory is rather far-fetched. As regards the hypothetical individual with an enormous stock of knowledge but no interest in the subject, there are questions about both the accessibility of this knowledge and the level of attention he will bring to bear, that would hve to be answered before one could make any claim about the relevance of (3) to him.

It is also important to note that interest alone will not make an utterance comprehensible: it will not determine disambiguation, reference assignment, implicatures, or any of the other aspects of utterance interpretation that our theory of relevance is designed to describe. For these, linguistic knowledge, background knowledge and some principles governing their development are required.

However, the interests of the hearer clearly do affect the interpretation process. Exactly how they do: how they affect acquisition of knowledge, accessibility of knowledge and level of attention, for example; is an interesting question, and one that it is quite appropriate to raise within our framework. In fact, if Gazdar and Good had spent as much time and ingenuity on raising and pursuing such general questions as they did on formalizing their straw man RELV, constructing objections to it, anticipating quite implausible replies to these objections and rebutting these anticipated replies, their paper might have been as valuable as it was entertaining and provocative.

NOTES

1. The two main inaccuracies in their formalization of RELV(P,C,M) (p. 89) are: first, their conversion of our claim that degrees of relevance "depend on a ratio of input to output" (our p. 74) to the claim that relevance *is* a ratio of input to output, as if establishing relevance were a matter of doing long division; second, their assumption that the main determinant of amount of processing is accessing time, and that the only other determinant is number of contextual implications (see below, p. 105, for further discussion). The two main inaccuracies in their formalization of our principle of relevance (p. 89) are: first, that as stated, it only applies to ambiguous utterances; and second, that it replaces our "try" with "intend". For us, trying involves doing one's best to achieve something: the difference between trying and intending is crucial in our treatment of examples (32)–(36).

2. Parallel remarks apply to the case of *and*-introduction. Gazdar and Good assume that a hearer who has processed the premises in (i) and (ii) and is given the information in (iii) would be unable to proceed to the conclusion in (iv) without first performing the step of *and*-introduction (iii'):

(i)	$(P \& Q) \to R$	Premise
(ii)	P	Premise
(iii)	Q	Premise
(iii')	P & Q	(ii), (iii), *and*-introduction
(iv)	R	(i), (iii'), MPP

We propose an alternative derivation in which given (i), the hearer immediately derives its non-trivial implication (i'); given (ii), he immediately derives (ii') by MPP; so that when given (iii), he can proceed directly by MPP to the conclusion (iv):

(i)	$(P \& Q) \to R$	Premise
(i')	$P \to (Q \to R)$	(i), analytical implication
(ii)	P	Premise
(ii')	$Q \to R$	(i'), (ii), MPP
(iii)	Q	Premise
(iv)	R	(ii'), (iii), MPP

Again, both derivations are formally adequate, but ours is psychologically more realistic.

3. We are grateful to Yuji Nishiyama for bringing these examples to our attention.

4. Gazdar and Good incorporate these mistakes into their formalization of our principle of relevance (p. 89). This has the absurd consequence that when $C = C'$, the amount of processing needed to access C' is zero, and if the proposition being processed has any contextual implications at all, it will be predicted as infinitely relevant.

Comments on Sperber and Wilson's Paper

Terence Moore

The paper approaches problems of language understanding within a broadly Gricean framework. In particular, the authors adopt the generally Gricean position that speakers are trying to conform to certain conventions for verbal communication. However, whereas Grice proposed informally a number of such conventions, this paper argues that a *single* principle, the principle of relevance, governs every aspect of comprehension. In reducing Grice's several principles to a single one, and in proposing that such a principle embraces *all* utterances, the authors would seem to be more Neo-Gricean than Gricean.

The major difficulty with judging whether the paper makes any contribution to theories of comprehension lies in the characterization of relevance itself. This is partly because the term is used in a number of different ways during the course of the paper. But more important, in discussing relevance in terms of such concepts as "amounts of processing", the authors appear to be referring to actual cognitive processes involved in understanding. However, nowhere in their paper is there any suggestion as to how expressions such as "amount of processing" or "measurement of relevance" are to be given empirical substance.

In illustrating the ways in which the principle of relevance operates, the authors appear to overlook the very real problems involved in reconstructing, on the basis of a hypothetical linguistic exchange, the contextual implications that are said to determine relevance. To take just one example, the dialogue:

Ann: Will you have a glass of brandy?

Omar: You know I am a good moslem. (=S&W (26), p. 79.)

where, it is claimed, if Ann knows that brandy is an alcohol and that good moslems do not drink alcohol, she can infer:

Omar will not have a glass of brandy.

One difficulty is that since Ann knows that Omar is a good moslem, we might wonder why she is offering him a drink. Must we assume that on some occasions Omar nevertheless drinks alcohol? If so, a more natural inference is not the inference that the authors claim, namely that Omar will not have a brandy, but rather that he will. A more general difficulty is that what people actually infer depends on a host of factors including their relations with one another, their past experience and expectations as well as linguistic and paralinguistic features such as intonation and facial expression associated with the particular exchange. It is not at all clear that the principle of relevance is yet sufficiently well delineated to throw light on the subtle and still largely mysterious processes involved in the comprehension of language.

Comments on Sperber and Wilson's Paper

Yorick Wilks

I find it difficult to comment on this paper, though I feel compelled to do so. I want to say quite baldly and without wishing to offend two distinguished colleagues that, in offering a new approach to relevance and understanding, they are rather like one who now, in all seriousness, offered a proposal for the planetary model of the atom. It is not so much that he would be wrong (and he might well have interesting and original details to add), but that he would have to say more, and catch up on what people had been doing for some years past, before he could command attention. In the present case, closely related work has been going on in artificial intelligence (AI) and psychology, which will explain why many (though by no means all) linguists encountering Sperber and Wilson's (SW for short) work are not aware of what I refer to, and may think me unfair.

I shall take for granted the following general claim:

In order to disambiguate and so understand, say, English we must postulate processing mechanisms in the hearer that select from among the possible interpretations of an utterance the most appropriate (or relevant) one. There can be some general single principle for choosing this interpretation, and it can be expressed in terms of the efficiency, or processing effort, of the understander. In concrete terms, this last will find expression in terms of the number of inferences, or implicatures in a chain linking the items whose relevance is to be tested, and upon which interpretations are to be imposed. The premises and inference rules are to be drawn from some form of structured background knowledge shared between speaker and hearer.

The above claim I take to express the broad form of what SW call "maximal relevance" (p. 74), and it leaves out their specific suggestions relating relevance to the utterance with the most implicatures from context (p. 74), as well as their distinction (p. 81) between the "most relevant proposition" (i.e. independent of the speaker's intentions) and the one the speaker *tries* to express. I put the general claim this way to distinguish it as far as possible from the Gricean background, as well as from the Schiffer-Lewis work on a simple definition of "mutual knowledge" to which neither SW nor the other work described in this note are much connected.

In addition, I have divided up the claims in this way because SW simply do not seem to realize that the main part of the claim is well known in AI. A particular version of the general claim concerns me personally (Wilks, 1972, 1975a,b): one which adds the sub-claim that, on efficiency of processing grounds, one will expect the most appropriate interpretation to be that which requires the shortest chain of inferences, that is to say which carries the least information. The suggestion in that work is that humans are lazy systems and will seek to impose interpretations on the assumption that their interlocutor is equally lazy. In more sophisticated computational and psychological terms this approach is now known as "resource limited processing" (Bobrow and Winograd, 1977). I make no great claim to originality for it, and indeed now believe it to be wrong in detail, even if right in spirit. It is certainly more plausible than its converse: that the appropriate interpretation is to be found by some maximum-processing strategy. This was advocated by Rieger (1975) and ably criticized by Charniak (1976), on the grounds that it is not only prima facie absurd (in that we could never know we had an appropriate interpretation because more inferencing effort could *always* produce yet another, more appropriate, one), and because the position has no defence against *contradiction*. A system with a contradiction will always, in principle, produce an infinite number of non-trivial inferences and so yield the simplest, if silliest, route to appropriateness and relevance.

On the face of it, SW's claim is closer to Rieger's, when they write "of two utterances that take the same amount of processing, it is the one with most contextual implications that will be the more relevant; and of two utterances which have the same number of contextual implications, it is the one which takes the least amount of processing that will be the more relevant" (SW, p. 74).

On the other hand, theirs seems to resemble the earlier work more in that, unlike Rieger, it is also a least effort hypothesis. The difficulty in the way of settling this is SW's utter naïvety about notions like *processing*. The quotation from SW above only makes sense if we assume that processing is independent of the number of implications. But on any serious view of processing, that is almost certainly not so. Suppose someone said "if processing a bank payroll is calculating the wages of each employee, then Barclays and Coutts require roughly equal amounts of processing"!

In fact their paper suggests they intend a least effort hypothesis (on p. 76 they write of the lower relevance of progressively wider contexts) but that must surely require fewer *not more* implications. Their example (19)–(21) is utterly vitiated by this confusion because the fact that (20) yields more contextual implications than (19) will *ipso facto* mean that it requires more processing (quite contrary to their assumption on p. 75).

I have no intuitions about the differences between SW's (19) and (20), but can make my point with respect to a familiar (to me) example: (Wilks, 1975b)

The soldiers fired at the women and we saw several fall

where I argue that, in the absence of further explicit context, and given the standard beliefs and inferences of a hearer, *several* refers unambiguously to *women* not *soldiers* because we can set up pragmatic inferences using such premises/rules as:

Things fired at may well be hit
Things hit may well fall/die/be wounded etc.

We could reach *soldiers* (instead of *women*) by similar inferences but that would be based on longer chains (i.e. more implications) such as:

Shots may miss a target and hit an unintended object
Those who fire may miss etc. etc.

In fact any normal reader understands this sentence by drawing the least number of such inferences, I argued, and he only constructs longer chains when shorter ones are blocked or not available.

I do not see that SW can have it both ways, given a sensible notion of processing: *either* they want least processing (in which case they want shortest inference chains and least implications), *or* they want longest chains and most implications like Rieger. The latter view is so implausible, if for no other reason, because it makes nonsense of the well-attested redundancy of natural languages: non-redundant utterances are so hard to understand precisely because they support so (unresolvably) many implications and interpretations.

Lest it be thought I am concerned to press my own thesis, may I emphasize that I now consider it false. Sparck-Jones has pointed out that a numerical theory (most/least inferences) is always highly suspicious not only because it is numerical, but because it is almost impossible to be sure that the numerical differences are not merely a function of the way the premises and inferences have been chosen and formalized, rather than because of anything inherent in the content. I produced (Wilks, 1975a) such counter-examples to my own claims as:

I was named after my father

which should have the least informative interpretation on those claims (i.e. that I was named at a point in time after that at which my father was named, which is conceivably false but only just). I think SW may be trying to make the same point in their

(36) My son has grown another foot

but cannot be sure because they simply assert that their amended principle of relevance can reach the normal interpretation in a way their earlier one could not. But they do not show this, and my worries about their notion of how you quantify processing do not reassure me that it has been worked out. The particular problem here is that their two principles switch from processing by the speaker to the putative hearer. It is quite unclear how or why the switch in principles requires a switch between processing entities.

I was inhibited from further analysis of their principles by their description (p. 76) of the hearer obtaining access to wider context by going first to utterances further back in conversation, then to more encyclopaedic knowledge in memory, and then to whatever is holding his attention etc. Reading all this was like being whisked back on a time machine to an easier, more relaxed and agreeable age, as if the last fifteen years had never happened. SW really must flip through a few years of the issues of *Cognitive Science* (many linguists write for it, as well as psychologists, philosophers and AI men), the biennial *Proceedings of the International Conference on Artificial Intelligence*, or two important US Conferences on *Theoretical Issues in Natural Language Processing* where they will find a host of articles on these issues, all far beyond the level of "my first thoughts on psychological or computational access to relevant information". Text linguists, too, have mined this material (with acknowledgements) and much of it can be found in a linguistic mode in (Metzing 1980).

These remarks may seem self-serving, and if so they must be discounted for that: one can always say, with the full authority of Wittgenstein behind one, that one is not concerned when developing one's ideas with what number of people have had similar ones before.

Nonetheless, if I am right, there are confusions in SW's paper that need to be cleared up quite independently of the relation of their work to the areas of study I have brought into the discussion.

Reply to Wilks

Dan Sperber and Deirdre Wilson

Wilks' comments are an excellent illustration of the sort of obsessive misinterpretation mentioned in our paper (p. 83, 84). To Wilks, the most important feature of our work is that it reminds him of his own. Its main implications for him are about him: for example, that we have either wilfully ignored his work or deliberately used it without acknowledgements. It does not seem to have occurred to him that to achieve these implications, he has had to engage in massive misconstrual of our text.

Wilks (1975a) proposes a method for assigning reference to pronouns with textual antecedents. According to Wilks, the hearer attempts to link the pronoun to its antecedent by a chain of inferences: where there is more than one possible antecedent, the one linked to the pronoun by the shortest chain of inferences is selected. The method is illustrated in (1):

(1) *The soldiers* fired at *the women,* and we saw several of *them* fall.

Here, *the women* can be linked to *them* by some such chain as the following: the women were fired at, things fired at may be hit, things hit may fall, therefore the women fell. *The soldiers,* on the other hand, can only be linked to the pronoun by a longer chain, involving the assumption that the soldiers missed the women and hit some of their own members, who fell. Thus *the women* is selected as the antecedent for *them.*

Wilks seems to believe that there are only two possible views of pronoun-resolution: his own, that it is the shortest possible chain that determines the antecedent; or the opposite, that it is the longest possible such chain. He is not sure which of these positions we adopt, and attributes this to some confusion in us rather than in himself. In fact, we adopt neither position. We are not concerned with linking a pronoun to its antecedent by a number of inferential steps: we are concerned with the deductive *consequences* of assigning one or other possible referent to a pronoun or other referring expression. Our claim is that reference is assigned so as to satisfy the assumption that the speaker has tried to maximize the relevance of the proposition being processed: that is, to maximize its contextual implications and minimize the amount of processing needed to derive them.

The two proposals have virtually nothing in common. To avoid further misunderstanding, we would like to draw attention to some of the major differences between them. An obvious difference between Wilks' position and ours is on the role of deductive inference in utterance interpretation. We are interested in a range of processes based on valid deductive inference, and in the type of deductive system underlying them. Wilks explicitly disavows such interest. He postulates processes which are "finally reducible to non-deductive pragmatic forms" (Wilks, 1975a). The inference in (2) is an example:

(2) Something here is yellow.

Buttercups are yellow.

———————————

Therefore the something is a buttercup.

In fact, he is often prepared to treat a proposition as logically equivalent to its own negation, so that not only the "inference chain" in (2), but also that in (3), is considered adequate (p. 71):

(3) Charles was liked.

If someone is liked, he is good.

———————————

Therefore Charles was not good.

Wilks claims that "It is the content and applicability of inferences like these (i.e. like (2)) that should be our concern in natural language analysis at present, and not the finding of strong systems of logic in which to represent them" (Wilks, 1975a, p. 55). We disagree. We see nothing to be gained by calling (2) and (3) "inference chains", or by postulating a "reasoning" device that is just as likely to emit a *non sequitur* as a rational conclusion. If, as seems fairly obvious, both deductive and non-deductive processes are involved in utterance interpretation, the reasonable approach is to try to distinguish them and to describe their interaction, not to produce, as Wilks seems to have done, a curious composite of part-rational, part-irrational principles.

A second major difference between our proposals and Wilks' is in their scope. Wilks deals only with the assignment of textual antecedents to pronouns. We are concerned with reference assignment in general, whether the expressions being dealt with are pronominal or non-pronominal, and whether they have textual antecedents or not. Wilks' method, as it stands, will invariably interpret *he* in (4) as referring to John:

(4) Look at John. Oh God, he's going to fall over the cliff.

This would be quite the wrong result if, after uttering the first sentence of (4), the speaker noticed her baby son Charles tottering towards the edge of the cliff. Clearly, to handle such cases correctly, some method must be given of accessing and evaluating information about a range of potential referents neither explicitly nor implicitly mentioned in the text. Our proposals about the various possibilities for extending the context[1] (p. 76), together with the principle of relevance (p. 75), are specifically designed to handle the problems that arise in this area, which text-based approaches to pragmatics are only now beginning to grapple with.

There is a more general point about reference-assignment which is often overlooked on the text-based approach. The assignment of textual antecedents to pronouns does not solve the problem of the interpretation of referring expressions, but merely defers it: the antecedents themselves are referring expressions, which also have to be interpreted. Wilks seems to feel that some references are so obvious as to need no explanation, and his method of pronoun resolution is in effect to insert plausible (or in the case of (3) highly implausible) additional material into the text, so that the references in the expanded text are self-evident. But this is not a theoretically defensible move. Referring expressions in natural language, whether they are proper names, definite descriptions or personal pronouns, almost invariably have more than one logically and linguistically admissible referent, and it is the job of an adequate pragmatic theory to explain how reference assignment takes place. From the hearer's point of view, of course, *all* the references in a well-constructed text are obvious: that is part of the datum to be explained. But to "explain" the assignment of reference to pronouns by reducing it to a further set of "obvious" cases that are equally in need of explanation is to beg the question.

Our claim is that what makes a reference obvious is the principle of relevance. In normal circumstances, a reference is obvious when assigning that referent to a referring expression makes the resulting proposition substantially more relevant than any alternative assignment would have done. This in turn depends on there being an easily accessible context of information about the selected referent, a context in which a wide range of contextual implications can be obtained. Consider (5), for example:

(5) Ronald Reagan tells lies.

In normal circumstances, *Reagan* would be interpreted here as referring to the President of the United States. This is not the only *possible* interpretation, even for an international audience: for example, most people know that the President of the United States has a son also called Ronald Reagan: what rules him out?[2] The answer, we claim, is the easy accessibility of a context in which (5), interpreted as referring to the President of the United States, will have an enormous number of contextual implications, and the absence of any such context for alternative assignments of reference. The principle of relevance thus deals in exactly parallel ways with a wide range of examples which Wilks makes no attempt to handle at all.

Even in the limited domain of text-based pronoun-resolution, Wilks' method is not fully general. All sorts of *ad hoc* constraints and extra machinery have to be introduced to make it work. Wilks notes, for example, that the shortest possible chain of inferences is of zero length, and that his chaining method would thus falsely predict that the hearer will attempt wherever possible to construe utterances as straight repetitions of earlier remarks, with consequent misconstrual of examples like (6) Wilks 1975a, p. 72:

(6) *John asked Fred to close the window. He did it.*

His solution is simply to add a constraint that the chain of inferences should not have zero length. Since Wilks' whole system is geared to *minimizing* the new information introduced by utterances, and since straight repetitions indeed minimize new information, this constraint is entirely unexpected. By contrast, our system expects the hearer to *maximize* new information of a certain type (the contextual implications of the utterance) and thus has no difficulty in dealing with the interpretation of examples like (6).

The chaining method of pronoun resolution is not the only one Wilks postulates: in fact, he postulates three. Apart from the "extended mode" chaining method, there is also a "basic mode" method which very roughly corresponds to a set of linguistic constraints on reference. There is a wide range of cases which can be handled in neither the basic nor the extended mode. Wilks gives (7) as an example:

(7) He put *the bicycle* in *the shed* and when he came back next week *it* was gone.

To handle these, he introduces a third principle: "Assume that whatever was being talked about is still being talked about", where "what is being talked about" (here the bicycle rather than the shed) is to be described in terms of a notion of focus which Wilks makes no attempt to define (Wilks 1975a, p. 65). The resulting system is a wildly disparate one, with an enormous amount of machinery and little explanatory value.

The notion of focus has been taken up in much recent AI-related work (seen for example Linde (1979) and references therein). But although it has a certain intuitive content, there is still a question about how focus is to be defined, what precise role it plays in utterance-interpretation, and why it plays this role. Our framework offers some insight into these questions. If an object is "in focus" (that is, if it has recently been talked about or thought about), on normal assumptions about accessibility, there will be a rich, easily accessible context of information about it, consisting of the propositions used in, and resulting from, the interpretation of those earlier remarks or thoughts. The fact that such a context exists will greatly increase the chances of relevance of an utterance which refers to an object in focus, as compared with an object linked to a less rich, less easily accessible context of information. Heuristics based on a notion of focus thus fit quite naturally into our framework, whereas their existence should be entirely unexpected in Wilks'.

Our framework offers an explicit account of pronoun resolution, based on a single general principle which also handles disambiguation, reference assignment and many other aspects of utterance interpretation. By contrast, Wilks offers three distinct and ill-defined methods for dealing with the single, limited domain of pronoun-resolution. Wilks accuses us of following where the pioneering footsteps of AI specialists have already been. On the contrary, by proposing an integrated, explanatory theory of utterance-interpretation, we are doing what some AI specialists have tried to do, and failed.

NOTES

1. Wilks takes us to be proposing three distinct, temporally ordered methods of extending the context, by looking first at earlier stretches of discourse, secondly at encyclopaedic knowledge, and thirdly at the physical environment. We certainly did not intend to suggest either temporal ordering or distinctness among these methods: we simply wanted to indicate some of the sources from which additional information may be introduced into the context. Similar remarks are quite commonplace among psychologists (see, for example, Clark and Marshall, 1981).
2. This example is adapted from a similar one which Katz (1972, p. 449) used to make virtually the same point.

The Relevance of Common Ground: Comments on Sperber and Wilson's Paper

Herbert H. Clark

In their paper "Mutual knowledge and relevance in theories of comprehension", Sperber and Wilson propose a new theory of relevance. They pit their theory against proposals by Catherine Marshall, Thomas Carlson and myself on the role of common ground in comprehension. They need not have. Their theory is not incompatible with our proposals. The reason it appears to be incompatible is that Sperber and Wilson, and we, mean different things by the terms "comprehension" and "context". Once these differences are made clear, the two proposals can live in peaceful coexistence: they are about different things.

These differences, however, count against certain claims that Sperber and Wilson make about their theory of relevance. I will make two brief arguments.

(1) Grice's co-operative principle, built as it is on his notions of speaker meaning, saying and implicating, does not encompass everything that Sperber and Wilson call contextual implications, even those that are maximally relevant. It encompasses only those contextual implications that the speaker "m-intended", as Grice put it. Grice is right to make this restriction, for hearers try to distinguish these implications from all others. In particular, Sperber and Wilson's principle of relevance doesn't make this distinction, hence it cannot be part of Grice's co-operative principle, as they want to claim.

(2) For the principle of relevance to be part of the co-operative principle, it must make reference to common ground. It must make use of just that part of our proposals that Sperber and Wilson wish to reject.

AUTHORIZED INFERENCES

One morning, my secretary tells me, "A strange man with an Alpine hat just stopped by". She tells me this to warn me that the man may stop by later. As it happens, I recognize her intentions to tell me and warn me of these things. But I recognize that her intentions are of a special kind, which Grice called "m-intentions". She intends me to recognize what she wants me to know and be warned of in part *by means of* my recognition of her intention that she wants me to know and be warned of these things. An m-intention is a speaker's intention that a hearer do something in part by means of the hearer's recognition of that intention. If I successfully recognize her intentions, I will have drawn the inferences she "authorized" me to draw. Any other inferences I draw, in the terminology I will use (see Clark, 1977b) are "un-authorized", not m-intended to be drawn. (In Clark (1977b), for the purposes of exposition, I unfortunately defined "authorized inference" as any inference that the speaker intended. I should have said "m-intended".)

The fundamental concept behind Grice's approach to language is speaker meaning. In 1957, he characterized it this way: "For some audience A, (utterer) U intended his utterance of x to produce in A some effect (response) E, by means of A's recognition of that intention." In his 1968 terminology, the utterer U "m-intended to produce in A some effect". In his William James lectures (1975), he divided what the speaker means into two parts: (1) what the speaker says (in a favored sense of say); and (2) what the speaker implicates. As the two parts of speaker meaning, what is said and what is implicated still both require m-intentions. In those same lectures, Grice proposed the co-operative principle, with its maxims of quantity, quality, relation, and manner. He proposed it as a way of accounting for what the speaker implicates: how the speaker can m-intend some effect that cannot be recognized directly in what he says. For Grice, therefore, the co-operative principle is a device for enabling hearers to draw the inferences that are authorized by the speaker. It isn't for enabling them to infer things that are not m-intended by the speaker.

In example after example, Sperber and Wilson make it clear that the principle of relevance they offer leads to contextual implications that are *not* authorized, not m-intended, by the speaker. "If someone walks up to you in the street and asks "What time is it?", you assume that the answer you give is relevant to him, that is, that it has a number of contextual implications, without knowing at all what they are and what the context may be." Later, "What exactly the context consists of, what these implications are, the speaker does not need to know in order to act in accordance with the principle of relevance". Sperber and Wilson do appear to require their principle to lead to implications that the speaker intended, but these are not restricted to the implications that the speaker *m-intended*. As a result, the implications that the principle allows go beyond what the speaker meant.

This poses an obvious difficulty for Sperber and Wilson. Grice proposed the maxim of relation, "Be relevant", as part of the co-operative principle in order to account for implicatures, which are *authorized* inferences. Sperber and Wilson have proposed the principle of relevance as a characterization of that maxim. However, it explicitly allows both authorized and unauthorized inferences. Whatever its other merits and faults, therefore, it cannot be used as a specification of Grice's maxim of relation. It does not belong in Grice's co-operative principle.

There are two types of comprehension under discussion here, what I will call comprehension$_1$ and comprehension$_2$. Comprehension$_1$ consists of trying to determine what the speaker means. Comprehension$_2$ consists of trying to determine the contextual implications that are maximally relevant to the hearer, whether m-intended or not. Comprehension$_1$ is solely concerned with authorized inferences. Comprehension$_2$ is concerned with unauthorized inferences as well. Our proposals have been about comprehension$_1$, and so have Grice's, Searle's, and those of many others in pragmatics. Sperber and Wilson's principle of relevance is concerned with comprehension$_2$. Their enterprise should not be confused with Grice's, Searle's, or our own.

THE ROLE OF COMMON GROUND

For Sperber and Wilson's principle of relevance to work even as they want it to work, it must itself be part of the common ground of the speaker and hearer. Recall that the principle is this: "The speaker tries to express the proposition which is the most relevant one possible to the hearer". Now imagine, as I talk to you, that you don't know this principle. Or imagine that you believe I don't know it. Or that you believe I believe you don't know it. Or that you believe I believe you believe I don't know it. With anything less than mutual knowledge or beliefs about this principle, you won't be able to decide whether or not I am trying to express the proposition most relevant to you, and you won't draw the appropriate contextual implications. The principle of relevance is of little use unless we both assume it is part of our common ground.

Surprisingly, the principle of relevance is mute on a crucial point about relevance itself: relevance with respect to what? "The speaker tries to express the proposition which is the most relevant one possible to the hearer". Depending on which of the hearer's views are taken into account, the proposition the speaker ought to express will change dramatically. From the hearer's standpoint, the contextual implications will change dramatically too. What must be taken into account, I suggest, is the speaker's and hearer's common ground.

To see this, consider Sperber and Wilson's example of Ann, who offers Omar a glass of brandy and receives this reply: "You know I am a good Moslem." Sperber and Wilson say, "If Ann knows that brandy is alcoholic and that good Moslems do not drink alcohol, she can infer (that Omar will not have a glass of brandy). She can also infer that Omar intended her to draw that specific inference, without which his utterance will not be relevant". Hardly. Imagine that Ann also believes that Omar believes that she thinks good Moslems *love* alcohol. From this expanded viewpoint, she will take him as accepting the glass of brandy. Or imagine that Ann also believes that Omar believes that she believes that Omar holds that good Moslems don't drink alcohol. From this even broader viewpoint, she will take him as refusing her again. With each expanded viewpoint, Ann is coming closer to using her and Omar's common ground. It appears, though this example is hardly proof, that the viewpoint Ann must take is her and Omar's common ground.

What this example suggests, as my colleagues and I, and others, have argued more directly, is that common ground is *necessary* for recognizing what the speaker implicated. The arguments that Sperber and Wilson raise against the necessity of common ground do not apply here, since they are concerned with comprehension$_2$ and not comprehension$_1$.

Sperber and Wilson, then, must ultimately do two things: distinguish authorized from unauthorized contextual implications; and make reference to common ground. Until they do, their principle of relevance seems fated to remain irrelevant to Grice's co-operative principle.

Reply to Clark

Dan Sperber and Deirdre Wilson

On p. 125 of his reply, Clark imagines his secretary making a remark to him with a certain set of communicative intentions. He adds "*As it happens* (our italics), I recognize her intentions". The question we would like to ask is: how?

According to the strict Gricean approach, the goal of pragmatic theory is to describe utterance-*comprehension,* where comprehension involves identifying an m-intended actual context and recovering all and only the set of propositions that the speaker m-intended to express and implicate. Griceans take it for granted that it is possible to achieve this goal. We think there is good reason to doubt it. First, although m-intentions may be necessary for successful communication, they do not always seem to us to be of the specific, propositional type that Griceans envisage. Secondly, it does not seem to us to be possible to identify *all* propositional m-intentions. Thirdly, it does not seem to us to be possible to identify *only* propositional m-intentions. Many of the reasons are given in our paper, and we shall review them only briefly here. We do not want to deny the existence or importance of m-intentions in communication: however, we feel it is both legitimate and necessary to question whether a pragmatic theory whose *sole* concern is the recovery of a speaker's m-intentions has any chances of success.

Let us assume that the speaker always has a well-defined set of propositional m-intentions. How are they to be recognized? How, given a potential context consisting of the common ground shared by speaker and hearer, is the actual m-intended context to be identified; and how, given an actual context, an utterance and Grice's co-operative principle and maxims, does the hearer identify the exact set of propositions that the speaker m-intended to express and implicate? Griceans are generally silent on this point. The only answer that seems to us at all promising at the moment is provided by our principle of relevance. Using the principle of relevance and a potential context even larger than the common ground, the hearer can, in the way described in our paper, identify the proposition expressed by the utterance, an actual context and a set of contextual implications. The m-intended propositions that he can identify with some certainty will be a subset of these: that subset which plays a necessary role in establishing the interpretation which satisfies the principle of relevance. Generally, this subset will include the proposition actually expressed by the utterance, since without it no contextual implications will be recovered at all. It may also include certain parts of the actual context, and certain contextual implications; in either case, identification will be possible because the propositions in question give access to a range of (further) contextual implications which, by its size and accessibility, establishes the relevance of the utterance.

If this approach is right (and it provides the only method of recognizing m-intended propositions that we know of) there are two unavoidable consequences. First, the m-intended proposition which can be recognized as such are at most a subset of the total set of propositions recovered during utterance-interpretation: they are identifiable precisely because they make it possible to recover further propositions which are not themselves so identifiable. Therefore the goal of recovering *only* m-intended propositions is misplaced. Secondly, only a subset of the speaker's m-intended propositions have a chance of being identified as such: that subset which plays a necessary role in establishing the relevance of the utterance. Of course, the speaker may *have* further m-intentions, and the hearer may suspect that he has. But if they fall outside that subset identifiable by the principle of relevance, we know of no way in which those suspicions might be confirmed. Some speakers, shy lovers for instance, m-intend their hearers to comprehend much more than they actually manage to convey. However, comprehension consists in retrieving only those m-intentions which have been made retrievable by the speaker. Therefore the goal of recovering *all* m-intended propositions is misplaced.

Finally, it is not even clear that the speaker always has a well-defined set of specific propositional intentions. In our framework, the crucial m-intention is a general one: the speaker has to m-intend his utterance to satisfy the principle of relevance. Usually of course, he will also m-intend to express a specific proposition, and he may have further m-intentions about the actual context and contextual implications of his utterance. However, it sems quite possible for successful communication to take place when only the general m-intention is present, and the speaker does not know which specific proposition he intends to express and implicate. Take the ambiguous utterance in (1):

(1) They gave us much valued advice.

In many circumstances, (1) would be not only ambiguous but equivocal: the hearer would be unable to tell whether the advice was much-valued or merely valued. In these circumstances, whatever the speaker's propositional m-intentions, they would go unrecognized. In fact in many circumstances, a speaker who was aware of the equivocality in (1) would not even bother to resolve it for himself, since either interpretation would quite adequately reflect his views. In such circumstances, a perfectly satisfactory exchange could take place even though the speaker had no specific propositional m-intentions, and no such intentions were recovered.

Note that we are not saying that the speaker in the above example has no m-intentions, but only that he has no *propositional* m-intentions. This suggests a more general remark. Clark draws our attention to Grice's characterization of speaker's meaning and m-intentions as aimed at producing "some effect" in the hearer. In current Gricean pragmatics, only a very specific type of effect is ever considered: the recognition of a proposition. What has been lost sight of is the fact that many m-intentions are intentions to produce a much vaguer type of effect. Often, the speaker m-intends the hearer merely to look at things in a certain light, to adopt a particular attitude to a range of facts, to draw conclusions with a certain drift, to derive any one of several contextual implications with the same general import, and so on. It is a mistake, then, to try to divide all the propositions which a hearer derives from an utterance into two mutually exclusive subclasses: those which were m-intended, and those which were derived on the sole responsibility of the hearer. In most cases, the speaker m-intends only one specific proposition: the one expressed by his utterance; but he takes some responsibility for some of the contextual implications he encourages his hearer to derive.

Thus Clark is quite correct in claiming that we do not mean the same by "comprehension" as he does. However, he misunderstands where the difference lies (probably through our own fault, since we were not explicit enough on that point in our paper). For him, comprehension is the recovery by the hearer of a set of propositions m-intended by the speaker. We believe that "comprehension" in that sense does not identify a natural domain of psychological processes. For us, comprehension is the attempt by the hearer to recover the speaker's m-intentions, whether propositional or not. We also believe that comprehension so understood is only one aspect of the overall process of utterance-interpretation, and must be studied as such rather than in isolation.

Clark is again correct in claiming that our principle of relevance "does not belong in Grice's co-operative principle". He is wrong in assuming that we intend it to. We believe that the principle of relevance should replace the co-operative principle and all the maxims in pragmatic theory (see Wilson and Sperber, forthcoming, for further discussion). Moreover, we feel justified in proposing this alternative framework largely because of Clark and his associates' own work. It is to their credit that they have brought out, quite ingeniously, the psychological implications of the Gricean view of mutual knowledge and its role in comprehension. Until then, we had tended to accept these views. But Clark's model, which we find both hard to accept and hard to improve, justifies the search for a radical alternative to views of comprehension as based on mutual knowledge.

Chapter 3

On Circular Readings

Michael Brody

I. INTRODUCTION

It is well known that there are a number of constraints determining what are the possible positions of a linguistic antecedent of a given anaphoric expression. (1a,b) for example are ill-formed on the reading indicated; they cannot legitimately express the meaning of (2a,b). (Co-indexing marks anaphoric relationship between constituents.)

(1) a. *He_x said Tom_x was ill
    b. *Tom_x saw him_x
(2) a. Tom_x said he_x was ill
    b. Tom_x saw $himself_x$

Consider now (3), which contains a structure where the antecedent includes the anaphoric expression:

(3) *I met [her_x childhood friend's wife]

The meaning that we should expect (3) to have is something like (4).

(4) I met the one_x who_x is her_x childhood friend's wife

Just as in the case of (1a,b) a structural constraint can be stated that rules (3) ungrammatical.[1] In this paper, I shall consider the further question of whether the effect of this constraint follows from some independent considerations. An account of such structures has recently been proposed in a paper by James Higginbotham and Robert May, (1979a), (henceforth HM), to which I shall refer as the pragmatic solution. This crucially involves a pragmatic principle that is often assumed

in some form in the different approaches to the problem of the interaction of content and context, represented at this conference. I should
like to argue below that this solution, although at first sight plausible, is
not tenable. I shall present an alternative explanation, one that involves what are probably not pragmatic principles but rules of
grammar.

According to the pragmatic solution, a structure like (3) with the
referential dependency as indicated (henceforth Circular Reading
(CR)) "is in a certain sense absurd, for the reference of some of the
terms that it contains is given only circularly" (HM, pp. 20/21). This
absurdity is due to the general condition of use "that speakers are expected to provide sufficient cues for the determination of deictic reference" (HM, p. 21). So in the case of a CR, the reference of a pronoun is
dependent on some NP, NP*, hence varying the context cannot, by
hypothesis, provide contextual cues for the determination of the pronoun's reference. On the other hand, it is assumed, that NP* is unable
to supply this reference, since the reference of NP* is itself dependent on
that of the pronoun. "Intuitively, the reference of a pronoun cannot be
"given" in terms of itself" (HM, p. 109)

This solution then rests on the truth of two claims: (a) that there is a
pragmatic condition that the reference of a pronoun must be identifiable and (b) that CR structures fail to satisfy this condition. The first of
these claims has an air of naturalness about it, which I think is misleading. Suppose that the reference of a pronoun P is not determinable in
some context. Why could not P be interpreted as a free variable? Since
there seems to be no *a priori* reason why there could not be expressions
with free variables in them in natural language, the pragmatic principle
is in need of independent motivation. The second crucial premise of the
pragmatic solution is that the reference of the pronoun in a CR structure is not determinable. I shall argue that this premise is false, and
therefore whatever the status of the pragmatic condition, it cannot provide an explanation of the unacceptability of structures like (3). But before doing this, I should like to present some more relevant data and
introduce some terminology with the help of which the problems the
new data gives rise to can be stated.

Consider (5) and (6):

(5) a. *[her$_x$ childhood friend's wife]
        b. *[the fact that you believed it$_x$]
        c. *Tom [wanted to appear to $\emptyset_x$]

(6) a. *[her$_x$ employer] respects [his$_y$ secretary]
           $\,_y$ $\,_x$

   b. *Everybody who says [Fred proved it$_x$] agrees [that Mike
                          $\,_y$
      denies it$_y$]

   c. *The boy who [mentioned that Bill will Ø$_x$] saw the girl that
                   $\,_y$
      [announced that someone had Ø$_y$]
      $\,_x$

(5b,c) show that the full explanation of the unacceptability of CRs will have to take into acount not only co-reference relationships but anaphoric connectedness in general. (The sense in which I shall use the term "anaphora" here is meant to exclude rules of sentence grammar.[2]) As (6) shows, the description of CR structures as ones in which the antecedent contains the anaphor, is not exhaustive: the same type of unacceptability results also if the antecedent of an anaphor A contains anaphor B whose antecedent contains A.

Let us call the relation in which the interpretation of an anaphor stands to that of its antecedent "anaphoric dependency"; and the relation in which the interpretation of some segment stands to that of its constituents "compositional dependency". Let us furthermore define the relation "a-c dependency" as holding between two interpretations A and B iff. A is anaphorically dependent on B, or A is compositionally dependent on B. The ungrammaticality of (5) and (6) could now be described by stipulating that (a) a-c dependency is transitive and that (b) the a-c dependency of an anaphor's interpretation on that of its antecedent is asymmetric, that if A a-c depends on B, and A is an anaphor's interpretation, then B does not a-c depend on A. The CRs now lead to contradiction. In (5a), for instance, the interpretation of the anaphor *her* is a-c dependent on that of the NP *her childhood friend's wife*. The asymmetry of this dependence (stipulation (b)) entails that the interpretation of *her childhood friend's wife* does not a-c depend on that of *her*. But it does in consequence of the compositionality principle. Given the transitivity of a-c dependence, we can similarly derive contradictions from the CRs of (6).

A-c dependence incorporates only anaphoric and compositional dependencies. The fact that these two are under a transitive "super-relation" cannot be a consequence of a general property of dependencies between interpretations. The interpretation of a variable, for instance, depends in some sense on that of its quantifier: its reference varies within the limits set by its binder. Nevertheless, this dependency must not be included under a-c dependency, if it was, (7) would be incorrectly excluded.

(7) a. Tom [kissed every girl Peter did $\emptyset_x$]
$\qquad\qquad x$

$\quad$ b. [Every girl Peter did $\emptyset_x$] Tom [kissed y]
$\qquad\quad y \qquad\qquad\qquad\qquad\qquad\quad \mathrm{VP}_x^*$

On some level of analysis (7a) will have to have a representation like (7b), evidence for Quantifier Raising and for the identity condition on VP-anaphora converge to support this.[3] Assume that the stipulations about a-c dependency made above refer to this level. Here the zero VP asymmetrically a-c depends on VP* by stipulation (b). VP* in its turn a-c depends on the variable (related to the extracted quantifier phrase), as does the quantifier phrase on the zero VP. Thus given the transitivity of a-c dependence, if the variable a-c depended on the quantifier, we should end up with a contradiction and the structure would be incorrectly excluded. VP* a-c depends on VP (by transitivity of a-c dependence) and VP* does not a-c depend on VP (by asymmetry of the a-c dependence of an anaphor's interpretation on that of its antecedent). Thus "behaving transitively" with respect to anaphoric or compositional dependence is not a general property of interpretive dependencies.

At least three questions arise at this point. First, why do anaphoric and compositional dependencies interact, and why in this particular way by forming a transitive chain? Note that described in these terms, the fact that the structures in (6) are just as ungrammatical as the apparently related ones in (5) is not a logical necessity, hence surprising in a linguistically interesting sense. Secondly, from what independently motivated consideration could it be made to follow that it is just these two and no other relations that form such a chain that can create contradictions with the entailments of the principle of asymmetry? Again it is worth noting that the grammaticality of (7a) seems to be an unexpected and genuinely puzzling fact when this structure is compared with (5) and (6). Thirdly, the same question could be asked about the principle of asymmetry. Could some independently motivated consideration explain the asymmetry of the a-c dependence of the interpretation of an anaphor on that of its antecedent? We shall see in the next section that this is not a property of dependencies between interpretations in general either.

The two stipulations concerning a-c dependency are *ad hoc*. Nevertheless, they are quite natural and it is not obvious if they should not be taken as axioms. But I shall attempt to search for explanations.

II. THE INADEQUACY OF THE PRAGMATIC SOLUTION

Returning now to the pragmatic solution, we note that in this only examples like (5a) and (6a) are considered, that is, ones containing pronouns and dependencies between referents. Given this limitation of the data, the problem of explaining why anaphoric and compositional dependencies interact does not arise. In (5a) and (6a), only referential dependencies (both anaphoric and compositional) occur. It is indeed difficult to imagine how this relation could fail to be transitive. However, the problem of explaining the asymmetry of anaphoric dependence does show up. Why is it that sentences in which the reference of some pronoun A depends on that of some segment B, where B's reference depends on that of A, are unacceptable? I shall return to the problem of explaining the interaction of anaphoric and compositional dependencies in later sections. First I should like to reconsider the explanation given by the pragmatic solution of the unacceptability of CRs with referential linkages. From our present point of view, this is an attempt to explain the asymmetry of referential dependence, i.e. to give a partial answer to problem (3) of section I. I shall then go on to examine the potential of this solution to serve as a basis for an explanation for the asymmetry of the a-c dependence of anaphors other than pronouns.

Recall that according to the pragmatic solution, the reference of a pronoun in a CR structure is not determinable, this being due to it "being given in terms of itself".

"In this respect, pronouns are no different from other singular or plural terms. If one wanted to know who the name *Cicero* refers to, it is of no use to be told that it refers to the person people refer to when they use that name, for what we wanted to know was *who* that was." (HM, pp. 19/20). HM appear to assume then that some principle like (8), call it the Circularity Principle, is logically necessary:

(8) If the reference of some segment A is given circularly, that is, if it is dependent on that of another segment B, and the reference of B is dependent on A, then the determination of the reference of A cannot be effected.

If this was indeed a necessary principle, then the asymmetry of referential dependence would be explained. Whenever the pronoun both depends on and is depended on by some segment, this leads to leaving the pronoun without a determinate referent and hence to the exclusion of the structure by the pragmatic constraint. However, the Circularity Principle is not logically necessary, and even if it was, the solution would not be generalizable to the whole range of data.

The "Cicero" example appears to be misleading. The absurdity there is not due to circularity, but simply to the uninformativeness of the answer. Thus someone who would like to know who the name "Cicero" refers to can be informatively, though "circularly", answered by stating that it refers to the person who just uttered the name "Cicero". The explanation can be proper and truthful in appropriate circumstances. The example is irrelevantly complicated since "Cicero" is being mentioned in it instead of used as pronouns in CRs are. To take another, perhaps more perspicuous analogy, consider (9):

(9) $c = 1/c$

Suppose that "c" may take values in the domain of integers. The specification that the actual value of "c" equals the value of "1/c" may be circular, but is perfectly adequate, picking out 1 and -1.

It is neither necessary nor sufficient for a proposition to be a syntactic definition in order for it to pick out determinate referents that satisfy it. Of course it can be assumed that the relation between antecedent and anaphor is that of definiens and definiendum, or that the interpretation of an antecedent must be computable independently of (without access to) the interpretation of the anaphor. If some such step was made, asymmetry of the dependence of the interpretation of an anaphor on that of its antecedent would follow. But these assumptions, although perhaps natural, are neither necessary nor independently motivated, so they represent no improvement on the equally natural axiom of asymmetry of a-c dependence of the anaphor's interpretation, which I set out to explain.

Circularity in and of itself does not make the computation of the anaphor's and the antecedent's interpretation a difficult or even unparalleled task either. Computing the interpretation of an anaphor participating in a CR could be similar to disambiguation. Thus in (10), one of the possible meanings of *ball* is filtered out by selectional restrictions.

(10) the ball's trajectory

In (10), the interpretation of *ball* depends on that of the whole NP, whose interpretation in turn depends on that of *ball*. CRs could be dealt with in an exactly parallel fashion. Take (5a) for instance. Here the reference of *her* depends on that of *her childhood friend's wife*; whose reference in turn depends on that of *her*. In both cases, the contained NP (*ball/her*) has a number of possible interpretations/referents from which that or those will be picked out that meet(s) further conditions imposed by the container NP. It will have to be checked, for each possible interpretation/referent of the contained segment, whether it meets these: the selectional restrictions of the whole NP's interpretation in the former case, the identity requirement with the whole NP's reference in the latter. We can then conclude that the Circularity Principle is not logically necessary, and neither is the asymmetry of the dependence of a pronoun's reference on that of its antecedent.

But even if the Circularity Principle was necessary or independently motivated, no satisfactory solution could be based on it for the full range of data in (5) and (6). Asymmetry of a-c dependence is a property of the interpretation of all anaphors, it is not characteristic only of pronouns' referents. To explain this in the spirit of HM's solution, a stronger version of the Circularity Principle would have to be necessary, which refers not only to referential dependencies but to dependencies between interpretations in general:

(11) If the interpretation of some segment A is given circularly, that is if it is dependent on that of another segment B, and the interpretation of B is dependent on A, then the determination of the interpretation of A cannot be effected.

But this revised principle is not just not necessary or motivated, it is false. As the cases of disambiguation and of the antecedent-contained VP-anaphor (7) show, it is possible to have circular dependencies between interpretations in grammatical structures.

Summarizing so far, I have argued that the pragmatic solution is unsatisfactory for several reasons. This account of the unacceptability of CRs with referential linkages makes use of two assumptions: the pragmatic principle that the reference of a deictic expression must be determinable, and the Circularity Principle according to which CRs fail to satisfy this condition. Neither of these assumptions seems to be necessary or independently motivated.

But even if the account was accepted as an answer to the problem of why referential dependency is asymmetric, it would not be generalizable to explain the asymmetry of anaphoric dependency in general. Hence at best, the pragmatic solution could only have been a partial answer to one of the three central problems of CRs. It does not contribute at all to the solution of the problems of why anaphoric and compositional dependencies, and only these, interact by forming a transitive chain.

III. REFERENTIAL CHAINS AND ASYMMETRY

I shall persist in trying to find an answer to the asymmetry problem, whose solution, as will be seen, provides the answers automatically to the other two problems posed in section I. I will approach this by gradually modifying the framework presented in Higginbotham and May's paper.

According to HM, structures with CRs have "referential chains" that may be infinitely long. Referential chains are hypothetical objects, part of a full semantic representation. Briefly, if the reference of a pronoun A depends on that of the NP B, then "A → B" may form part of the chain representing that B is the antecedent of A. Furthermore, if a segment C *contains* another, D, where C and D are in the referential chain by virtue of being on the right-hand side and on the left-hand side respectively of an arrow, this will be shown by linking C and D in the following notation: "C ⊃ D".

So for example the referential chain of (6a) "[her_x employer] respects [his_y secretary]" on the reading marked may contain "her_x → [his_y secretary]" and "his_y → [her_x employer]". Since both "[his_y secretary]" and *his_y* are in the chain they are linked by " ⊃ ":

   (12) her_x → [his_y secretary] ⊃ his_y → [her_x employer]

        "[Her_x employer]" includes *her_x* so (12) can continue as (13):

   (13) her_x → [his_y secretary] ⊃ his_y → [her_x employer] ⊃ her_x

But now the reference of the last *her* in (13) again depends on that of the NP "[his secretary]", so the construction of the chain need not stop here.

Let us make the following natural assumption:

   (14) All pronouns and pronoun containers in the referential chain must initiate an element of the form "A → B" or "A ⊃ B" respectively.[4]

Now the chain of (6a) appears to have to be infinite. Referential chains and (14) can be generalized as anaphoric chains in the obvious way. Since the chain is part of the semantic representation, structures on CRs can be excluded by the assumption that grammars must not assign an infinite representation to a finitely long sentence. Semantic representations must be accessible. This it would seem should be considered as a necessary property of grammars. Asymmetry of the a-c dependence of an anaphor's interpretation on that of its antecedent seems to fall out now.

This solution, however, does not work as it stands. Note first that even if it did explain asymmetry, it would not be satisfactory. It offers no hope of an explanation to the first two problems of section I: why do anaphoric and compositional dependencies interact transitively, and why is it just these two dependencies between interpretations that do so? Anaphoric chains only stipulate and do not explain this. It would be, for instance, incorrect to include the dependence of the interpretation of a variable on that of its quantifier in the anaphoric chain (cf. (7)), but no motivation independent of the present problem can be given against this. But asymmetry is not explained either. The idea that referential chains for CRs will be infinite is crucially used (and generalized to anaphoric chains). But in HM's framework, this is incorrect even if (14) is accepted. This is because according to HM, the annotations of the chain only relate entities: "The items themselves in the referential chain are definite occurrences of NPs in the logical form". (HM, p. 19)

To see the problem, with this in mind, reconsider the referential chain of (6a). At the stage where the first four steps have been constructed, it may look like (13). But under the present assumptions about the status of the items in the referential chain, there will be no fifth step, since the last item in (13) is the same as the first: a definite occurrence of an NP in the logical form. The last *her* in (13) must of course initiate an element of the form "A → B" under (14), but it already has. This is the one that the first *her* in (13), with which the last one is identical, has initiated. It seems then that if the explanation of the unacceptability of CRs based on the infiniteness of the relevant anaphoric chains is to be maintained, then it must be ensured that the first and the last *her* in (13) are not identical. To do this, the assumption that the annotations of the anaphoric chain only *relate* entities must be given up; they have to create new ones.

IV. ANAPHORIC EXPANSION

Is there any independent evidence for such a modification? To show that there is, I have to describe some data first noted and analysed by Jacobson (1977). She pointed out the difference in acceptability between (15a) and (15b) and the fact that it can be accounted for under the assumption that the first pronoun in (15a,b) (*her*), is represented at some level as a full NP identical to the pronoun's antecedent, as in (16a,b).

(15) a. [The man who$_y$ y loved her$_x$] kissed [his$_y$ wife]

b. *[The man who$_y$ she loved y] kissed [his$_y$ wife]

(16) a. [The man who$_y$ y loved [his$_y$ wife]] kissed [his$_y$ wife]

b. [The man who$_y$ [his$_y$ wife] loved y] kissed [his$_y$ wife]

(17) a. *[the man who$_y$ y loved [his$_y$ wife]]

b. [the man who$_y$ [his$_y$ wife] loved y]

Some constraint will have to differentiate between (17a) and (17b) marking only the latter as deviant. Assume that it will be sensitive to the relative order of the variable (related to the *wh*-phrase) and the co-indexed pronoun. But whatever the precise formulation of this condition, it can automatically account for the difference between (15a) and (15b) provided that it has access to the level at which (15a,b) are represented as (16a,b) respectively.

HM build this into their framework in the following way. They stipulate what I shall call the Target Condition:

(18) the target of an annotation entry (i.e. the right hand side of an arrow "A → B") must not "contain a free variable, as such targets have reference only relative to an assignment of values to variables. In general a target NP$_i$ which gives the reference of a pronoun$_j$ must be *closed*, where NP$_i$ is closed iff. every anaphor contained in NP$_i$ has a c-commanding antecedent in NP$_i$ (understanding containment as a reflexive relation)." (HM, pp. 18/19)

(Keep in mind that "anaphor" in this quotation refers to dependent elements participating in sentence grammar binding processes. This is in contradistinction to the way the word is used elsewhere in this paper to mean the dependent members of "discourse grammar" associations.) Furthermore, it is stipulated that there is to be an exception from the Target Condition: annotations that violate it are permitted "where their semantic interpretation is determined by the result of substituting the target for the pronoun" (HM, p. 25), in other words, where the substitution will result eventually in a well-formed semantic representation.

In the derivation of (15a), the annotation that associates *her* with *his wife* has a target that violates the Target Condition; *his* is not bound from within the NP *his wife*.[5] Therefore this annotation is only legitimate if *his* can end up bound when *his wife* is substituted for *her*. After substitution, as in (16a), *his* can be properly bound. (15b) is not similarly derivable since the pronoun *his*, in the substituted NP *his wife*, cannot have the same index as the variable that is linked to the *wh*-phrase and is to its right in consequence of the constraint that excludes (17b).

This analysis relying on substitution presupposes just like Jacobson's the existence of a level where certain pronouns are represented *in situ* by their antecedents, and not in abstraction from the rest of the structure. This is necessary in order to check whether conditions of proper binding are met by the substituted segment. Here we have evidence, then, for reinterpreting, at least in some cases, the annotation "A → B", relating logical form entities as a rewriting rule expanding A as B. It is natural to think of this rule as part of the mapping to a full representation of meaning.[6] Note that the analysis creates unmotivated distinctions between the interpretations of parallel structures. For instance, different structures are assigned to (15a) and (19). Since in (19), *her* has a closed target (*Mary*) there is no substitution:

(19) The man who loved her$_x$ kissed Mary$_x$

Suppose that the generalization is made that *all* anaphoric pronouns (i.e. those not bound by some antecedent in a sentence grammar process) have to be expanded when they have linguistic antecedents. (15a) and (19) will now have parallel mappings. The expansion of the first pronoun in (15a,b) will fall out from general principles: all anaphors expand. Note that the second pronoun in (15a,b) need not expand since the relation between it and its c-commanding antecedent is not anaphora in our sense, but that of sentence grammar binding.[7] The Target Condition becomes superfluous here as does its *ad hoc* exception covering the case of substitution. Since the "all expansion" account does not have recourse to anything not assumed in HM's theory, it is also more parsimonious in being able to dispense with anaphoric chains.

V. SOME CONSEQUENCES

Equipped with evidence that all anaphoric pronouns must be substituted by a copy of their antecedents at some level of representation, I can return to the three problems that were posed at the outset. This theory can explain the asymmetry of the dependence of the pronoun's reference on the reference of its antecedent. It is now genuinely a consequence of the inadmissibility of inaccessible semantic representations. Given that an antecedent has to be copied in for all anaphoric pronouns, no fully expanded semantic representation will ever be reached for a CR. In (5a) for example, the anaphor *her* expands as *her childhood friend's wife*; in which *her* expands again as *her childhood friend's wife*, and so on.

The arguments originally advanced for the syntactic treatment of a great number of anaphoric processes (Grinder and Postal, 1971; Hankamer, 1973; Ross, 1969; etc.) do not stand up when turned against more sophisticated interpretive theories. But they are as yet unrefuted if constructed as showing the necessity of countenancing the existence of some level where anaphors are expanded, represented by a copy of their antecedents. These arguments taken together with Jacobson's, discussed briefly in section IV, would seem to argue strongly for generalizing the expansion treatment to all anaphoric processes of discourse grammar (in the sense of Williams 1977).[8] If so, then the generalization of the explanation given for the ungrammaticality of (5a) to examples like (5b,c) is independently motivated. This solves the third problem of section I, the asymmetry of the anaphor's interpretation on that of its antecedent.

Why does the ungrammaticality of CRs extend from the self-embedding patterns of (5) to the crossing ones of (6), the first of the three problems posed at the outset? The present theory provides an answer to this too. Anaphoric dependency interacts transitively with compositional dependency because expansion rules translate, as it were, the former into the latter. So to take (6a) for example, the interpretation of *her employer* compositionally depends on that of *her*, the interpretation of *her* anaphorically on that of *his secretary*. But at the level where the expansion rule has applied to *her*, it is represented as *his secretary* (copy). So *her employer* will simply compositionally depend on *his secretary* (copy). The makeshift notion of a-c dependency becomes superfluous.

This solution automatically provides an answer to the second problem of section I, for which, just like for the first, anaphoric chains held no promise of an explanation. Only anaphoric dependency interacts with compositional dependency because expansion is motivated only for anaphors. There is no syntactic motivation for the substitution of a variable by a copy of its quantifier or of course for the expansion of a lexical item in the shape of a segment whose selectional restrictions disambiguate it. Expansion in these cases would also produce semantically nonsensical results.

In summary, I have argued that the condition that deictic expressions must have determinable referents has no role to play in the explanation of the unacceptability of CRs. An alternative explanation was put forward that was based on independently motivated rules and which was able to account for some interesting properties of CR constructions.

I am grateful to James Higginbotham, Robert May, Geoff Pullum, Neil Smith and Deirdre Wilson for helpful conversations on this material.

NOTES

1. A number of such constraints have been proposed in the linguistic literature to exclude structures of this type. (For example cf. Postal, 1972; Vergnaud, 1974; Jacobson, 1977). These proposals are conspicuously *ad hoc* and do not cover or generalize naturally to the whole range of relevant data.
2. For example cf. Williams, 1977, for the distinction between sentence and "discourse" grammar rules.
3. Cf. Sag 1977; Williams, 1977.
4. In an earlier version of this paper, this assumption was incorrectly attributed to HM. I am grateful to James Higginbotham and Robert May for pointing this out to me.
5. I ignore a number of interesting questions that relate to the derivation of these and similar structures since they are not directly relevant to the present discussion. I should note that HM assume that in the derivation of (15a), Quantifier Raising applies to the subject NP, and that the target of the annotation entry for *her* is not closed, not simply because it contains a pronoun, but because it contains a pronoun related to a quantifier/variable.
6. As (i)–(iii) show in HM's framework, expansion must apply *after* the level L at which the condition C that excludes (iii) is stated (in HM L = logical form).
   (i)   Who$_x$ x said [his$_x$ mother] thought she$_y$ liked Tom
   (ii) Who$_x$ x said [his$_x$ mother] thought [his$_x$ mother] liked Tom
   (iii) Who$_x$ x said Mary$_y$ thought Mary$_y$ liked Tom
   The target of *she* in (i) is not closed in the sense of the Target Condition. If the pre-

dicted substitution applies not later than L producing (ii), this structure will be excluded by C. (Expansion in (i) will not be necessary in the framework I propose below.)

7. I assume along with much current work that some structural condition like c-command between antecedent and anaphor is necessary for the association to belong to sentence grammar, hence to be exempt from expansion.

Stating C of note (6) after expansion would entail that pronouns that have a c-commanding linguistic antecedent never expand; that they are related to their antecedents by a rule of sentence grammar. This would have certain advantages: it would eliminate the possibility of assigning an infinite number of representations to structures like (15a). Strict ordering here leads to a paradox however. Quantifier Raising has to be able to apply before expansion for (7a) to be derivable. But as pointed out in Brody (1979), in order to exclude "she$_x$ liked [some of the boys Mary$_x$ met]", C must apply before Quantifier Raising which might convert this structure into "[$_y$some of the boys Mary$_y$ met] she$_x$ liked y". This will not violate C any more, as the grammaticality of "[$_y$Which of the boys Mary$_x$ met] did she$_x$ like y" shows.

8. It is not clear how and whether this should be extended to anaphors whose antecedents are non-linguistic. In the same way, no position is taken here on the treatment of anaphors with antecedents that are inferred on the basis of some linguistic segment as for example in the case of "Every man who owns a donkey beats it".

Chapter 3

Comments and Replies

Comments on Brody's Paper

Keith Brown

Brody is concerned with two types of structure: those illustrated in his (5) involving "compositional dependency", where an anaphor is contained within its own antecedent, and those illustrated in his (6), involving "crossing dependencies", where one constituent contains an anaphor to a second and the second constituent contains an anaphor to the first. These problems have usually been considered to be distinct, but Brody rightly sees them as interrelated and seeks a unitary account of some of the problems that arise in these structures. The explanation he provides is along the right lines, though I shall argue that his solution should properly be part of a "discourse" component rather than lie within the semantic component of a sentence grammar, as he proposes.

The model he adopts assumes a number of distinct components. For our purposes, we need only note that there will be (i) a set of rules of syntax which will, *inter alia*, introduce pronouns and other anaphors through rules of the base; (ii) a set of rules which determine the "logical form" of a sentence: these will, *inter alia*, co-index anaphors with other constituents which can be their antecedents and, through the use of syntactic configurations involving notions of "c-command" and the like, identify syntactic configurations in which co-indexing is held to be obligatory, impossible, optional and so on; (iii) a further set of rules which map logical form to a full representation of meaning and (iv) a set of pragmatic rules, presumably including rules of discourse. If this account is correct, Brody is surely right to distinguish between "co-indexing", in (ii), and the establishment of referential dependencies, in (iii) (on this subject, see the remarks of Bach and Partee, 1980). As I have remarked above, I believe that his rules for establishing co-reference are more properly treated along with other discourse rules, and that if this were done, then many of his problems would disappear, since some of them may be an artefact of his model.

We may assume that the rules of syntax will generate all the strings shown in Brody's (5) and (6) without the marked co-indexing; indeed they must, since the strings shown are all perfectly acceptable without the compositional or crossing dependencies shown. We may further assume that the rules yielding logical form will permit the co-indexing shown in the examples; indeed we must assume this, since although he spends some time setting up a constraint of "a-c dependency" which might have been used to exclude such structures, he eventually rejects this as insufficiently general. Furthermore, as we shall see, not all the structures, co-indexed as in the examples, are impossible. Brody's solution is to develop machinery in his component "mapping logical form to a full representation of meaning" to account for the purported ill-formedness. This machinery, developed from Higginbotham and May (1979a) involves a level of representation in which anaphors are substituted by a copy of their antecedents, the expressions to which they are co-indexed. If this expression itself contains an anaphor, then this too must be substituted until no unsubstituted anaphors remain. This process will, of course, be impossible in some of the structures shown since it can never be concluded: an anaphor being substituted by a constituent containing an anaphor to itself, which will be substituted by a constituent containing an anaphor to itself and so on. Brody declares that it is not clear whether this "should be extended to anaphors whose antecedents are non-linguistic" (fn. 8), so called "exophoric" anaphors, but the machinery must surely be extended in this direction, since it is the only way out of the circularity, when this is possible. Brody himself appears to recognize this when he remarks (page 144) that "these arguments . . . argue strongly for generalizing the expansion treatment to all anaphoric processes of discourse grammar."

Given Brody's general model, one might wonder why he rejects a straightforward "configurational approach" to the problem: i.e. why does he not have a configurational condition, parallel to c-command and the like, which would simply disallow in logical form the sort of co-indexing shown in his (5) and (6). He does consider this solution with his notion of a-c dependency, but he rightly rejects it as insufficiently general. There are further reasons why this is not the correct solution. First, not all constructions involving compositional or crossing dependencies are impossible. Brody himself supplies an example in his (7) of an apparent compositional dependency that must be allowed to go through, and similar examples have been discussed in the literature (Bouton, 1970). The most famous case of crossing dependencies are the

Bach-Peters sentences, and these too have been extensively discussed. A second reason is that configurational approaches are not problem free: for example, both the "precede and command" and the "c-command" conditions, widely discussed in this connection, mark as impossible constructions that do in fact occur in appropriate discourse contexts; and mark as possible, constructions which are in fact impossible in certain discourse contexts (cf. Wasow, 1979; Bolinger, 1979; Kuno, 1972). As we shall see, some configurations that Brody declares to be ungrammatical are perfectly acceptable in appropriate circumstances. A final reason may well be that the scheme that Brody proposes, which seems to be along the right lines, should in fact be considered to be a part of the pragmatic, discourse, component and not part of the semantic component at all. We will return to this point, but in this connection, it is interesting to note that over the years we have seen this problem being passed from the syntactic component as such (Ross, 1967; Langacker, 1969) to the semantic component (Jackendoff, 1972), to the rules for determining logical form (Chomsky, 1980a). Perhaps we shall eventually see it in the pragmatic discourse component, where some have considered that it has always belonged (Kuno, 1972; Bickerton, 1975; Bolinger, 1979).

The syntactic and co-indexing potential of the sets of sentences Brody examines are slightly different, and one virtue of Brody's approach is that it attempts to unify the problems found in these various constructions in one common solution. For reasons of space, I will confine my remarks, as Brody and Kempson do, to a consideration of some of the properties of the structures involving anaphoric pronouns, illustrated in his (5a) and (6a).

Let us first consider the structure shown in his (5a). The first, and obvious, observation is that it is grammatical and acceptable on a non-co-indexed and non-co-referential interpretation: [$_x$ her$_y$ childhood friend's wife] to use Brody's notation, which I will preserve in my comments. Here we assume that the antecedent for *her* is outside the constituent of which it is a constituent, or it is exophoric.

Next observe that strings like his (5a), co-indexed as shown by Brody, are perfectly acceptable when they occur in complement constructions. Thus:

1. Mary$_x$ became [$_x$ her$_x$ childhood friend's wife].

Within the framework Brody adopts, complement constructions involve co-referentiality, and hence presumably co-indexing. Thus May and Higginbotham observe of the sentence (2) their example:

2. The singer of his song was Fred

"Many have noted examples like (2) where, apparently, co-reference is possible all round. But notice that in this case, *Fred* and the subject *can* be co-referential. Thus, the possibility of a non-circular annotation, giving the reference of *Fred* as the reference of *his*, also allows in this case co-reference between the pronoun and its container" (Higginbotham and May, 1979a, p. 23). It is not clear that either co-indexing or co-reference, unless suitably qualified, is an appropriate solution to this old problem, but this is not the place to pursue this matter (cf. the discussion in Lyons, 1977, 177ff).

Structures of this sort can obviously also contain pronouns: when Cain was asked where Abel was, he replied (Genesis 4.9):

3. Am I my brother's keeper?

It will be correctly observed that first person pronouns are necessarily exophoric, to the speaker. Structures like this also occur with third person pronouns:

4. He is his own worst enemy

and not surprisingly other complement constructions show a similar pattern of co-indexing:

5. He considers himself his own worst enemy

6. He elected himself his own company's chairman

In all these examples, of course, it is assumed that the subject pronoun is exophoric, and thus a chain of reference can be satisfactorily concluded. The point at issue here is that Brody claims that structures like his (5a) are "ungrammatical", and this is clearly not the case.

I turn now to sentences like Brody's (6a), repeated below as (7).

7. Her employer respects his secretary

We may first observe that if both of the pronouns are exophoric, clearly no problems arise, as can be seen if we substitute proper nouns for the pronouns:

8. Mary's employer respects John's secretary

furthermore that if the first pronoun is exophoric, the sentence is still acceptable even if the second pronoun cross-refers, as can be seen if we substitute a proper noun for the first pronoun:

9. $[_x$ Mary's $_y$employer] respects $[_y$ his$_x$ secretary]

If, however, the second pronoun is exophoric, then problems do arise, as can be seen if we substitute a proper noun for the second pronoun:

10. $[_x$ her$_y$ employer] respects $[_y$ John's$_x$ secretary]

This problem is not new, though it is perhaps more familiar in considering the differences in acceptability between examples like:

11. John$_x$ respects [his$_x$ secretary]

12. [her$_y$ employer] respects Mary$_y$

The former is agreed by all to present no difficulty. The latter, which incidentally the precede and command condition will disallow, but the c-command condition will permit, is generally held to be only properly interpretable in an appropriate context. The properties of such sentences have been discussed by, *inter alia*, Kuno (1972), Bickerton (1975) and Bolinger (1979). Kuno, for instance, offers the following generalization to cover the circumstances which he described, in 1972, as involving "backward pronominalisation":

"Backward pronominalisation is possible in English only when the rightmost of the two co-referential NPs represents old predictable information" (p. 302). He compares the distribution of the two sentences

13. John's brother visited him

14. His brother visited John

and remarks: "Let us examine these two sentences in contexts in which *John* is old information on the one hand, and in which it is new information, on the other:

15a. Who visited John and Mary? His brother visited John, but no one visited Mary.

15b. Who visited who? *His brother visited John.

Note that in (15a) . . . *John* represents old predictable information. Hence the acceptability of backward pronominalisation. On the other hand, in (15b) . . . *John* represents new, unpredictable information, hence the ungrammaticality of these sentences" (1972, pp. 303–304). In passing we may note that Kuno's generalization is too absolute. Bolinger (1979:293ff.) notes many plausible counter-examples, for instance: "No antecedent is necessary if the noun in question is CHARACTERISED:

16. Their pride has been the undoing of tyrants.

This could start a discourse. Tyrants are assumed to be noted for their pride." Kuno's generalization does, however, seem to be along the right lines, and it is echoed by many linguists (cf. Kempson, p. 170 below). In this case, at least part of the problem of sentences like (7) has nothing to do with co-indexing or co-reference as such, but is rather a discourse problem.

Let us now return to structures like Brody's (6a). As before, we find that if the subject NP contains a "first" or "second" person pronoun, no problems arise:

17. [$_x$my$_y$ wife] loves [$_y$her$_x$ husband]

18. [$_x$ your$_y$ children] love [$_y$their$_x$ father]

even though all the examples can have the crossing dependencies shown. To be sure, *my* and *your*, also refer exophorically to speaker, hearer etc. and this permits well formed referential chains to be established. Similarly, sentences with third person pronouns in the subject NP are unexceptionable under crossing and exophoric reference:

19. [$_x$ his$_y$ children] don't respect [$_y$ their$_x$ father]

etc.

However, we may observe that if we reverse the order of the pronouns, acceptability judgements change: sentences like

20. Her husband loves my wife

21. Their father loves your children

are extremely difficult, if not impossible, to interpret under the intended crossing interpretation. It is discourse considerations rather than semantic considerations as such that make cross reference difficult or impossible here.

There is a further curiosity about such sentences, which has to do with the semantic relationships between the lexical items concerned. Note that the examples all involve lexical pairs like *secretary-employer*, *husband-wife* etc. together with verbs like *love, respect* etc. Lexical relatedness surely has some part to play in their interpretation: thus even in a context where the hearer knows that the speaker is a "greengrocer" and that his wife loves him, a sentence like:

22. My wife loves her greengrocer

seems bizarre!

As before, the point is that the structures we are concerned with do permit cross-indexing and cross-reference. The question of the interpretability of these structures has to do with the possibility of establishing adequate referential chains; Brody is correct in this. However, the constraints on referencing are surely imposed by discourse and not by a semantic component independent of discourse.

The conclusion to which I am led, then, is this: Brody is wrong to suppose that his examples (5a) and (6a) are inevitably ungrammatical on readings in which they are understood to have compositional or crossing dependencies. He is right to suppose that anaphors must be linked to antecedents, either linguistic or exophoric, and that in examples like his (5a) and (6a), some anaphor must also have a referential dependency outside of the structures illustrated. He is, however, wrong if he supposes that this process can be performed in the semantic component alone: it must involve discourse considerations.

This is not to suggest that "syntactic" and "semantic" considerations play no part in resolving questions of anaphora, as some have implied (cf. the first paragraph of Bolinger, 1979) merely that such considerations must interact with discourse considerations. This is true not only in the examples discussed by Brody, but in other areas involving pronouns. For example, while many of the problems associated with the distribution of reflexive pronouns can be handled insightfully in the sort of grammar envisaged by Brody, there remain some problem areas. I will briefly mention two: one involving cases where a reflexive pronoun has no "clause mate", and the second where two "co-referential" pronouns occur as clause mates, but the second is not reflexive.

The first case involves the sort of reflexive pronouns adduced by Ross to support his performative verb analysis (1970). An example is:

23. This paper was written by Anne and myself

We don't need to rehearse Ross' arguments here, but it is worth pointing out that some of the sentences that Ross needed to find unacceptable in order to support his thesis, sentences like

24. The paper was written by Anne and himself

do not seem unacceptable if embedded in a suitable discourse context. Leech (1976, p. 92) discusses examples like:

25. Klinkhorn left Miami in 1953. For some time there had been an estrangement between his wife and himself.

Whatever the rules are that govern "pseudo" reflexives in sentences like (25), they clearly involve discourse considerations. The second sort of example is briefly mentioned by Bach and Partee (1980, p. 6): "Consider Quintus the war hero who is suffering from amnesia. He is discussing the war hero with a friend. We report "He (=Quintus) admired him". Further examples of a similar sort discussed in the literature involve the distinction between pairs of sentences such as

26. I can't imagine me playing the piano

27. I can't imagine myself playing the piano

(cf. Cantrall, 1971) or the necessary failure of reflexivization in a sentence like:

28. I dreamt I was Brigitte Bardot and I kissed me

The point at issue is that discourse and contextual matters affect the interpretation of these sentences, as they do in the cases we are primarily discussing.

The conclusion is not that structural considerations do not play a part in determining the potential for co-indexing or the establishment of referential dependencies, they clearly do, but that the rules for the establishment of referential dependencies interact with discourse considerations, and cannot be kept apart from them, a point noted by Chomsky (1980b: 167) with respect to the rule of focus.

Reply to Brown

Michael Brody

"Given Brody's general model one might wonder why he rejects a straightforward "configurational approach" . . . which would simply disallow in logical form the sort of co-indexing shown in his (5) and (6). He does consider this solution with his notion of a-c dependency, but he rightly rejects it as insufficiently general." (p. 149)

It is not clear to me why Brown takes the description in terms of a-c dependency to be a configurational account. As for such an account, Brown notes that HM claim that structures like (1) below in which the referent of the subject can be the same as that of the NP *Fred* provide an empirical reason for rejecting it.

(1) $[_\alpha$ The singer of his$_x$ song] was Fred$_x$

(2) *$[_x$ The singer of his$_x$ song] met Fred$_x$

The argument depends on the assumption that in (1) α is x, in which case a configurational condition could not distinguish (1) from the impossible (2). Since the identity relation between the subject and the postverbal NP is different in the two cases (say stipulated *vs* presupposed); the correctness of this assumption seems to be an open question (pertaining to the theory of proper interpretation of indices).[1]

The main reason for choosing a description in terms of a-c dependency *instead of* index configurations is that this description seems to be more perspicuous and it leads quite naturally to what I think is the explanation of the curious properties of CRs, and thus to the explanation of the *ad hoc* constraints designed to describe these. I did not "reject [the constraints stated in terms of a-c dependency] as insufficiently general" (neither did I question the possibility of providing a *description* in terms of index configurations[2]), but attempted to give a principled explanation for the set of phenomena described by them.

Brown suggests that "There are further reasons why this [i.e. constraints in terms of a-c dependency or of index configurations which he conflates] is not the correct solution." (p. 149). He takes the grammaticality of sentences like (7) and (15a) in *On Circular Readings* as one reason, but the a-c dependency description was set up precisely in such a way as to take account of these (and it is unclear why a configurational description could not do the same).

His second reason for this conclusion is that discourse considerations interact with configurational conditions to determine patterns of acceptability in what he takes to be CR structures. As a third argument, the suggestion is offered that "the scheme that Brody proposes, which seems to be along the right lines, should in fact be considered to be a part of the pragmatic, discourse, component . . ." (p. 150). Perhaps what is meant here is that this is a possible consequence of the previous point.[3]

Brown discusses structures where "crossing interpretations" are possible but do *not* exhibit circular dependencies and are not therefore CRs in the sense that I used the term. Thus e.g. in (1) above, the reference of the pronoun *his* may depend on that of *Fred*, but the reference of this NP does not depend on that of the subject. He gives further examples of non-CRs with "crossing interpretations", where one of the pronouns has a non-linguistic antecedent, and thus again do not exhibit circular dependencies. (For example in "[my_x wife] loves [$_\alpha$ her$_y$ husband]", the reference of the pronoun *my* is not given by/does not depend on that of the NP *her husband*.) Hence the point that "Brody claims that structures like his (5a) are "ungrammatical", and this is clearly not the case" seems unwarranted. The claim is that these are ungrammatical on a certain reading, i.e. with a certain structure of dependencies between interpretations.[4]

Brown exemplifies the interaction of pragmatic and configurational constraints in these structures and concludes that "the rules for the establishment of referential dependencies interact with discourse considerations and cannot be kept apart from them . . ." (p. 155). But the examples show the effect of pragmatic conditions only in those "crossing interpretation" structures where the dependencies between interpretations are not circular: a domain that is irrelevant for the concerns of *On Circular Readings*.

In a sense, this answer is beside the point, though. Consider the argument that the law of gravitation is incorrect since it interacts with considerations of, e.g. friction resistance, in accounting for the observed phenomena, and therefore cannot be kept apart from these. Care must be taken in denying the legitimacy of abstractions in general since rather serious consequences follow.

NOTES

1. Arguments based on other "predicational-type" structures (e.g. "he considers himself his own worst enemy" or "his wife, Mary, saw her husband") invite the same comment.
2. Although I did suggest that certain descriptions in these terms did not cover the whole range of relevant data.
3. Possibly the proposal that the expansion treatment must be extended to pronouns with non-linguistic antecedents is related to this, but I fail to understand why this follows from the fact that it is possible for pronouns to have non-linguistic antecedents.
4. There are a number of terms that are used in a significantly different sense in Brown's comments and in *On Circular Readings*. Most importantly from the point of view of possible confusion: "dependence of an interpretation on another" seems to mean sameness of interpretation for Brown, but is a more restrictive notion in *On Circular Readings*. Another term that appears to be used in a sharply differing sense is "compositional dependency".

Problems of Co-reference and Logical Form: Comments on Brody's Paper

Ruth Kempson

I. PRELIMINARIES

MB's paper contains three main sections. In the first part, he puts forward a so-called super-relation of a-c dependency (a = anaphoric, c = compositional). This a-c dependency is a relation which explicitly correlates anaphoric dependency and surface compositionality of a string. In order that a-c dependency will lead to the conclusion he wishes, MB must argue for an absolute distinction between quantifier-binding and anaphora, and this is the other main burden of section I. In the second section, he criticizes Higginbotham and May (H-M) for their pragmatic explanation of the deviance of circular readings. In the final part (in fact sections III–V of the written paper), he criticizes some of the mechanics of H-M (in particular their use of an "anaphoric chain"), and argues for replacement of their analysis with one which differs from theirs only in that the anaphoric chain is replaced by an "expand" rule which applies to all anaphoric pronouns (implicitly all anaphoric dependencies). He then claims that his notion of a-c dependency and the deviance of circular readings fall out as an automatic consequence of this account of pronouns expanding to the full form of their antecedent. It is at this point that the difference between quantifier-binding and other forms of anaphora are critical. For if on the contrary, all pronouns have to be given both a compositional account and a bound-variable account, then the explanation of the deviance of circular readings will only apply to one type of pronoun, and not the other. Hence the "naturalness" of the explanation evaporates.

My arguments will fall into four sections. First I shall argue that MB's attack on H-M's pragmatic explanation is spurious. Secondly, I shall argue that the account of VP anaphora implicit in the logical form for MB's example (7a), if suitably enriched, leads to the conclusion he seeks to avoid by this very example: namely that there is no radical difference in principle between variable-binding and pronominal anaphora, and that all pronouns must have two logically equivalent representations, (a) as bound variables, and (b) as a constant, referentially interpreted in the context. Only this latter corresponds to MB's "anaphoric" use. Thirdly, I shall argue that the position adopted by all trace theorists, MB included, is inconsistent with the Leftness constraint. Finally, I shall argue that the revision I propose for the H-M constraint against anaphoric circularity correctly prohibits all crossed referential dependencies.

II. ON THE DEVIANCE OF CIRCULAR READINGS

H-M propose a pragmatic explanation for the deviance of circularity which is approximately that if the reference of some segment A is given circularly, then it is indeterminable. MB attacks this on several grounds. The chief of these are (a) an argument concerning the necessary and harmless circularity in the disambiguation of the expression *a ball's trajectory*; (b) an argument that the H-M principle has to be generalized to one that is false. These do not seem to me to be convincing. MB's argument concerning *a ball's trajectory* runs as follows. The interpretation of *ball* depends on the whole NP since it is this which disambiguates it, and the NP in its turn depends for its (compositional) interpretation on *ball*. Hence circularity does not lead to difficulty in processing. But there is no circularity here. The interpretation of the phonological sequence *ball* as to which linguistic element is intended ($ball_1$ or $ball_2$) is dependent on relevance criteria and contextual factors, in this case provided by the pragmatic processing of the entire NP. The semantic interpretation of that NP depends on $ball_1$, or separately on $ball_2$. In the one case, we have a relation between a phonological sequence *ball* and its disambiguation by processing of the linguistic context. In the other case, we have a compositional relation between the NP and either the linguistic element $ball_1$ or the linguistic element $ball_2$, but invariably separately. No circularity. Finally, we come to MB's generalization of H-M's solution, generalized to include the interpretation of all anaphors. It runs, approximately, "No interpretation of any segment may be given circularly" (cf. Brody's (11), p. 139 above for his precise version). This MB says is false. The generalization, however, is uncharitable. If the generalization is restricted to anaphoric segments only, then it is surely correct. Thus the restriction should read, and I give it in full:

> If the interpretation of some anaphoric segment A has to be made circularly, that is, if it is dependent on that of another anaphoric segment B, and the interpretation of B is dependent on A, then the determination of the interpretation of A cannot be effected.

According to the intentions of H-M, this is a pragmatic constraint. It is not intended as a definition of anaphora, so it is not itself circular. Quite simple examples confirm this. The following are quite unacceptable:

(1) A Who is that?
   B That's him.

(2) *[What Sue did to Mary]$_i$ was what Mary did to her and what Mary did to her was [that]$_i$.

Indeed MB himself wishes to invoke something equivalent to my reformulation. The only problem is whether this restriction should be tightened to allow the crossing co-reference cases. I shall return to this problem at the end, where I shall argue that as a pragmatic constraint, what I have stated is correct.

III. VP ANAPHORA

We come now to MB's semi-logical notation. Much turns on the logical form for his example (7a) with its logical form (7b), for it is upon this that the distinction between quantifier-binding, a sentence-grammar process, and anaphoric interpretation, a discourse-grammar process, depends. His logical form 7b is at best incomplete. It should be (3), according to his conception of logical form:

(3) [Every girl who-y Peter [did y]$_{a_1}$]$_x$ Tom [kissed x]$_{a_2}$

That is to say, I have put in the trace caused by relative clause formation on *every girl*. There are many mysteries about this notation. First, it is not clear to me what principle determines that x and y are necessarily identical. Secondly, it is not clear what principle determines that it does not have the interpretation "Peter kissed every girl". Thirdly, it is not clear how this intermediate logical form with predicative elements still incorporated into the NP, which has undergone quantifier extraction, maps onto what I take to be a more standard logical form with a conditional:

$(\forall x)$ $[x$ a girl & Peter kissed $x \supset$ Tom kissed $x]$

But if we leave all those problems to one side, then what we have with all the trace-variables in evidence looks very much less like VP anaphora, and more like verb anaphora. For all that we require is did_V expanding as $kissed_V$. But if we assume this is the process required, then there is no inconsistency in a-c dependency, for we do not have the crucial containment relation between a_2 and the trace variable x left after $kissed$ by this process of quantifier-raising.[1] If there is no inconsistency, then there is no demonstration of the difference between quantifier-binding and anaphora.

Suppose, however, and more plausibly, MB argues that this is indeed a case of VP anaphora, on the grounds that VP anaphora is known to be insensitive to the variables contained in the VP. This is because of examples such as (4)

(4) All professors turn down every book they are asked to review, but a student doesn't.

Here the binding of the pronoun is particular to the second VP, despite its being anaphorically dependent on the first. On the evidence of such examples as these, Sag postulates a condition of identity which allows what is called "alphabetic variance" on his rule of VP-deletion (roughly speaking the VP predicate in general picks out the predicate, ignoring the binding of the variables in that antecedent predicate). Suppose on analogy with this, MB invokes a rule of VP anaphora which has built in a reconstruction which allows alphabetic variance,[2] then his analysis will be forced into the consequence which follows directly upon Sag's own analysis: that sentences containing pronouns must be treated as having two logical forms: one with the pronoun analysed as a bound variable, the other (MB's anaphoric interpretation) with the pronoun assigned a referential index. (For details cf. Sag, 1977, ch. 2.2; but the evidence turns on the ambiguity of sentences such as *John washed his dog and so did Bill.*) But this is the very conclusion which MB would presumably wish to avoid, for two reasons: (i) it interferes with his acceptance of a division between S-grammar and discourse grammar, (ii) it severely restricts the explanatory force of his account of the circular readings, since the bound variable account of pronouns will still require mechanisms corresponding to those he rejects as *ad hoc*, to explain their non-availability for circular readings. It is of course open to MB to argue for an analysis of VP anaphora which allows for alphabetic variance without logical ambiguity of pronouns, but Sag's arguments are to my mind persuasive. And in any case, there is independent evidence that sentences containing pronouns must be analysed in terms of two equivalent logical forms. Consider sentence (5):

(5) Only John washed his dog

This sentence is ambiguous: either John is asserted to be the only dog-owner to have washed the dog he owns, or John is asserted to have been the only one to have washed John's dog. It is only if we have two analyses of the sentence *John washed his dog* that (5) can be explained: one in which the subject has a predicate of a form equivalent to "x washes x's dog", and one which has a predicate equivalent to "x washes John's dog".

As I see it, the general problem which underlies MB's arguments is twofold: (i) the attempt to state anaphoric dependencies on surface sequence alone and with no regard to logical form is misguided; (ii) the attempt to state as logical forms, a weird mixture of surface structure and a representation which has undergone quantifier extraction (a format which is common in trace theory) leads to a spurious inter-level. It is to this second part of the problem that I now turn.

IV. PROBLEMS WITH THE LEFTNESS CONSTRAINT

Consider a sentence identical to MB's (7a) except that the universal quantifier is replaced by the definite article:

(6) John kissed the girl Bill did

I shall argue that the two possible analyses of this sentence within MB's framework are fraught with problems which cast doubt on the conclusions of his own paper. The two possible analyses are either that Quantifier-raising applies to the definite NP or that it does not. Assume first that it does not. It should accordingly have a logical form (6a):[3]

(6a) John [$_a$ kissed [the girl$_x$ wh$_x$ Bill [did x]$_{a'}$]]

If we assume a rule of VP anaphora (as in MB's analysis of (7a)), we get immediately into an obviously pernicious circularity problem, for the antecedent contains the anaphor in a way which is not rescuable by substitution. So we turn to the (admittedly plausible (!)) possibility that definite NP's are quantified expressions and therefore subject to Quantifier-raising (as in fact assumed by MB in expounding H-M). The logical form for (6) is therefore (6b):

(6b) [The girl$_x$ wh$_x$ Bill [$_{a'}$ did x]]$_x$ John [$_a$ kissed x]

The circularity problem is now avoided, but problems arise with other sentences containing definite noun phrases. Consider first (7)

(7) The man who died loved the woman who nursed him

According to the pattern of (6b), this would have (7a) as its logical form.

(7a) [The man$_x$ who$_x$ x died] [the woman$_y$ who$_y$ y nursed him] x loved y

But now recall the leftness constraint invoked by MB* to explain the deviance of his (17b) "[The man who his$_y$ wife loved]$_y$". This according to Chomsky (1976) states that no pronoun can have an antecedent involving a trace to its right. The leftness constraint therefore predicts that (7) cannot have an interpretation in which *him* is co-referential with the subject. Incidentally, this criticism applies to the logical forms of H-M as well,[4] and also to Chomsky's analysis of the leftness constraint examples if we assume his own analysis of definite NP's.

There are four possible ways out of this that I can think of, two of them not compatible with the facts, and two of them theoretically quite unsatisfactory. The first is to say that the leftness constraint as applied by H-M and MB does not exclude the possibility of a co-referential trace variable to the right of a pronoun, as long as there is a trace variable to its left. This would allow in (7a) co-reference between *him* and the subject, on the strength of the x in the initial quantifying expression. Even if this were a plausible move, it seems to be factually wrong. Consider (8)–(10):

(8) Which student that she loved did the professor report t to the authorities?

(9) Which student did the professor he seduced report t to the authorities?

(10) Which student that she loved t did the professor he seduced report t to the authorities?

On the assumption that quantifier-raising has applied to the definite NP we have as logical forms for (8)–(10) (8a)–(10a):

---

* The leftness constraint was mentioned in the preliminary version of MB's paper, but not in the revised version published here, cf. below, p. 177 (ed.)

(8a) [Which student$_x$ wh$_x$ she loved x] [the professor]$_y$ y reported x
to the authorities

(9a) [Which student]$_x$ [the professor$_y$ wh$_y$ he seduced y] y reported
x to the authorities

(10a) [Which student$_x$ wh$_x$ she loved x] [the professor$_y$ wh$_y$ he
seduced y] y reported x to the authorities

(8a) is predicted to have no co-reference with the professor and *she*, on
the basis that there is only one trace variable y which is to the right of
she. Incorrect. (9a) with one trace variable x to the right of *he* also, this
time correctly, predicts no co-reference between *he* and *which student*.
But in (10a), where there is a preceding and following instance of x
around *he*, this version of the leftness constraint predicts incorrectly
that *he* can be co-referential with *which student*. Even if we assume that
definite NP's are not subject to quantifier-raising, this weakened version of the leftness constraint makes incorrect predictions. The only
way to achieve the correct results is to have a leftness constraint prohibiting any occurrence of a trace variable to the right of a pronoun
sharing its antecedent with no extraction of the definite NP's by quantifier-raising. This allows co-reference between *she* and *the professor* in (8)
but disallows co-reference between *he* and *which student* in both (9) and
(10).

The second alternative is to restrict the leftness constraint so that it
only applies within what H-M call the restriction of the quantifier, i.e.
within the relative clause inside the extracted quantifying element.
Though this would certainly save the prediction required for (7), it is
quite implausible, since it would no longer account for the examples
(11) and (12), for which Chomsky (1976, p. 342) set up the leftness constraint:

(11) Who did the woman he loved betray?

(12) Who was betrayed by the woman he loved?

In these cases, the logical forms Chomsky assigns are (11a) and (12a):

(11a) (For which person x) the woman he loved betrayed x

(12a) (For which person x) x was betrayed by the woman he loved

Only (12) allows a co-referential reading between *he* and *who* and only
in (12a) is the trace variable not to the right of *he*. If however we assume
quantifier-raising in the form MB assumed,[5] we have (11b) and (12b):

(11b) [For which person x] [the woman$_y$ wh$_y$ he loved y]$_y$ y betrayed x

(12b) [For which person x] [the woman$_y$ wh$_y$ he loved y]$_y$ x was betrayed by y

In none of these forms is there a variable x to the right of the pronoun *he* in the restriction of the quantifier itself, and so none of them would be excluded if we restrict the application of the leftness constraint to the restriction on the quantifier. So this restriction of the leftness constraint to within the complex quantifiers themselves cannot be upheld. Thus, neither of the two possible modifications of the leftness constraint at the level of logical form makes the predictions required.

The third alternative is not to modify the leftness constraint, but rather to assume that quantifier-raising, like all other rules in the trace-theoretic framework, is an optional rule. In the case of definite NPs, we then have two types of case. Quantifier-raising can apply without the intervention of the leftness constraint in such cases as the proposed logical form (6b) for example (6). It can also apply in cases such as (7), where its output (7a) will be filtered out by the leftness constraint; since in this latter case, there will also be a logical form identical in sequence to the surface string, in which quantifier-raising has not applied.[6] This solution is unsatisfactory for two reasons. On the one hand, on the basis of the optionality of quantifier-raising, it will allow as a well-formed logical representation, the circular reading of (6), which it is the burden of MB's paper to exclude. On the other hand, for the same reason, it will provide for all sentences containing quantifiers, a representation at logical form identical in sequence to that of the surface string. For example, one logical characterization of the sentence *Someone loves everyone* will be "Someone loves everyone". It is, of course, open to anyone suggesting this alternative to invoke "a straightforward algorithm", which maps logical forms of the trace-theoretic framework onto a more transparent semantic notation. But in all these cases, any such algorithm would have to map surface structure sequences on to genuine logical forms. It would therefore render the intermediate trace-theoretic level of logical form entirely redundant. While I suspect this would be the correct move to make, it is not likely to be one that any trace-theorist would accept lightly.

The fourth and final alternative, advocated by Chomsky at Pisa in 1979, is that the leftness constraint be weakened to say that a sentence may have a reading in which a trace variable has an antecedent identical to that of the pronoun as long as *at some stage* in the derivation, the pronoun is to the right of the variable. This is a cheat. There are only two rules which leave variables (i.e. traces that become variables bound by a quantifier), the rule of *wh*-movement and the rule of quantifier-raising. This move is therefore equivalent to a filter which ignores quantifier extraction while wishing to treat it as forming a natural class with *wh*-movement. If both these rules leave traces (by a syntactic process) which become variables at the level of logical form, then any filter is only substantial if applied to the class as a whole and not to a (semantically arbitrary) subset. Such a revision of the leftness constraint is also unsatisfactory in that any constraint on the richness of interpretation a sentence may have is something that *ought* to be captured at the level of logical form, the level that purports to represent what is in some sense said. It is theoretically inadequate to capture the generalization at a stage in the derivation which is not even a well-defined level of the syntax, let alone of the logic. We are faced with one of two conclusions within MB's framework. Either the leftness constraint has to be abandoned, or quantifier-raising in the form MB has it must not apply to definite NPs (or indeed at all, if we take H-M's examples into account as well!).

There is independent evidence, however, that quantifier-raising must apply to definite NP's, in order to capture the data of VP anaphora. Recall the discussion of section III on anaphora, and the requirement of identity of predicates allowing alphabetic variance of variables. With some such analysis of VP anaphora, we require quantifier-raising to apply to definite NP's in a construction such as (6) not only because of circularity problems, but because the condition of alphabetic invariance is only met if the definite NP is analysed along the lines of Chomsky (1975) as involving universal quantification (cf. fn. 5 and Sag, 1977, ch. 2.3). Thus if Sag's argument is correct, we have independent evidence that the list of quantifying expressions must be extended to include definite NP's. Moreover, the data of the leftness constraint are not altogether clear. Compare (11) with (13):

(13) It was John that the woman he loved betrayed.
According to Chomsky (1977), clefts involve *wh*-movement into the position of *that*, so there would be a trace variable left following *betrayed*. Yet co-referentiality between *John* and *he* (and hence between *he* and the trace variable) seems clearly possible. It looks as though the leftness constraint may have to be abandoned. But this leaves part of MB's analysis unexplained.

V. NO CIRCULAR READINGS?[7]

In section II, I proposed a revision of H-M's pragmatic constraint as a constraint that no anaphoric segment may be dependent on another anaphoric segment which is dependent on the first. An immediate apparent counter-example is any crossing co-reference sentence which people find acceptable: e.g. (14):

(14) [The woman who touched him$_j$]$_i$ shouted at [the man who was near her$_i$]$_j$

MB assumes (following Jacobson) that these are acceptable on a crossing co-referentially dependent reading, and are, moreover, synonymous with (15):

(15) The woman who touched the man who was near her shouted at the man who was near her.

I now wish to suggest that both of these claims are false.

First consider the matter of crossing co-reference. I have so far assumed that this way of referring to the problem is unexceptionable. It isn't. The question of relevant acceptability is not whether such examples allow crossing co-reference, for of course they do. Even MB's (6a) is acceptable as long as the pronouns are not referentially dependent on each other, as witness (16):

(16) In our office, there is just one employer and one secretary, a girl called Ruth. Her employer respects his secretary, which never ceases to surprise her.

The concept we must operate with is Evans' "referential dependence" (Evans, 1980). What I wish to argue is that though there is a semantically consistent analysis of any sentence containing cross-dependent pronouns, such an interpretation is invariably excluded by a pragmatic constraint. According to this analysis, crossing co-reference sentences are only acceptable if at least one of the anaphoric elements is referentially dependent on the context and not from within the sentence itself.

I shall return to this shortly. But before doing so, I wish to establish the non-equivalence of (14) and (15).

W: a set of women
M: a set of men
→ touch
← near

In the domain listed, there are eight people in all. Three of the women touched one man who was near the one woman who did the shouting. Under these circumstances, where the uniqueness of the first noun phrase is not satisfied, the sentence cannot be true (it is false, unsatisfiable, call it what you will): it is not possible to determine which individual is indicated by the subject expression of whom to evaluate the predicate. (15) however is true. (14) only becomes true if the domain is restricted to just two people with the matching properties, number one touching number two, and number two being near number one with number one shouting at number two. If this is correct, then the truth conditions of MB's (15a) and (16a) are not identical either. (15a) and (16a) are merely misleadingly similar for entirely non-linguistic reasons: in our culture, one is not married to more than one person at a time. It is of course possible to dispute truth-value judgments and in any case, they are not always relevant to determining interpretations. But if we form a *wh*-question on MB's (15a) and (16a), the difference between them is brought out more clearly.

(17) Which man who loved his wife kissed his wife?

(18) Which man who loved her kissed his wife?

(17) is straightforwardly paraphraseable as "Of all the men who loved their wives, which kissed his?"; but (18) has no coherent, circular, paraphrase. It only has "Out of all the men who loved some identified female, which kissed his wife?". Similarly (19) and (20).

(19) Which woman who touched the man who was near her shouted at the man who was near her?

(20) Which woman who touched him shouted at the man who was near her?

But if, in parallel to these, Brody's (15a) and (16a) are not semantically identical, then we cannot expect to explain (15a) in terms of (16a): MB's explanation must be wrong. Indeed MB's decision to follow the Jacobson analysis and explain the first pronoun in terms of expansion but the second as a bound variable is really quite arbitrary. For in equivalent cases, either NP can be acceptably expanded. Thus it is possible to expand (21) as either (22) or (23):

(21) The man who loved her kissed the woman who was married to him.

(22) The man who loved the woman he was married to kissed the woman he was married to.

(23) The man who loved her kissed the woman who was married to the man who loved her.

Furthermore, as pointed out in H-M (1979b), there are cases where both pronouns must be treated as a bound variable, and where the truth-conditional divergence is much greater: (24)–(25):

(24) Many pilots who shot at them hit many Migs that chased them.

(25) Many pilots who shot at many Migs that chased them hit many Migs that chased them.

As a preliminary to an alternative explanation, consider (14) in the following environment (14'):

(14') There were forty men and women touching each other in a very small room. In other words, they all had several people near them and they were all in one way or another touching quite a lot of people more or less simultaneously.

Under just this background, with no other information, (14) is to my mind uninterpretable. The only way to process it is to fix on a referent either for the first occurrence of *the woman* or the first occurrence of *her* and then predicate the content of the other NP of that individual. Notice the improvement in acceptability in (26):

(26) The woman$_i$ shouted at [the man who was near her$_i$]$_j$, who she$_i$ was touching.

(26) is equivalent to (14) except that the first restrictive relative clause has been postposed as a non-restrictive relative clause. In (26), the first NP has consequently to be assigned a referent independently of the linguistic context the sentence itself provides. The interpretation of the relative clause as a non-restrictive relative clause in crossing co-reference cases invariably has this effect, since non-restrictive relatives are well known to be equivalent to conjunctions. But in making any such move to interpret any one of the NP's without reference to the other, one is no longer processing the sentence by circular means, even though the result may be that of crossing co-reference. In Evans' terms, whichever expression is taken referentially is then *not* referentially dependent on the remainder of the sentence. Any pragmatic constraint which excluded all cross-referential dependency would lead to the prediction that in a context where no other dependency is provided, the sentence will be unacceptable. It is only possible to interpret it acceptably if in fact the context is boosted to include such a dependency. This prediction seems to be correct. Thus I suggest that in all crossing co-reference

sentences, the sentence is never interpreted with crossing dependency, either where there is co-reference or even where the sentence may be true under such a semantic analysis.

Let me take one more example-plus-context, this time involving a plural NP, where the truth conditions of restrictive relative clauses are easier to distinguish from those of a non-restrictive relative.

(27) The students who had stoned them were attacked by the vandals who were behind them.

(28) There was a large student demonstration outside Brixton Town Hall last night.

The sequence (28) plus (27) does not seem to me to be an acceptable part of the 8 a.m. news. It only becomes so if the relative clauses are differently understood as non-restrictive relatives. This is the prediction made by an analysis which pragmatically forbids cross-referential dependency.

What then is the semantic analysis of these sentences under a cross-dependency interpretation? As I see it, their truth conditions are only satisfied as uniquely matching pairs. That is to say MB's (6a) is true just in case there is in the domain just one employer and just one secretary such that he respects her. Indeed it is for sentences of this general type for which H-M motivate a double binding of quantifiers: quantification over pairs of variables. Similarly in (14). (14) is true just in case there is a unique pair of man plus woman, the woman touching the man, who is near her, and she shouted at him. In other words, both pronouns must be taken as bound variables and bound simultaneously to a pair of quantifiers. It is however significant that it is precisely in these very restricted domains that the NP's in question are in any case uniquely identifiable in the context. Thus these cases have truth conditions which are only satisfiable in contexts where they are non-distinct from contextual uniqueness. It therefore follows that the very considerable increase in descriptive power involved in using double quantification need not and (according to the pragmatic constraint proposed) should not be invoked.

On this analysis, not only is MB's (6a) unacceptable on a crossed dependency reading: so too are all other circular dependencies such as (29):

(29) The man who loved her kissed his cousin

(I have replaced MB's example with *wife* with the less unique matching relation of *cousin*.) One immediate riposte might be that such an account is unable to distinguish the difference between (30) and (31), a distinction which many feel to be considerable:

(30) The man who employed her kissed his secretary

(31) Her employer kissed his secretary

The answer, I submit, is that a possessive pronoun in subject position, despite the possibility of co-reference with a following object NP, cannot be referentially dependent on it. Thus *His mother loves John* is to my mind only acceptable with prior reference to John. Notice how much odder (32) is:

(32) His mother loves the man who lives upstairs.

One very frequently refers to people repeatedly by name. One does not, however, refer to people by descriptions such as *the man who lives upstairs* if their identity is independently established. Thus an analysis of (32) which disallows referential dependency between *his* and the following NP has an obvious explanation for its oddity. Compare also the three following sequences:

(33) Mary walked into the room with Sue holding her hand. When his wife saw John, she turned and ran.

(34) Mary walked into the room with Sue, John's wife, holding her hand. When his wife saw John, she turned and ran.

(35) A Mummy, tell me a story about when you were young.

      B O.K. dear. His mother was cruel to your great-uncle.

(34) is of course acceptable, but neither (33) nor (35) are. The formal statement of this restriction is of independent theoretical interest, for it appears to provide evidence in favour of a semantic account of restrictions on referential dependence (cf. Bach and Partee, 1980), rather than the more orthodox syntactic account (in terms of c-command: cf. Reinhart, 1976, 1979). For Reinhart's constraint could not simultaneously disallow referential dependence between the pronoun *his* and the definite NP in (32) and yet allow referential dependence between pronoun and definite NP in (36).

(36) In his cave, the wizard keeps a dragon.

In both cases, the definite NP is not in the syntactic domain of the pronoun (cf. Reinhart, 1979, for details). On the contrary however, the restriction is relatively simple to state as a function-argument restriction, as long as we assume definite NP's are quantified expressions. The restriction is in the form suggested by Bach and Partee (p. 17ff. and fn. 13):

A pronoun whose interpretation is free in the argument of a function cannot be bound by a quantifier which "came from" a position within the function.

According to this restriction, (32) would only be acceptable if the pronoun is interpreted as referentially dependent on some entity outside the linguistic context provided by the sentence itself. And this restriction, together with the Higginbotham and May, pragmatic constraint on crossing co-reference, guarantees that the crossed interpretation of (31) is prohibited for two reasons: one semantic, and one pragmatic.

It may seem that there are some very obvious counter-examples to a constraint prohibiting crossed anaphora, such as (37)–(38).

(37) Many white collar workers that have strong opinions about them criticize most politicians that ignore them.

(38) A boy who had dropped one took a sweet that another one had put on his desk.

But neither of these are genuine counter-examples. The only natural reading of (37) is with the first *them* equal to *politicians*, the second equal to *white collar workers*. This is not a circular dependency, and so is not a counter-example. Similarly in (38). The first *one* is only anaphoric to *a sweet* and crucially not to *a sweet that another one had put on his desk*. Nor is the second *one* anaphoric to *a boy who had dropped one*. More generally, anaphora with *one* appears to be invariably lazy in this way in not picking up the total semantic content in any context where to do so would lead to circularity. This is consistent with the analysis suggested here. *One* anaphora allows its content to include the entire predicative content of the preceding NP as in one of the possible interpretations of (39):

(39) Jo bought a book on Chomsky and Bill bought one too.

Thus there is nothing in the semantics of *one*-anaphora to exclude a circular reading of (38). It is the pragmatic constraint that predicts that it will never be interpreted in that way, which indeed it never is.

An apparently more serious counter-example is (40):

(40) A boy who was fooling her kissed a girl who loved him.

However, it must be remembered that restrictive and non-restrictive relative clauses are indistinguishable with indefinite singular noun phrases. A crossed reading of (40) is logically indistinguishable from either (41) or (42):

(41) A boy, who was fooling her, kissed a girl who loved him.

(42) A boy, who was loved by a girl he was fooling, kissed her.

In other words, in view of the existential quantification representing the indefinite NP, the logical form of (40) involves no crucial binding be-tween *him* and the complex NP *a boy who kissed her* but only between *a boy* and *him*.

If what I have tentatively suggested is even in outline correct, then the problem that faces MB's analysis disappears. Within his account, though the circular dependencies are predicted to be unacceptable upon a compositional interpretation of the pronouns, there have to be additional mechanisms to explain why bound variable readings are im-possible. On this account, no crossed dependency is acceptable. Crossed referential interpretations are acceptable only if the depen-dency is assumed to be provided outside the linguistic context of the sentence itself: i.e. in the background context.

NOTES

1. There is some slight evidence in favour of analysing this e.g. as sub-VP anaphora. Like other cases of sub-VP anaphora, backward anaphora is impossible (cf. Sag, 1977, p. 34, fn. 32). The string corresponding to this logical form in surface sequence is unacceptable on the required anaphoric understanding.
2. Notice that even this weakening of the statement of identity cannot be stated as a compositional expansion rule operating on a surface string, for the reconstructed VP in the second antecedent of (4) is not stringwise identical to the first.
3. In all the logical forms that follow, I shall assume identity of indexing between the head NP and the binding within the relative clause, since presumably the identifica-tion has to be made as part of the mapping onto logical form.
4. The logical form of H-M's (36) ((i) below) is (ii):
    (i) Every student that took it passed some test he dreaded.
    (ii) (Every x, some y:x a student that took it & y a test he dreaded) x passed y.
   In (ii), y is to the right of *it* even within the restriction of the quantifiers and x in the matrix predicate is to the right of *he*. Furthermore, *it* has no occurrence of y to its left within the quantifier's restriction. Thus on any of my suggested analyses of the left-ness constraint, this logical form should be excluded as a possible interpretation.
5. In Chomsky (1975, p. 100), it is argued that definite NP's involve universal quantifi-cation. A more complete rendering of Chomsky's logical form for (11) and (12) would accordingly be (11c) and (12c).
    (11c) (For which person x) $(\exists W_1 \, \forall_{\substack{w \\ w \in W_1}} (\text{he loved } w \supset w \text{ betrayed } x))$
    (12c) (For which person x) $(\exists W_1 \, \forall_{\substack{w \\ w \in W_1}} (\text{he loved } w \supset x \text{ was betrayed by } w))$
   W is a restricted set variable ranging over women
   W_1 is a set whose cardinality is I; W_1 a member of W
   w is a restricted individual variable ranging over any individual w ε W_n
   Notice that here too, the leftness constraint in any of the forms I have suggested makes wrong predictions.
6. This alternative was proposed to me by MB (personal communication).
7. This section is the result of extensive discussions with Annabel Cormack.

Reply to Kempson

Michael Brody

Kempson comments on the grounds of my disagreement with H-M's pragmatic explanation for the deviance of circular readings in the following terms: "The chief of these are (a) an argument concerning the necessary and harmless circularity in the disambiguation of the expression *a ball's trajectory*; (b) an argument that the H-M principle has to be generalized to one that is false. These do not seem to me to be convincing" ("the H-M principle" here refers to the assumption made by HM that is named the Circularity Principle (8) in *On Circular Readings* (OCR)).

As reiterated several times in the paper, the reasons why I do not find HM's solution satisfactory are the following: (a) it has no contribution to make to two of the three basic problems of CRs, that a-c dependency involves only anaphoric and compositional dependencies and that these interact transitively; (b) the two assumptions it makes use of to account for the unacceptability resulting from the asymmetry of the dependence of a pronoun's reference on that of its antecedent (the Circularity Principle for referential linkages and the pragmatic principle that the reference of a pronoun must be determinable) are neither independently motivated nor necessary; (c) even if the Circularity Principle had given an explanation of the asymmetry of referential dependence, this explanation would not be generalizable to the whole range of data.

The point concerning the disambiguation example relates to the claim that the Circularity Principle is not logically necessary. I argued that it is in principle possible to compute the interpretation of anaphor and antecedent in a CR and suggested that the way this may be done is parallel in relevant respects to the way the interpretations are computed in the disambiguation case. Kempson disagrees then with (c) and with the appropriateness of a particular exemplification of how the computation of the interpretations might proceed in a CR, hardly the chief points of the argument against the "pragmatic solution".

As for the disambiguation case, it was stated in the paper in what way the computation of the interpretations could be similar in these and in CRs. Kempson gives essentially the same description of this computation for the *ball's trajectory* example and gives no reason why the parallel I suggested could not hold. This does not amount to an argument. Kempson's claim that in the disambiguation case there is "no circularity" because the interpretations are computable is only an unfortunate terminological proposal. In the same sense, there is "no circularity" in CRs.[1]

Kempson rejects (c) on the grounds that it is possible to state a constraint to the effect that the dependence of an anaphor's interpretation on that of its antecedent is asymmetric.[2] This confuses description and explanation. The question I addressed was whether the constraint (of which several alternative formulations were offered in OCR) could be *explained* as being the consequence of the logical necessity of a circularity principle generalized to all dependencies between interpretations ((11) in OCR). Since this principle is false, as shown among other things by the disambiguation case, it is not necesary, and thus cannot provide the explanation which was then looked for elsewhere.

In section III, Kempson concludes on the basis of sloppy identity type facts "that sentences containing pronouns must be treated as having two logical forms: one with the pronoun analysed as a bound variable, the other (MB's anaphoric interpretation) with the pronoun assigned a referential index." (p. 162) This would cause problems for the solution in OCR since "(i) it interferes with [my] acceptance of a division between S-grammar and discourse grammar, (ii) it severely restricts the explanatory force of [my] account of circular readings since the bound variable account of pronouns will still require mechanisms corresponding to those [I] reject as *ad hoc* to explain their non-availability for circular readings." (p. 162–3) Kempson assumes that the bound variable reading in e.g. "Only John likes his dog" involves a sentence grammar rule, and the other reading involves a process that belongs to discourse grammar. Although not unnatural, the step is gratuitous; this seems to be a matter for research not for decision. (A pronoun interpreted as a bound variable might be considered to have a variable as its antecedent and it may expand accordingly as a variable. As for sentence grammar linkages, no claim was stated or intended that all dependent elements involved in these must be interpreted as bound variables.)

Suppose that pronouns interpreted as bound variables are invariably linked to their antecedent by a sentence grammar rule. C-command of a pronoun by its antecedent (or some similar structural configuration) was considered in OCR to be a necessary condition for the linkage to belong to sentence grammar. The data that Kempson cites do not appear to pose difficulties for this, since they motivate an account in terms of the bound variables only for pronouns whose antecedents c-command them. For the same reason (ii), is equally unwarranted; no circular structures are constructible using such pronouns.[3] The assumption that c-command of a pronoun by its antecedent entails that it is treated by a rule of sentence grammar is not used in the explanation of the properties of CRs. Hence, whether the relationship between the pronoun and its antecedent in the "referential" reading of "Only John likes his dog" belongs to discourse grammar or not, the phenomenon shows no problems with the distinction between the two components of grammar assumed in OCR.[4]

Kempson concludes this with some admonitions concerning what she considers to be the general problem. The relation of these to the foregoing more concrete remarks seems loose. She expresses dissatisfaction with proposals about levels of representation made on the basis of empirical evidence, on the grounds that they do not conform to the demands of some extrinsic consideration (whose identity incidentally is left vague by her appeal to "more standard" and "genuine" logical form. I am unable to see the merits of this admittedly quite popular objection to the empirical approach to grammatical theory construction.[5]

I shall refrain from commenting on Kempson's discussion of the leftness constraint, since it is irrelevant to the problem of CRs. In OCR, reference is made to a constraint, call it D, that distinguishes (17a) and (17b). For the purposes of the paper, it does not matter what the formulation of D is, only its existence is assumed: a fact that is difficult to deny.

In the last part of her comments,[6] Kempson puts forward the claim that not only structures like (5) and (6) but also ones like (15a) and, presumably, (7a) (numbering from OCR) are unacceptable. She wishes to extend the principle which describes the asymmetry of the anaphor's interpretation on that of its antecedent to sentence grammar relationships. The distinction between (5) and (6) *vs* (15a) and (7a) was accounted for in OCR with the help of the independently motivated distinction between sentence and discourse grammar. Extending the Circularity Principle from discourse to sentence grammar linkages re-opens the problem. Kempson's suggestion is that (6a) "*[her_y employer] kissed [$_y$ his_x secretary]" is worse than (15a) "[the man who loved her_y] kissed [$_y$ his_x wife]" because "a possessive pronoun in subject position, despite the possibility of co-reference with the following object NP, cannot be referentially dependent on it"; hence (6a) is excluded for two reasons. This seems to be somewhat less than a full-fledged alternative, since it ignores all the other contrasts between members of (5), (6) and (15a) or (7a). (The opposition between "a friend of his_x mother talked to Tom_x" and "*[$_y$ a friend of his_x mother] talked to [her_y secretary]" suggests that the contrast between (6a)-type and (15a)-type structures is not due to such a constraint either.)

More importantly, it is unclear why Kempson considers the extension of the Circularity Principle to sentence grammar linkages and/or the assumption that this is a pragmatic constraint[7] as an alternative explanation of the problems of CRs. Contrary to her assertions, her judgements on the data do not seem to change the nature of the basic problems that need explanations: why is anaphoric (for Kempson in the wider sense, incorporating sentence grammar associations) dependence asymmetric, why do only anaphoric (again for Kempson in the wider sense) and compositional dependencies interact and why do they form a transitive chain?

NOTES

1. Note that even if the parallel turned out to be non-existent, this in itself would have no consequence for the crucial claim here: that the Circularity Principle for referential linkages is not logically necessary.
2. I am not sure what Kempson means by saying that this constraint is "pragmatic". She attributes this assumption to H-M. The way I understand these authors, they assume that the Circularity Principle is logically necessary, and it *interacts* with a pragmatic constraint to rule out CRs.
3. If H-M's Absorption analysis is correct, then there will be a class of marked crossing interpretation structures in which a pronoun interpreted as a bound variable will not be c-commanded by its antecedent in surface structure. There are a number of ways in which this could be integrated into the framework of OCR, but as far as I can see, no conclusions like Kempson's (i), (ii) in the text, can be drawn on the basis of these phenomena either.

4. But cf. note 7 of OCR for some speculations that would entail that both readings belong to sentence grammar.
5. In section III, she cites a number of other "mysteries", which do not seem to me to be real, being based on this and other misunderstandings.

The suggestion that the rule in (7a) in OCR is the (highly marginal) process of "sub-VP anaphora" also seems wrong; cf. "Tom wants to kiss every girl Peter wants to" *vs* "*Tom wants to kiss Mary and Peter wants to Betsy". (The alleged "slight evidence" in fact also argues against the proposal, if anything can be based on such marginal data.) There is not much difference between (i) and (ii) whereas in the cases of verb deletion (iii, iv) the contrast between forward and backward deletion seems greater:

(i)?   Every girl Peter kissed Tom did also
(ii)?   Every girl Peter did Tom kissed also
(iii)?   Mary hasn't met Tom but she has Harry
(iv)   *Mary hasn't Tom but she has met Harry

In any case, since the distinction between sentence grammar binding and discourse grammar anaphora is equally well motivated by (15a) of OCR, even if Kempson's point was right, its importance for OCR would be minimal.
6. Kempson also argues here on the basis of evidence from synonymy relationships that the analysis of OCR "must be wrong". But in order for the explanations in the paper to be correct, it is not necessary for the levels of representations involved to have semantic import in this sense at all. (This is why as far as OCR is concerned, Quantifier Raising could be an optional rule.) What kind of "semantic" properties these levels have is again a matter for empirical research, not for stipulation. Assuming that the synonymy data is relevant, it seems to be good methodology to let the clear facts determine the theory and to let the theory determine the status of the less clear ones. That semantic judgements of the type involved here are notoriously unreliable is well documented in the literature (cf. Jacobson, 1977 for a review).

In stating that the decision to "explain the first pronoun in terms of expansion but the second as a bound variable is really quite arbitrary", Kempson forgets that this was made on the basis of the fact that the first but not second behaves as if it was its antecedent under constraint D (cf Jacobson, 1977).
7. Cf. note 2 above.

Chapter 4
Mutual Beliefs in Question–Answer Systems

Aravind K. Joshi

I. INTRODUCTION[1]

Man–machine interactive systems are usually designed to serve some helpful function. As in the corresponding human conversational situations, a certain amount of co-operative behavior is expected in these systems, i.e. the system (S) is expected to help the user in a variety of ways such as correcting possible misconceptions of the user (U), helping U to formulate the appropriate question, providing U with the requested information (which may involve straightforward retrieval or more complex computations on the information in the knowledge base of the system), explaining to U the structure of the knowledge base, possibly even demonstrating to U how to carry out certain procedures, etc. A number of systems have been proposed and/or designed in the past several years which exhibit one or more of these aspects (e.g. Hobbs and Robinson, 1977; Grosz, 1978; Kaplan, 1979; Mays, 1980; McKeown, 1980; and others).

   Such helpful behavior depends both on the knowledge of the domain of discourse as well as a variety of rules, conventions, postulates, etc. that allow the communication of intentions and beliefs in addition to the literal meaning of the utterances. These rules and conventions are principles of co-operative interaction and largely independent of the domain of discourse. Shared beliefs about the domain, mutual beliefs[2] that are discerned during the course of interaction, and mutual expectations of the system and the user, all enter into the design of such systems in a variety of ways. We will distinguish general knowledge about the domain that is shared by S and U from mutual beliefs. *In this paper, we will use the term mutual beliefs (MB) to refer to those beliefs that are discerned by a participant only as a result of the interaction, more precisely a certain segment of the interaction.*

Co-operative or helpful behavior defined in this general way is a very worthy goal to keep in mind while designing such interactive man–machine systems. However in this paper, we will deliberately limit ourselves to some very particular aspects of co-operation, and relate them to the more technical definitions of mutual knowledge. We will be particularly concerned with the case where co-operativeness involves both giving a truthful and informative response and "squaring away" the relevant mutual beliefs (Section II). In this context, we will suggest that the "squaring away" contribution of the interaction can be explained by a suitable modification of one of the maxims of co-operative conversation.

Finally, we will discuss another related topic which has to do with excess (or surplus) information and how and when the system should assimilate this information, i.e. implicitly update itself without being explicitly told to do so (Section III). These considerations require that mutual beliefs should not be regarded just as a set of propositions, but rather with some structure over them where the structuring of information itself is a mutual belief.

In summary, we have discussed briefly the role of mutual beliefs with respect to some specific aspects of man–machine interactions.[3]

II. MUTUAL BELIEFS AND CO-OPERATION:

The type of co-operative behavior we will be concerned with can be roughly characterized as follows. There are two participants: S (system) and U (user). U interacts with S in order to seek some information from a knowledge base (KB). In a given interaction between U and S, there is a set of relevant mutual beliefs that can be associated with U, i.e. those beliefs which U thinks that U and S share (of course relevant to the given interaction). If P is such a belief, we denote this mutual belief by MB(U,S,B) where

$$MB(U,S,P) = UB(P) \wedge UBSB(P) \wedge UBSBUB(P) \wedge \ldots$$

UB stands for U believes, SB stands for S believes, UBSB stands for U believes that S believes, etc. Similarly, for the same interaction between U and S, there is a set of relevant mutual beliefs that can be associated with S, i.e. those beliefs which S thinks that S and U share. If P' is such a belief, we denote it by MB(S,U,P') where

$$MB(S,U,P') = SB(P') \wedge SBUB(P') \wedge SBUBSB(P')$$
$$\wedge \, SBUBSBUB(P') \ldots$$

These definitions are essentially the same as in Clark and Marshall (1981) and Perrault and Cohen (1981). MB(U,S,P) can be better described as one-sided mutual belief. There is no implication here that each one of the potentially infinite set of conjuncts has to be individually assessed when P is assessed to be a mutual belief by U (similarly for S). Clark and Marshall (1981) have given a detailed discussion of the problem of assessing mutual beliefs. We are not going to worry about this issue in this paper. Certainly, regarding the type of examples we have considered in this paper, there is no real difficulty. Also, the justification of regarding MB as a potentially infinite set of conjuncts is the same as in Clark and Marshall (1981) and others: namely, that a finite *a priori* fixed number of conjuncts will not be adequate because a belief could be embedded arbitrarily deep in the belief spaces of the participants.

We now require the following conditions to hold for the interaction to be judged as co-operative:

(i) S truthfully and informatively answers U's question (i.e. provides the requested information).

(ii) At the end of the interaction (with respect to the given request), the mutual beliefs of S, i.e. MB(S,U,P') and the mutual beliefs of U, i.e. MB(U,S,P) are "squared away", i.e. if S has discerned any misconceptions on behalf of U about the content of the knowledge base (KB) (with respect to the given request), then S informs U about it, and similarly U informs S.[4]

There are two situations we would like to consider:

(1) S discerns that there is a possibility of some misconception on the part of U (e.g. about some entity in MB), and unless the resulting mutual beliefs are "squared away", there is no way S can truthfully respond to the request. Thus S must first engage in an interaction with U to clarify the situation (e.g. determine unambiguously who U is talking about) and then respond to U's request. Thus the interaction will consist of U's initial request followed by a "clarification dialogue" between

S and U and then S's response to U's initial request.

(2) Although S has discerned that there is some misconception on the part of U, it is possible for S, based on the information provided by U, to truthfully and informatively answer U's request. At this point, S has responded to U's request and the interaction could end. In fact, following certain conventions of co-operation, it would be quite appropriate for the interaction to end at this point. However, according to our criteria, the relevant mutual beliefs have not been "squared away". Hence, it will be necessary for S to provide information to U and then possibly for U to provide information to S, etc. to square away the mutual beliefs. Thus the interaction will consist of U's initial request, which is truthfully responded to by S, followed by a "squaring away dialogue" between S and U.

We will give examples of both situations. However, it is the second situation in which we will be more interested in this paper.

Example 1

Clarification dialogue: dialogue before the question can be answered at all.
Clarification may be needed for a variety of reasons, but we will limit ourselves to the case of clarifying the referent and the description used to refer to it. The examples below are variants of the Donnellan-type examples (1966). Our treatment here is very much like that of Perrault and Cohen (1981) in their paper on "inaccurate reference". However, we will consider the situation of inaccurate reference in the context of question–answer systems and the needed clarification.

1.1 Suppose there are two women (say W_1 and W_2) called Jane and Mary respectively. S and U are two participants. Furthermore, S knows that W_1 is the Mayor of Chicago (MC). Now, U asks S:

    U: Is Jane the MC?

    S: Yes

No clarification is required here.

1.2 Let us assume that W_1 and W_2 tell U that since last week, they have swapped their names. Again, U asks S:

    U: Is Jane the MC?

    S: Yes

Again no clarification is required.

1.3 Let us assume that W_1 and W_2 tell S and U separately that since last week, they have swapped their names. U asks S:

   1.U: Is Jane the MC?

   2.S: Do you know that since last week Jane and Mary have swapped their names? Are you referring to the one who was called Jane last week or to the one who is called Jane this week?

   3.U: I am referring to the one who was called Jane last week. I knew that they had swapped their names but I didn't know that you knew that.

   4.S: In that case, the answer is yes.

Here, 2–3 is the clarification dialogue.

1.4 Let us assume that W_1 and W_2 tell S and U separately that since last week they have swapped their names. They also told S that they have told U about it. (Note that U does not know that S knows about the swap.) U asks S:

   1.U: Is Jane the MC?

   2.S: You know that Jane and Mary swapped their names last week? Perhaps, you didn't know that I knew about it. Are you referring to the one who was called Jane last week or to the one who is called Jane this week?

   3.U: I am referring to the one who was called Jane last week. I knew that they had swapped their names, but I didn't know that you know it.

   4.S: In that case, the answer is yes.

Here 2–3 is the clarification dialogue.

1.5 Let us assume that W_1 and W_2 tell S and U separately that since last week, they have swapped their names. They also told U that they have told S about it. (Note that U knows that S knows about the swap, but U cannot assume that S knows that U knows that S knows about the swap.) U asks S:

   1.U: Is Jane the MC?[5]

   2.S: Do you know that Jane and Mary swapped their names since last week? Perhaps, you don't know about it. Are you referring to the one who was called Jane last week or to the one who is called Jane this week?

   3.U: I am referring to the one who was called Jane last week. I knew about it and I also knew that you knew about it, but I didn't know that you knew that I knew about it.

4.S: In that case, the answer is yes.

Here 2–3 is the clarification dialogue.

Clearly, these situations can be made more and more complicated in some obvious ways. The clarification dialogue will invoke beliefs embedded at greater and greater depths in the belief spaces of the participants. Another situation where clarification will be necessary is as follows. S discerns from U's request that there is some misconception on the part of U (about either the structure or content of KB or both) and it is not possible for S to give a direct response to U's request, although a logically correct response can be given; however this response will mislead U, making him continue to believe in something which S knows to be false. In this case, instead of giving the logically correct but misleading response, S will let U know about the misconception. U may then reformulate his/her question which S may then be able to answer. Kaplan (1979) and Mays (1980) have studied such corrective responses in the context of KB systems. For example, if U asks "How many students got the grade A in CIS 500 in Fall, 1979?" and assume that it is the case that CIS 500 was not offered in Fall, 1979. In this case, S could give a logically correct response "None (or zero)", but it would be misleading because it will confirm U's false belief that CIS 500 was offered in Fall, 1979. S should rather let U know about his/her misconception. Note that it is not possible for S to give a direct response to U's request. S must first clarify the situation. U may then reformulate his/her question which S may be able to answer.

In Example 2, we will look at the situation where indeed it is possible for S to give a direct response even though S has discerned some misconception on the part of U.

Example 2

Now we will be concerned with the situation where S can truthfully and informatively answer U's request, although S has discerned some misconception on the part of U. In such cases, besides answering U's request, S (and U) will continue the interaction until the *relevant* mutual beliefs are squared away.

Suppose there are two women (say W_1 and W_2) called Jane and Mary respectively. Furthermore, W_1 is a blonde and W_2 is a brunette. S and U are two participants. As before, S knows that W_1 is the Mayor of Chicago (MC). The hair color attribute is introduced here to provide unique identifications for W_1 and W_2. W_1 and W_2 may not change hair colors but they may change their names.[6]

The examples below are variants of some of the traditional examples (e.g. Donnellan, 1966; Kripke, 1977) and their variants as in Perrault and Cohen (1981), of course, suitably modified for our context of question–answer systems.

In some of the traditional examples (e.g. Kripke, 1977) unique identification of the referent is achieved by some explicit or implicit deictic expression such as "the man over there". For example, two people (A and B) see a man with a woman. One of them (say, A) says to the other (B), "Her husband is kind to her", which is short for "the man over there, her husband, he is kind to her". A may have mistakenly taken the man to be the husband of the woman, yet it is clear which man is being talked about.

We can now proceed with our examples. It is always assumed now that U will refer to W_1 or W_2 by their respective names (as he believes them to be the case) and the color of the hair.

2.1 U: Is Jane, the blonde one, the MC?
   S: Yes.
No squaring away of mutual beliefs is necessary in this case.

2.2 Let us assume that W_1 and W_2 tell U that since last week, they swapped their names. Again U asks S:
   U: Is Jane, the blonde one, the MC?
   S: Yes.
Again no further response is necessary. Of course, if we want the squaring away interaction to be symmetric, then at this point, U should initiate the squaring away dialogue and tell S about the swapping of their names, etc.

2.3 Let us assume that W_1 and W_2 tell S and U separately that since last week, they have swapped their names. (Note that U knows about the swap, but U does not know that S knows that U knows about the swap.) U asks S:
   1.U: Is Jane, the blonde one, the MC?
   2.S: Yes. However, are you aware that Jane and Mary have swapped their names since last week?

3.U: I am aware of that, but I didn't know that you knew that.
Part of 2 and 3 help square away the relevant mutual beliefs.

Let us represent this in more detail so that one can see how the misconceptions could be resolved systematically.

Let P stand for "W_1 (the blonde one) is called Jane".
After U's question, one can associate with U

(1) $MB^1(U,S,P) = UBSB^1(P) \wedge UBSBUB^2(P) \wedge UBSBUBSB^3(P)...$

where the superscript on MB indicates that the first conjunct in

$MB(U,S,P) = UB(P) \wedge UBSB(P) \wedge UBSBUB(P) \wedge ...$

has been omitted. $MB^i(U,S,P)$ would mean that the first i conjuncts have been omitted. (The indices on the conjuncts in (1) are only for easy reference.)

There is no difficulty for S in answering the question because S knows who U is talking about (namely, W_1) and S always answers truthfully and informatively.[7] However, the relevant mutual beliefs have to be squared away. We can certainly associate with S

(2) $MB^1(S,U,P) =$
$\qquad\qquad SBUB^1(P) \wedge SBUBSB^2(P) \wedge SBUBSBUB^3(P) \wedge ...$

From U's question, S can assert for itself the conjuncts 1, 2, 3, ... in (2) above. But in order to go from $MB^1(S,U,P)$ to $MB(S,U,P)$, it must be the case that $SB(P)$, which S knows to be false. Of course, we also assume that S knows that this was not the case last week, i.e. S knows that the falsity of $SB(P)$ is due to the fact that the name attribute, associated with W_1 has been "updated", and it also has access to the "history of the updates" (to use technical jargon of the knowledge base systems). Hence, S gives the corrective response.

On account of S's corrective response, conjuncts 2, 3, ... in (1) are fine, but there is a problem with the conjunct 1. We can certainly associate with U

(3) $MB^2(U,S,P) = UBSBUB(P) \wedge UBSBUBSB(P) \wedge ...$

In fact in this case, we have

(4) $MB^2(U,S,P) = UB(MB^1(S,U,P))$

The two mutual beliefs by U, and S respectively can be "squared away" if S informs U of the false conjunct in $MB(S,U,P)\text{-}MB^1(S,U,P)$ and U informs S of the two false conjuncts in $MB(U,S,P)\text{-}MB^2(U,S,P)$.

In general, we will have the following situation. In order to "square away" the mutual beliefs, S will have to inform U about a *finite* number of false conjuncts in $MB(S,U,P)-MB^i(S,U,P)$, for some i, and U will have to inform S about a *finite* number of false conjuncts in $MB(U,S,P)-MB^i(U,S,P)$ for some j. There are no disparities between $MB^i(S,U,P)$ and $MB^j(U,S,P)$. P will, of course, in general be a set of propositions.

2.4 Let us assume that W_1 and W_2 tell S and U separately that since last week, they have swapped their names. They also told S that they have told U about it. (Note that U knows about the swap but U does not know that S knows that U knows about the swap.) U asks S:

1. U: Is Jane, the blonde one, the MC?
2. S: Yes. You are aware that Jane and Mary swapped their names since last week but perhaps, you didn't know that I knew it.
3. U: I knew about it but I didn't know that you knew about it.

Again part of 2 and 3 help square away the relevant mutual beliefs.

2.5 Let us assume that W_1 and W_2 tells S and U separately that since last week, they swapped their names. They also tell U that they have told S about it. (Note that U knows about the swap and U knows that S knows about it but U cannot assume that S knows that U knows about the swap.) U asks S:

1. U: Is Jane, the blonde one, the MC?
2. S: Yes, however, are you aware that Jane and Mary swapped their names since last week? Perhaps, you didn't know that I knew it.
3. U: I knew about it and also I knew that you knew about it, but I didn't know that you knew that I knew that you knew about it.

Once again part of 2 and 3 help square away the relevant mutual beliefs.

Clearly, these situations can be made more and more complicated in some obvious ways, requiring more and more prolonged responses for squaring away the relevant mutual beliefs.

Remarks

In Example 2, especially in 2–3, 2–4 and 2–5, after answering U's question truthfully and informatively by saying "Yes", S could have ended the interaction at that point. In fact, in normal conversational situations, principles of conversation perhaps dictate that it would be appropriate to end the interaction at that point, and S should avoid giving more information than necessary (Grice, 1975, maxim of quantity). It would thus appear that our criteria of co-operativeness are not in accord with the usual ones. Rather than permitting an *ad hoc* violation of the usual convention, we will try to see whether we can suitably modify one of Grice's maxims (not of course, the maxim of quantity which is being violated here), so that there is no violation of any of the conventions.

The maxim we will modify is the one Grice calls the maxim of quality. In our context, this maxim dictates that S should not say anything that is false. That is, if S says Q, then it must be that $SB(Q)$. Let us modify this maxim as follows: if S says Q, then it must be that $SB(Q)$; further based on S's assessment of the mutual beliefs, it should not be possible for U, from what S has said (i.e. Q), to infer some other fact (say Q^1) which S knows to be false. If there is such a possibility, then after saying Q, S should add further information to "square away" the mutual beliefs. Otherwise, S is likely to mislead U by possibly making him continue to believe in Q^1 which is false in the knowledge base. In other words, S should not say anything which may imply (for U) something which S believes to be false.[8]

With this modification of the maxim of quality, there is no violation of the maxim of quantity. The extra corrective information provided by S is now called for by the revised maxim of quality. We may now ask what is the justification for the proposed revision. I will offer a few suggestions ranging from reasonable to somewhat wild.

(i) In the man–machine interaction for information-seeking from a knowledge base, it is important that S (System) is sensitive to U (User)'s misconceptions and inform U accordingly especially when by not informing U, it is likely to mislead U, and next time when U interacts with the system, he/she is likely to communicate the same misconception to the system again. In the context of such information-seeking man–machine interactions, the user (U) comes to expect such corrective co-operative responses, although in normal conversational situations, such expectations may not be valid, and hence it is appropriate to give the reduced responses.

The point I want to make is that one should not always model a man–machine interaction as one or another type of man–man interaction, although there will be obviously a close relationship between these two types of interactions.[9] There will be a need to elaborate or modify the conversational conventions for man–man interactions. Certain apparent violations of some normal convention could be accommodated by a principled modification of some other normal convention as we have done earlier.

(ii) Now a somewhat wild suggestion. How do the normal conventions of conversation arise anyway? It may very well be the case that at least certain conventions (rules) are *reflexes* of certain processing constraints. In the past few years, it has been suggested that certain grammatical rules (e.g. certain so-called island constraints, certain phenomena associated with resumptive pronouns, etc.) might be looked upon as *reflexes* of processing constraints, i.e. if one assumes a certain processing model, then these rules would turn out to be the result of some processing constraints in the model, i.e. the rules are abstractions of the processing constraints.

Analogously, we may speculate that certain conventions of conversation may also be related to some processing considerations. I would like to suggest that the maxim of quality which says that the speaker should not say anything which he knows to be false may be such a case. The speaker is not expected to worry (at least not too much!) about the possible implications of what the speaker says for the hearer, which the speaker knows to be false. If the speaker were to worry about it too much, it would require more figuring out (more computation) for the speaker. In the man–man interaction, we may not expect responses that require deep[10] inferencing because each participant is limited in this capacity and each is "aware" of this limitation of the other participant, and hence the convention. In the man–machine interaction, we may come to expect the machine to do deep inferencing more rapidly and therefore behave according to the modified maxim of quality.

In fact, there may be an asymmetry in this regard in the expectations on behalf of U and S. That is, U's expectations of the system's (S's) behavior need not parallel S's expectations of U's behavior. Thus, U may expect the system (S) to be more "co-operative" than U expects himself/herself with respect to S. For example, in Example 2 (2.2), S is not aware of any disparity in the relevant mutual beliefs, hence, S does not say anything beyond the direct response. U is aware of the disparity, but U does not attempt to square away the mutual beliefs. U got his answer and U expects S to truthfully and informatively answer the question and not mislead him/her, so there may be no need for the interaction to continue. (Of course, in this example (2.2), if U were to ask: Is Mary, the blonde one, MC? then a different interaction would ensue.)

III. SURPLUS INFORMATION

In Section II, we discussed a particular type of co-operative behavior, in particular, a situation where S (system) is able to respond truthfully and informatively to U (user)'s request, even though part of the description (of the entity talked about) as specified by U did not agree with what S believes to be the case. S is able to answer the question because the presence of a unique identifier in U's request left no doubt about the entity under consideration. The direct response was then followed by an interaction between S and U to square away the relevant mutual beliefs. Thus in Example 1.3, S knew that W_1 is being talked about; however S knows that in the knowledge base, W_1 has the name Mary, while U's request suggests that U believes that W_1's name is Jane. Thus there is a *mismatch* between the value of the attribute "name" in the knowledge base and the value assigned by U (as assessed by S). We use the term *mismatch* when S discerns that there is a disagreement between the values of some attribute of the entity under consideration.

We will now consider the situation which is similar to the one we have been talking about except that S simply does not have a value for the given attribute, i.e. S discerns that there is some surplus information which is not inconsistent with S's knowledge about the value of the attribute. There is no mismatch here, but S simply lacks the value. There is thus some surplus information with respect to S. (For some earlier work see Joshi, 1978.)

Example 3

Let us assume that our knowledge base has information about cars. Each car is characterized by a set of attributes such as the *registration number* RN, (Z578, P235, . . .) *type* (Chevy, Volvo, . . .), *color* (blue, red, . . .), *owner* (John Anderson, Mary Smith, . . .). RN would play the role of the unique identifier. Let us assume that it is not necessary that in the knowledge base, each attribute for each entity has a value (except, of course, the unique identifier, RN for which there must be a value).

3.1 Assume that for a particular car (say C1), with RN Z578, there are values for the attributes *type* (= Volvo) and *owner* (John Anderson), but there is no value for the attribute *color*. Suppose U asks S:

1.U: Does the blue Volvo RN Z578 belong to John Anderson?
2.S: Yes.

S has truthfully and informatively answered U's request because S knows which car is being talked about, and S can check to see whether or not the owner is John Anderson.

Let P1 be: C1 is a Volvo and P2 be: C1's color is blue.

It is not the case that P2 is false for S, but rather S simply lacks the information. As in our previous examples, S could follow up the direct response in 2 above by further information in order to square away the mutual beliefs. But since there is no *mismatch* here, there are some other possibilities.

(a) After the mutual beliefs are squared away, S could ask U whether the color attribute should be "updated" and do so only if confirmed by U.

(b) S could go ahead and update the color value (implicitly[11]), (perhaps even only under the scope of U, i.e. SBUB(P2), so that later, if necessary, consistency checking for this attribute can be relativized to U).

It is the second alternative which we would like to examine in some detail. The main question is under what circumstances one should allow such implicit updates. How does one process such "surplus" information in normal conversational situations?[12]

Let us look at our previous example.

1.U: Does the blue Volvo RN Z578 belong to John Anderson?

Note that P1: *C1 is a Volvo* and P2: *C1's color is blue* are not the only two mutual beliefs discerned by S. We should also add

P3: Cars have the color attribute.

In the knowledge base we have now, P3 is also true for S. As a matter of fact, strictly speaking, P3 is not a mutual belief according to our definition, but it is rather a piece of general knowledge shared by the participants. However, if we consider the situation when the knowledge base has only the attributes RN, type and owner, then P3 is a belief that is discerned by S as a result of the interaction, hence it is a mutual belief.

In the first case (i.e. when P3 is a piece of general knowledge shared by the participant), S has the appropriate structure available in the knowledge base to integrate the new information that C1's color is blue.

In other words, S only has to "update" the value of the color attribute; S does *not* have to "update" the structure of the information associated with each car (or cars in general).

In the second case (i.e. when P3 is a belief discerned as a result of the interaction, and it is "surplus" information for S), if S wants to integrate the surplus information, it must essentially make two updates. First S must update the structure of information associated with cars, i.e. set up a color attribute for cars (at least for C1 certainly) and then assign a value to this attribute, namely, blue.

Let us call the first type of update the "content update" and the second type the "structure update". In the context of man–machine interaction, structure updates will be more serious and should certainly not happen implicitly, i.e. without some further interaction and confirmation. I will speculate (with absolutely no hard evidence) that structure updates should be harder than content updates in normal conversational situations; harder, in the sense that in the case of a structural update, the flow of conversation would be interrupted to clarify the situation, while a content update may take place without any such interruption.

There is another important point to note here. It is necessary to characterize mutual beliefs as not just a set of propositions, but with some structure over them, at least classified into subsets of propositions (e.g. those dealing with content, P1 and P2, and those dealing with the structure, P3; those that are specific and those that are generic, etc.). Studies of mutual belief have not been concerned with the need to impose structure on the set of beliefs assessed by the participants. For example, information in the belief space could also be organized around (centered around) specific entities, the organization to be discerned as a result of the interaction. Such structuring would be relevant to the pragmatic notion of aboutness and the notion of topic of a sentence in a discourse.[13] I believe that such attempts at structuring the belief space will be necessary to understand the exchange of information in linguistic communication.

Remarks

One interesting question to look at is as follows. Does the ease or difficulty of an implicit update depend on the position where the surplus information appears? For example in Example 3, the noun phrase *the blue Volvo RN Z578* appears in the subject position which is a default position for "topic" (or old information, to the extent this notion coincides with the notion of topic). What would happen if the surplus information appeared elsewhere? For example, let us assume that it is understood which car is being talked about (assume that John Anderson owns exactly one car). U asks S:

U: Is John Anderson's car a blue Volvo RN Z578?

The surplus information is now in a non-topic position (focus or new information to the extent these notions coincide). Is there a difference in the ease or difficulty of the implicit update between the case when the surplus information is in the topic position and when it is in the focus position? It appears to me that in the latter case, implicit update should be harder (in the sense described earlier). Since topic and focus are discourse notions, the above example suggests that discourse structure also affects the ease or difficulty of updates.

IV. CONCLUSION

Certain aspects of co-operative behavior in man–machine interaction were considered, in particular where co-operativeness involves both giving a truthful and informative response and also "squaring away" the relevant mutual beliefs as a result of recognition of disparities among the mutual beliefs of the system and the user discerned during the interaction. A modification of the maxim of quality was proposed to give a systematic explanation of the "squaring away" contribution of the interaction. The role of mutual beliefs (treated not just as a set of propositions, but rather with some structure over them) in the assimilation of surplus information by the system was also discussed. A particular aspect of co-operation and the treatment of excess information were used as two specific aspects of man–machine interaction to illustrate the role of mutual beliefs in question–answer systems.

A larger issue (no doubt very controversial) has also been raised, concerning the treatment of man–machine interactions as systematic modifications of the conversational conventions for man–man interactions, rather than just some *ad hoc* approximations of them. Such a treatment may lead to an asymmetric characterization of man–machine interactions. The suggestion here is that this characterization is not prescriptive but rather a descriptive one. It is hoped that the issues raised in this paper will make some contribution to man–machine pragmatics.

This work was partially supported by NSF Grant MCS 79-08401.

NOTES

1. I want to thank Jerry Kaplan, Eric Mays, Kathy McKeown, Ellen Prince, Candy Sidner, Bonnie Webber and Scott Weinstein for their valuable comments. I would also like to thank Paul Grice for his comments during the colloquium. Of course, I have immensely benefitted from the remarks of Rose Maclaran and Geoffrey Sampson who were the rapporteurs for my paper. Their remarks are published in this volume. I could have substantially revised the paper in view of all the comments I received. However, a thorough revision of the paper at this time would not be fair to the rapporteurs as their remarks were based on my original draft. I have therefore followed the following strategy. I have made small improvements in the original text itself and added some footnotes at various points in the text to cover some important issues raised by all the comments I received on my initial draft. A brief reply to some of the remarks by the rapporteurs appears after their remarks.
2. Notwithstanding the well-known problems in equating knowledge and belief, in this paper we will use the terms knowledge and belief interchangeably.
3. The examples in Sections II and III are not from any particular system. They are hypothetical and contrived, but they illustrate some of the issues involved in these systems and suitably generalize them. There is no claim here that practical systems should always produce elaborate responses of the kind discussed here. Also in actual systems, there are many practical details to worry about, which have been conveniently ignored here.
4. The "squaring away" of the mutual beliefs need not be completely symmetric. For example, the "squaring away" interaction could always start with S to be then followered by U, etc. U may never initiate such interaction. In the examples in this paper we have assumed this to be the case, although there is no specific reason to do so in general.
5. Note that U could have posed the question: *Is Mary the MC?* Clarification is still required since S knows about the swap but S does not know that U knows about the swap.
6. This fact is a piece of general knowledge shared by S and U. We use the term MB only for those beliefs that are discerned as a result of a given interaction (see Section I). Perhaps, some readers would be more comfortable with W_1 and W_2 changing their hair color rather than their names. All we need is an attribute that can be used as a unique identification. Other attributes may be stable or updatable, i.e. likely to have different values on different occasions. There is no claim here (as one rapporteur seems to think I am saying) that misconception about names are more likely than some other attributes!
7. Note that there is no claim here that MB has to be assessed first in order to make a successful reference but rather that as a result of establishing the reference (based on partial information) MB has been assessed. However, because of this assessment, S

discovers some disparity between MB(U,S,P) and MB(S,U,P) which has to be squared away.

8. Of course, these implications could be embedded arbitrarily deep in the belief spaces of the participants.

9. This sentence was modified in response to a comment by Sampson.

10. In the sense of requiring more computation.

11. Implicitly, because U has not explicitly asked S to make the update.

12. I am not aware of any information concerning this aspect. Loftus (1979, Loftus *et al.* (1978)) talk about how extra information (both consistent and misleading) introduced via questions is integrated in memory; this is in the context of integration of visual and verbal information.

13. For example see Reinhart (forthcoming), Prince (1980), and Joshi and Weinstein (1981).

Chapter 4

Comments and Replies

The Economics of Conversation:
Comments on Joshi's Paper

Geoffrey Sampson

Joshi's paper deals with problems that arise in conversational interactions involving questions and answers. These problems have to do with the fact that participant A's contributions may suggest to participant B that A lacks some piece of knowledge which is relevant to the discussion in the sense that, without it, B's contributions are liable to be misunderstood. Joshi discusses strategies that may be used by the participant who detects the possibility of misunderstanding. In order to avert such misunderstanding, he goes on to raise the question of how to reconcile the use of such strategies with Grice's principles of conversational co-operation, which on the face of it forbid these strategies. Further, he suggests a particular modification to one of Grice's principles as the best solution to this difficulty.

Joshi's conversational interactions may be between man and man or between man and machine, meaning a computer system; and the first point I should like to take up is a certain unresolved tension which seems to me to exist in Joshi's paper between the issue of man–man interaction, where the problem is a descriptive one (What strategies *do* people in fact employ when they find themselves in the kinds of situation Joshi discusses?), and the issue of man–machine interaction where the problem is, rather, prescriptive (How ought we to design a mechanical question-answering system?; What will it be most convenient to arrange for the system to do in these circumstances?: a problem which would in turn raise further questions about the reasons why we were building the system in the first place, which is an issue that Joshi ignores completely, and reasonably enough since after all, he has to set some limit to the scope of his paper).

When I talk of tension between these two issues I do not mean to suggest that Joshi is unaware of the distinction between them. For instance on p. 190, he explicitly says that "one should not always model a man–machine interaction as one or another type of man–man interaction", from which it is clear that he is alive to the distinction. Nevertheless, what Joshi writes does not always respect the difference between the two categories of interaction. For instance, in the paragraph immediately preceding the one from which I have just quoted, he writes: "In the context of such information-seeking man–machine interactions, the user comes to expect [a certain kind of] corrective co-operative responses, although in normal conversational situations, such expectations may not be valid . . ." Now this to me suggests that Joshi is, at least momentarily, thinking of question-answering machines as a fixed fact of life and saying, descriptively, "if we look at how people behave with these systems, we find them coming to expect these responses even though in man–man interactions they usually do not get them". (This interpretation is given further support by the penultimate sentence of Joshi's Conclusion section, added after his paper had been delivered orally.) But in reality, it is up to computer specialists to *decide* how to organize their question-answering systems, and surely what expectations the human users come to form will depend very much on what routines the designers decide to build into the systems.

Another illustration of the confusion of which I am claiming Joshi is guilty, and one which touches the central point of this paper more closely, comes as early as p. 182, where Joshi announces part of what his paper is intended to achieve in these words: "we will suggest that the "squaring away" contribution of the interaction can be explained by a suitable modification of one of the maxims of co-operative conversation". The word "explained" here surely implies that Joshi is talking descriptively about how people achieve the "squaring away" function in discourse. So far as I can see, the only sense in which one could "explain" how a hypothetical question-answering machine achieved the squaring-away function would be by pointing to some aspect of its program, not by modifying one of Grice's principles, which are intended to describe how *humans* use language. Yet, earlier in the same paragraph, Joshi suggests that he is dealing with man–machine systems; and indeed the passage I quoted earlier from p. 190 explicitly argues that this squaring-away function is relevant to man–machine interaction in a way that it is *not* relevant to man–man interaction. So there does seem to be a genuine confusion here between the two categories of dialogue.

Once we insist on drawing a sharp distinction between descriptive treatment of man–man interactions and prescriptive treatment of man–machine interactions, we then have to make a policy decision about which of the two sets of problems to pursue. Here I have to say that my own interests may well be the converse of Joshi's. I am interested in the descriptive question of how people interact linguistically with one another, and I am interested in Joshi's thought-experiments with mechanical systems only insofar as they may be able to shed light on how people operate; whereas I suspect that Joshi may be more concerned with the practical problem of making these mechanical question-answering systems actually work, and that he investigates people's behaviour in order to get ideas about how to make his machines behave. The comments I shall go on to make will be guided by the fact that I am primarily interested in man–man interactions; but this is, obviously, no more than a personal preference.

From my point of view, the obvious danger in conflating the two categories of conversational interaction is that this may lead us to construe the nature of man–man interactions too much on the model of the kinds of interaction which a programmer might plausibly be able to allow men to have with computers. Part of the point of my remaining comments will be to suggest that Joshi has indeed fallen into this trap. To be specific, it seems likely to me that it is Joshi's preoccupation with the man–machine question which has allowed or encouraged him to accept Grice's co-operative principle and conversational maxims as a true descriptive theory of how people organize their linguistic interactions with other people.

Grice's theory of conversational implicatures (Grice, 1975; though circulated and discussed in draft form long before that date) was put forward as an attempt to account for various mismatches between the logical status of utterances and the appropriateness of those utterances in practical conversational situations. For instance, if I ask you "Will you be away tomorrow?", and the truth is that you will be away, then it would be inappropriate for you to answer "I'll be away if it's a fine day", despite the fact of logic that when q is true then $p \supset q$ is true too, and despite the fact that the $\supset$ symbol in logic is supposed to represent the English word *if*. Grice argued that we should interpret this sort of phenomenon by saying that conversation is governed by a "co-operative principle" according to which each contribution must be such as is required (at the stage at which it occurs) by the accepted purpose or direction of the talk exchange in which it occurs. This principle does imply (according to Grice) that contributions ought to be true, but it implies a number of further requirements as well; the various specific implications of the general principle, as Grice sees them, are spelled out in a series of "maxims", for instance "be relevant", and "do not make contributions either less or more informative than is required".[1] The particular example I used, in which someone says "I'll be away if it's a fine day", when the truth is that he will be away anyway, although it does fulfil the requirement of truth, would fall foul of (I suppose) both the other maxims I quoted; mention of the weather is irrelevant, and the statement is less informative than required since it does not specify what will happen in case of bad weather.

Now there are problems at several levels with this theory of Grice's. At the most basic level, it can be argued that his maxims fail to predict conventional usage correctly even with respect to the special class of problems about logical words such as *if* and *and* for which the theory was designed. For instance, Jonathan Cohen (1971) argues that Grice's theory fails in this way, and he suggests that it is just a mistake for Grice to equate English words with logical connectives such as horseshoe and ampersand. But even supposing that Grice can answer Cohen's objections, which are somewhat technical and *recherché*, there is a much more obvious problem: with respect to conversational choices that do not involve the special logical problems that interest Grice, people often manifestly flout his maxims. To anyone who knew, for instance, my old scout at Oxford, or a certain one of the shopkeepers in the village where I live, it would be ludicrous to suggest that *as a general principle* people's speech is governed by maxims such as "be relevant"; "do not say that for which you lack adequate evidence" (!); "avoid obscurity of expression, ambiguity or unnecessary prolixity" (!!). In the case of the particular speakers I am thinking of (and I have no doubt that any reader could supply his own counterparts), the converse of Grice's maxims might actually have greater predictive power. Yet, if Grice's maxims are claimed not to be generally operative, but to come into play only in the special cases where they are needed in order to rescue Grice's claim that the logical words of ordinary English are synonymous with the connectives of the propositional calculus, then surely his theory becomes unreasonably *ad hoc*?

However, neither of these objections to Grice's theory are the most crucial ones in connection with Joshi's paper. The central problem with Grice lies not with his specific maxims but with his general co-operative principle, from which the maxims allegedly follow. This principle embodies assumptions which I think are very widely shared by students of language, but which imply a profoundly false conception of the nature of social life. Speech is one category of interaction between individuals in society; but this particular category happens to be unusual in that those who have thought about it have been almost wholly uninfluenced by the theories of economics that have been developed over the centuries in order to make sense of other categories of social interaction. In the field of economics proper, the analogue of Grice's co-operative principle is a mediaeval fallacy, the wrongness of which was most famously expressed in the words of Adam Smith in *The Wealth of Nations*: "It is not from the benevolence of the butcher, the brewer, or the baker that we expect our dinner, but from their regard to their own interests . . .".

What Smith meant by this remark was that we must not think of economic interaction by the members of a society as governed by a sort of conspiracy to promote some generally-accepted set of aims which we all share. Real life is much too complicated for that; in practice individuals have very diverse aims and interests, and it would be impossible for us to know more than an insignificant fraction of everything there is to know about the aims of other people, even if we were anxious to go out of our way in order to help them fulfil their aims. But, as Smith more than anyone showed, this inevitable ignorance of each other's interests does not matter, because it is in the nature of a free society to evolve cultural institutions which function so as to co-ordinate individuals' activities in such a way that they unknowingly promote *each other's* aims in the process of knowingly promoting their *own* aims.

If I walk into an off-licence to buy wine, I do not know whether the proprietor wants to use the profit he is going to make from the transaction in order to be able to eat more luxurious food, or to buy books on theoretical linguistics, or to help his local church to cure its dry-rot problem; and similarly, he does not know whether I want the wine in order to lay on a good meal for some old-age pensioner friends who do not get invited out very often, or in order to help an orgy go with a swing, or perhaps just in order to drink myself into oblivion. But it does not matter; the cultural institutions of money, and shops which open at regular, conventionally agreed hours and stock known categories of goods, enable the two of us to get together and promote one another's unknown aims in seeking to promote our own interests.

Now, what is true of economic interaction is equally true of linguistic interaction. When people talk to one another, in general it simply is not true that the conversation has some "accepted purpose" shared by both participants, which they jointly conspire to promote. Admittedly there will be special cases where it is accurate to think of the participants as co-operating to achieve a common goal, but in very many cases, the relationship will be more akin to that between shopkeeper and customer. For instance, if a detective is talking to a member of the public, it may be that the detective thinks that the other man could have been a witness to the crime he is investigating, and is trying to elicit clues, or he may suspect that the man is the criminal and may be seeing whether he can trap him into a contradiction or a damaging admission, or the detective may know that the man has nothing to do with the crime, but he may be seeking to find out about the general milieu in which it occurred. Furthermore, the man answering the questions may be motivated chiefly by fear of getting into trouble with the police, or he may be fascinated by the intellectual task of reconstructing in his memory exactly what did happen on the night of the 27th, or he may be a garrulous type who just loves the sound of his own voice. It *may* also be the case that both detective and his interlocutor share the same aim of trying to discover who the criminal is and bring him to book, and if so then the dialogue between them will be a particularly co-operative one; but this is only one possible case, and there is no reason to treat it as the norm for all dialogues between people.

Asa Kasher (1977) has pointed out this fallacy in Grice's co-operative principle, but as far as I know, he is the first writer to have done so. Kasher suggests that Grice's principle ought to be replaced by a principle which Kasher calls the "principle of rational co-ordination", which runs: "Given a desired basic purpose, the ideal speaker chooses that linguistic action which, he believes, most effectively and at least cost attains that purpose".

It seems to me undeniable that Kasher's approach is superior to Grice's as a foundation for the descriptive pragmatics of man–man linguistic interaction. But it is true that man–*machine* interaction, in a computer question-answering system, would be a case to which Grice's co-operative principle might be relatively appropriate. If such a system were set up in practice, then obviously the two participants would not have independent aims: the programmer would arrange for the machine to serve the purpose of the human users as far as possible; and presumably any question-answering computer system that could actually be programmed would have to be geared to some rather well-defined range of practical purposes, so that the problem of the two sides being ignorant of each other's aims in man–man interactions would not arise to the same extent in the case of man–machine interactions. This is why I suggest that Joshi's preoccupation with man–machine systems may encourage him to give Grice's theory of *human* conversational interaction more credence than is warranted.

If the analogy between linguistic and economic interaction is a worthwhile one, then the next point that it suggests is that we may be wrong to think of a general principle of rationality, such as the one that Kasher states, as yielding a fixed set of conversational maxims. That is, it may be that Grice is wrong not only in the detailed contents of the maxims he proposes, but in his belief that we use any fixed set of maxims at all. Joshi makes it clear that he takes Grice's maxims to be correct for the case of man–man interaction. On p. 190, it bothers him that his machine system has to act in a way that does not conform to the usual conventions applying to man–man interactions, and on p. 191, he suggests that these "normal conventions", or some of them at least, may reflect what he calls "processing constraints", which I take to mean that he thinks they may be a consequence of some sort of Chomskyan innate limitations on our human mental machinery. (Joshi does call this "a somewhat wild suggestion".) Now, if we were thinking about the actions of a computer question-answering system, this general approach would seem quite appropriate. A computer system can act only in ways provided for in its program; so a system of the kind envisaged by Joshi would need to be equipped with some well-defined set of principles controlling the nature of its output in various circumstances, and it certainly could not dream up new guiding principles in response to novel situations.[2] Furthermore the Chomsky-like idea that the "intellectual" behaviour of the system was limited by a fixed, built-in mechanical structure would be obviously true in the case of a computer system: the fixed structure would be the details of the computer's hardware, together with the program supplied by the programmer (to the extent that this is fixed rather than self-modifying).

Consider, on the other hand, the case of human economic interaction. Arguably this is governed by a fixed general rationality-principle, according to which each agent acts in the ways which he believes will do most to fulfil his goals at least cost to himself. Indeed, many philosophical economists would regard that principle as an axiomatic truth rather than as a correct empirical generalization. And it is also true that this general principle has given rise to various relatively specific conventional patterns of behaviour which serve to implement the general principle, in much the way that Grice claims his maxims serve to implement his co-operative principle. I shall take just one example, which is trivial in itself, but will do as well as any other to illustrate the point.

Among shopkeepers there is a convention that shops open between fixed hours, nine to five or so on every day but Sunday. (In modern Britain, this is more than just a convention because to some extent shop-hours are regulated by law, something to which there is no analogue in the domain of conversation; but I am sure that a system of conventional shop-hours existed long before they were regulated by law.) Now of course, if Noam Chomsky were with us here, I have no doubt that he would tell us that the reason why shopkeepers keep conventional hours (even when there is no law forcing them to do so) is because we are all born with innate circuitry in our brain which is triggered into action by a small amount of impoverished and degenerate experience, such as contact with a cash-register, and which thereafter forces people willy-nilly to unlock the door at nine and pull the blind down again at five: "How else could various shopkeepers all unerringly converge on the same hypothesis about the best hours to open their shops?". But in this case, the answer to the rhetorical question is obvious: it is entirely redundant to postulate specific innate machinery in order to explain a social convention of this sort, because it is so easy to explain it in terms of cultural evolution with natural selection between alternative practices.

It could well be that when there first were several shops in one place, some of their owners would open them quite irregularly, or that one owner would keep regular hours different from those of his neighbour. But people who opened irregularly would soon find themselves losing trade to the regular shopkeepers, because customers would prefer to go where they could be sure of getting in; sooner or later the irregular ones would either become regular or go out of business. Similarly, a shopkeeper who kept regular hours different from most of his neighbours' would find that it was a waste of time to wait in his shop during the hours when almost everyone else was shut, because customers would aim to do all their shopping in one trip. So in due course the overriding principle of doing most to fulfil one's goals (which for a shopkeeper must involve maximizing trade) at least cost (which would include hours worked in the shop) will force the various shopkeepers to converge on conventional hours (that is, to govern their shopkeeping behaviour by a maxim such as "Open from 9 to 5"), even if they had quite different plans in mind originally. Surely one does not need to be a Hayekian, in the sense of necessarily accepting all of Friedrich Hayek's political prescriptions, in order to agree with his views about the evolution of this sort of cultural rule or maxim.

And if maxims relevant to economic life can come to be generally adopted in this fashion without being grounded in any specific innate mental constraints, surely just the same will be true for other aspects of human interaction? So, for instance, insofar as it is true that the behaviour of members of our society is governed by the maxim "Do not say what you believe to be false" (and clearly that maxim needs to be heavily qualified before it corresponds to an accurate statement of how we behave in real life), then I would suppose that that situation arose through a quite comparable process of Hayekian cultural evolution. It is easy to imagine that there could long ago have been a time at which some individuals or some circles of society paid much less attention than others to the criterion of truth when choosing what to say, but one can also imagine that life would have proved less satisfactory in all kinds of ways for the relatively untruthful individuals or cliques (after all, they would presumably lose much of the benefit of language as a medium for the exchange of information); so, gradually, the principle of truthfulness would spread because of its success at giving people what they want out of life.

All this is just to argue against Joshi's "wild suggestion"; so far I have been urging that Gricean maxims will be products of cultural evolution rather than consequences of innate mental equipment (Grice does not suggest that they are the latter). But, if the maxims of behaviour are indeed cultural rather than Chomskyan, biological products, it surely follows that they will never be fixed (as Grice apparently believes them to be). People will always be experimenting with modified or different maxims in response to their changing external situation. In the economic case, this is clear. To continue with the example of shop-hours: when I was a boy, so far as my own experience went, 9–5 was a more or less universal rule, but now that in large towns most women work, and more people live on their own than in the old days, it has turned out to be profitable for some foodshops to remain open late into the evening: people who work in the day and cannot shop then provide enough custom to make this worthwhile even though such shops usually charge high prices. Or, again, it is more common nowadays in the country to find small and quite specialized craft shops, and often they open only half a day at a time so that the owner can spend the other half of the day making more stock. An ordinary shop like a grocer's could not get away with half-day opening because it would lose too much trade, but a craft shop can, either because there are not so many competitors, or perhaps because it turns out that customers are typically tourists who mostly do not drive out from town till the afternoon.

Of course these are trivial examples; but they make the point that our conventions of behaviour in the economic sphere are subject to constant revision, even though they are always guided by the general principle of maximizing income and minimizing costs. The conventions of behaviour which implement that principle most successfully will be different in different economic circumstances; and anyway, since economic life is so complicated that the only real way to discover the consequences of adopting a novel economic practice is to try it and see what happens, people would always be experimenting with new patterns of economic action even if the circumstances within which they were acting were not subject to constant change.[3]

Exactly the same, it seems to me, is true for Grice-type conversational maxims. For instance, just suppose it were true that Englishmen at present uniformly obeyed the maxim "Do not say what you believe to be false", or for that matter, suppose they obey a maxim such as the one Joshi discusses for his mechanical system, which bids them avert foreseeable misinterpretations of their own true statements. Even if either of these maxims were obeyed at present, one would certainly hope that in the event of, say, a Russian invasion, the maxims would rapidly be abandoned in the context of conversational interactions with members of the occupying forces.

This is an extreme case, obviously, but it makes the general point: people playing different roles in a society will conform to different sets of conversational maxims (even though there will doubtless be strong family resemblances between the maxim-sets adopted by members of a single society), and none of the maxims are sacrosanct; it will always be open to us to experiment with a modification to any one of our maxims (though presumably not to change all of them at once).

For Joshi's question-answering system, clearly, these considerations are not applicable. Unless Joshi has the foresight to build a Russian-invasion subroutine into his program, his machine will blabber on, oblivious of the red star in its interlocutor's cap. But, just because we are now able to make machines do some surprisingly human-looking things, let us not be too quick to assume that humans do nothng more than our machines can do. Speaking as a human being myself, I have to say that I would by far prefer to see myself reduced to a Skinnerian pigeon or rat, than to a Chomskyan or Joshian computer.

NOTES

1. To say that Grice claims the maxims to be "implied" by his co-operative principle is to commit him to a claim which he might find unduly clear and specific. What he actually writes is: ". . . one may perhaps distinguish four categories under one or another of which will fall certain more specific maxims and sub-maxims, the following of which will, in general, yield results in accordance with the Co-operative Principle . . . it is just a well-recognized empirical fact that people *do* behave in these ways [sc. in accordance with Grice's maxims]".

2. This point is independent of the fact, often stressed by Artificial Intelligence scholars (e.g. Boden, 1977: 7), that a programmer will frequently be unable to foresee everything that his program will do in various circumstances.

3. Readers knowledgeable about economics will recognize that I assume the "Austrian" approach to be broadly right.

Comments on Joshi's Paper

R. Maclaran

Joshi's paper raises the interesting problem of how a computing system should be designed not only to give truthful and informative replies to users' questions, but also to correct the user when it discerns a mismatch between the user's and its own beliefs. To accomplish this latter goal, he proposes a modification of one of Grice's maxims, and suggests that this modification reflects an important difference between man–man and man–machine interaction. The superior computing ability of machines, he speculates, allows them to be more "co-operative", i.e. more sensitive to their interlocutor's misconceptions, than is a human. As a linguist I find this to be an interesting claim about the limits of human interaction. I shall argue, however, that it is false, not because humans *are* good at solving the kind of problem that Joshi sets for the machines, but because they are good at avoiding this kind of problem.

I'd like to begin by looking at some of Joshi's early examples which lay the groundwork of the problem. In example 1.2, Jane and Mary have swapped names and told the user (U), though not the system (S), that they have done so. U asks, "Is Jane the MC?"; S, not knowing about the change of names, says "yes". What bothers me is why U asks this question in the way he does. For U to be certain that he is being given the right answer to his question, he must be sure (a) that S has the facts right, and (b) that it has understood what question it is being asked. Now, U can presuppose that S's knowledge base is accurate. But how can he be sure that S has understood what question it is being asked? Since the two women have just exchanged names, he can only be sure who S thinks the question is about either if S has no idea about the change in names or if it knows about the change, and knows that U knows, and knows that U knows S knows etc. In the former case, where S does not know about the change, it will take U's question to be about the woman who *was* called Jane. In the second case, where S knows, and knows U knows it knows etc., it will take the question to be about the woman who is *now* called Jane. If U does not know whether or not S knows about the change, then he cannot be sure which question S is answering, whether it has understood the question to be about Jane or about Mary. This, of course, is the problem J. is raising. My point, however, is that if U does not know how S is going to understand his question, there is no point in his asking it, for a simple yes/no reply will be quite uninformative. Clearly what he should do is make sure that he and S agree on the referents of the names Jane and Mary and *then* ask his question. This will obviate the whole problem J. gets into; and it is typically the strategy humans use. Suppose that John has just got a new girlfriend Cathy, but I'm not sure if you know about her. I am unlikely to ask you, "Do you like John's girlfriend?", for I will not know if you are talking about the same person as I am. More likely I will ask, "Do you like John's *new* girlfriend?", "Do you like John's girlfriend Cathy?", or simply tell you that he has got a new girlfriend and then ask you if you like her. That is to say, typically, if we think there is a potential source of confusion, we make it clear who or what we are talking about. In terms of Grice's conversational principles, perhaps this can best be explained by the maxim "Be perspicuous", one of the maxims of manner.

This first example of J.'s is particularly surprising in light of his analysis of the following one, 1.3. Here Jane and Mary have swapped names and told U and S separately that they have done so. Once again, U asks S, "Is Jane the MC?", but S, so J. says, is unable to reply until it has found out who U is referring to by the name Jane. It therefore initiates a clarification dialogue, asking U if he knows about the name change and who he means to refer to. Now, it seems that there is a line of argument missing here. U asks, "Is Jane the MC?" S knows that Jane is the name of the second woman, who is not the MC. In this case, surely it should just answer "no". Why does it even question that U is referring to the present Jane? To use Kripke's terminology, why does it suspect that the semantic referent, i.e. what the name refers to, is different from the speaker's referent, i.e. what U intends by his use of the name? Presumably S does not give the straightforward answer "no", because it has a routine built into it that says: "If someone or something has recently changed its name, make sure that anyone using the name uses it in the same way you do". This is a perfectly sensible principle of communication, and one that is observed in human interaction. If you ask me, "Do you like John's girlfriend?" and I know he's just got a new one, I'll probably ask you who you are talking about. The point is that J. is here presupposing that the system, in clarifying the question before it answers it, follows just the principle I proposed should guide the human user in asking a question. In both cases, there is a potential for misunderstanding which needs to be straightened out before the interaction continues. My question is why J. thinks that U would, without elaboration, deliberately misuse a name in this confusing situation, especially when he requires that S be more circumspect here in its use of names.

I have rather belaboured this point because it seems that all the other examples simply compound the initial misdescription of the way humans proceed in these situations. The more complex examples of mismatch of belief appear to be artificial precisely because humans typically avoid them by spotting potential confusion and clarifying what they mean at the outset of the interaction.

The second set of examples is only different from the first set in that S does not just *suspect* but *knows* that U is using the names differently from the way it is. Here hair colour provides an unchanging way of uniquely identifying the women. S therefore always knows who U is referring to. U, however, refers to the women by both name and hair colour, and uses the names to refer to their previous bearers. Although S can straightforwardly answer U's questions without asking for further clarification, J. rightly requires that it should correct U's misconceptions about who the names refer to. How can it do this, he asks, without violating Grice's maxim of quality "Do not give more information than necessary"? His answer is that the maxim of quality must be revised so that S is required not to say not only anything that it believes to be false, but also it must not say anything which may imply something that it believes to be false. The maxim of quantity will then no longer be violated, as the amount of information necessary will include correcting the suspected false belief of U.

I have the same reaction here as in the previous examples. The communicative difficulties are due to the fact that U, although he knows that Mary and Jane have changed names, refers to the present Mary by her old name Jane, presumably because he is not sure if S knows about the change. But as I said before, this is a counterproductive way of asking a question, and something humans typically do not do. In a potentially confusing situation, they normally begin by saying who they are referring to. They normally follow some kind of conversational principle which says, "If in doubt, check your references".

It is now clear why J. sees an asymmetry in the interaction he describes between man and machine. As seen in the earlier examples, he implicitly applies more rigorous standards of co-operation to the machine than to the human user. In the situation of a change of names, U asks a question using a name, while in the same situation, S has to ask for clarification before it can reply. Thus from the outset, J. has decided to require machines to act in a way that he thinks humans do not (though I claim they do). It is not surprising, then, that this asymmetry becomes very apparent in later examples.

J. speculates that this asymmetry is due to the superior ability of computers to do "deep inferencing". While I agree that machines can do this kind of computation better than humans (I for one had great difficulty in processing the more complicated examples), I disagree that this enables computers to be "more co-operative" than humans, to be better at correcting interlocutors' misconceptions. It seems that the argument should, if anything, go the other way round: we are effective communicators precisely because, not having the ability to work out what we think the hearer thinks we think the hearer thinks we are referring to, we have effective strategies to avoid such confusion. Nor can I agree with J.'s statement that: "[t]he speaker is not expected to worry (at least not too much!) about the possible implications of what the speaker says for the hearer, which the speaker knows to be false" [p. 191]. I think we do hold people accountable for the false implications of what they say, especially when these implications are important enough. Several times when I have been with my brother at a party I have been taken for his wife. Suppose a guest were to ask him, "How many languages does you wife Rose speak?" My brother would know who they were referring to and could answer quite straightforwardly. If he were to do this, however, I think the guest would rightly be annoyed when he discovered later that I was not Michael's wife, especially if Michael's wife Pauline were at the party too. The more the implications are going to affect the interaction, the more the speaker will worry about them. If the above guest were to ask my brother to dinner and tell him to bring his wife, it would be quite outrageous of Michael not to point out the guest's mistake at this stage. It would be totally unacceptable for him to turn up with his wife Pauline, when the guest was expecting to see me. People *are* responsible for the false implications of what they say.

Now, I do not want to claim that humans are always perfectly co-operative and that human communication always runs smoothly. This is the simplistic view that Sampson criticizes. He is right that humans are not always co-operative, they lie and dissimulate, they have differing goals. In the above example, my brother might not initially correct the guest's misconception: he might not want to embarrass the guest by pointing out his mistake. People often allow mismatches of belief to continue: because they gain from the deceit, because they want to be diplomatic, because they do not want to disabuse someone's naïve beliefs, or simply because they think the misconception is too trivial to be worth the bother of sorting out. However, if we take the ideal of communication as being where the interlocutors try to maximize their common set of beliefs relevant to the task at hand, then the cases where we allow a mismatch of beliefs to continue can be explained in terms of the conflict of the participants' goals. Inasmuch as I refer to Santa Claus when talking to a child, I am being unco-operative, but this is because I have the competing goal of fostering the child's pleasure in a make-believe character. Sampson seems to think that examples like this cast doubt on the whole Gricean programme; and yet I doubt whether he would allow the existence of shopkeepers who are not out to maximize profits to prejudice Adam Smith's principle of economics. The exceptions are best viewed as such, and explained in terms of the ideal. It is especially interesting to apply Gricean principles to man–machine interaction since here the goal of co-operative behaviour is more nearly realized: we do not have to worry about deceit, politeness or any of the other interfering factors in man–man communication. It therefore provides an excellent testing-ground for a theory of conversational interaction.

If, as J. envisages, machines are to be designed which are as helpful as humans in correcting their interlocutor's false beliefs, there is a related case of miscommunication which needs to be looked at more carefully. I have criticized J.'s examples of the purposeful misuse of a name because I think that humans just do not behave like that. There are, however, plenty of cases where people unwittingly use the wrong name or misdescribe a referent, with the result that the semantic referent of the name or description is different from the speaker's referent. These are the cases Donnellan and Kripke have discussed. To use the example I introduced above, suppose a fellow guest comes up to my brother and says, "Your wife tells me she's a linguist". My brother can easily work out that the man is referring to me, although the description picks out my sister-in-law. But how is it that the guest succeeds in expressing a proposition about me and not about my sister-in-law?

There are two separate problems here, though they often coalesce. First, the hearer has to realize that the semantic referent may not be the intended referent; and then, if indeed it is not, he must work out what the intended referent is. The latter problem, that of identifying the intended referent, has been quite widely discussed, particularly in relation to examples in which there is no semantic referent, e.g. non-unique definite descriptions. Here the hearer has to supply a referent if the speaker's utterance is to make sense at all. Suppose I come home and say, "We must take the cat to the vet tonight". We may have more than one cat, in which case the singular definite description does not have a unique referent; but if you know that there is only one cat that needs to be taken to the vet, you can easily supply the intended referent. It is the other half of the problem that has not received much attention, as far as I know. That is, if there is a semantic referent, how does the hearer work out that it may not be the intended one? How does the hearer recognize that the speaker is trying to express a different proposition than the one he seems to be expressing? In J.'s examples of the change of names, S suspects that U might not be saying what he means to say because it has been programmed to check up on the referents of names in just this kind of situation. But in the situation I discussed before, where a guest comes up to my brother and uses the description "your wife", my brother would not automatically suspect that the guest has got the description wrong. Rather, it is as a result of what the guest appears to be saying that Michael would suspect the guest was mistaken. The guest says, "Your wife tells me she's a linguist". Since Michael's wife Pauline is not a linguist, this is a surprising statement. And it is just because it is a strange thing to say about Pauline that Michael would hypothesize that the guest is trying in fact to assert a more expected proposition about me.

Take another example. The central university computer has a listing of students with the courses they are enrolled in. I ask the computer, "Is Jane Smith enrolled in Linguistics 601"? The computer searches under

Jane Smith and finds she is registered for Ling 401, Ling 700, French 200 and Psych 416. It answers "No" to my question. Suppose it were to look down and find she was registered for Constitutional Law 100, Case Law 203, Jurisprudence 212 and Ethics 101. Again it would answer "No", but in this case any competent human would wonder why I should even consider that this student, who is evidently in beginning law, might be taking an advanced linguistics course. The human might then check the list of students and find that there is also a Jean Smith, who is indeed a linguistics student, and realize that this is who I meant to ask about. This kind of hypothesis about a user's misconception requires that we can judge which questions are appropriate or relevant. My question to the computer appears inappropriate because, given the contents of the system's knowledge base, it is extremely unlikely that the question will receive an affirmative answer. It is for this reason that the system should check whether the question I have in fact asked is the question I intended to ask. In order to identify such miscommunications, it is thus necessary to have an explicit theory of conversational interaction, which can match what is actually said against what would be relevant or appropriate. If something irrelevant is said, it can be reprocessed to see if more sense can be made of it.

Conversational relevance is also important to the final part of J.'s paper, which looks at the difference between content updating and structure updating in the processing of surplus information. U asks S, "Does the blue Volvo RN Z578 belong to John Anderson?" Since the registration number provides a uniquely identifying description, S can pick out the car, even though it may not have a value in its data base for the colour attribute of the car. But since the question identifies the car's colour, S can update the content of its data base. On the other hand, if it does not already know that cars have the attribute colour, it has to do two things. First, it has to restructure its beliefs about cars, and then it can supply the value "blue" for the new colour attribute slot of John Anderson's car. These latter structure updates, J. claims, should not be done implicitly and are harder to process in normal conversation than are content updates.

I think these claims are essentially correct, but I do not think it is as simple as saying that content updates work one way and that structure updates work another. Some content updates do require explicit processing. If I ask you, "Does the gold-plated Rolls Royce RN Z578 belong to John Anderson?", you only need to know the registration number to be able to answer my question; but if you did not already know the rest of the information, you will almost certainly remark on it. Similarly, I could ask you, "What do you think of my cousin Noam's book *Syntactic Structures*?" Once again, your reaction is likely to be not to answer the question, but to say, "Is Chomsky really your cousin?" My being Chomsky's cousin is much more interesting than the question, so that is what you're going to attend to. Just as we may or may not let a mismatch of beliefs go by in the case of misdescriptions, depending on how important the mismatch is, so here too we are likely to pick up on those bits of surplus information that are particularly relevant or interesting but ignore the uninteresting bits. Not all structural information is very interesting. Suppose you are moving away and trying to store your furniture. You might ask me, "Do you have room in your attic for my Swedish waterbed?" Now, I may not have categorized waterbeds as coming from different countries, but the fact that they do is relatively trivial. In this case, it is the storage of the bed which is probably most important, and so that is what I will react to. However, structural information is generally more relevant than content information, since it affects more of our knowledge and beliefs. It should not be surprising, then, that surplus structural information is more likely to be explicitly commented upon than surplus content information. This distinction between content and structural information should simply fall out of an adequate theory of conversation that gives an explicit account of conversational relevance. (See Sperber and Wilson above.)

To sum up then, I believe that the particular principles that J. proposes for machines are better treated in terms of a general theory of conversational relevance rather than being built into the machine as specific routines. I do not see the need to assume an asymmetry between man–man and man–machine interaction. A theory which successfully describes human interaction should be adequate to explain the kind of co-operation we expect from machines.

A Brief Reply to some of the Remarks by Sampson and Maclaran

Aravind K. Joshi

I will respond very briefly to some of the remarks by Sampson (S) and Maclaran (M). Each section below will be a response to an issue raised by either S, M, or both, which will be indicated at the beginning of the section by (S), (M), or (S,M).

1. (S,M) Both S and M are greatly concerned about my asymmetric characterization of man–machine interaction. Some of their remarks are due to a genuine disagreement with my position, but some others are due to a possible misunderstanding of the goals of my enterprise. My comments in this section will deal with the latter situation.

First of all, I am concerned with those interactions where the system (S) is expected to help the user (U) and be co-operative in a variety of ways as outlined in Section I of my paper. S is expected to play the role of a helpful agent for U. Even in man–man interactions, where one participant plays the role of a helpful agent (as in many "service" functions, e.g. the ticket agent at the box-office, the secretary in the registrar's office dealing with class schedules, grades, etc.), we see asymmetry in the interactions. The agent is usually expected to be more "helpful or co-operative" (both qualitatively and quantitatively) than the human participant. With computer systems as helpful agents, the service functions become more sophisticated and their scope is immensely expanded, and will continue to be so. However, I believe, the essential asymmetric characterization of the interaction will continue to hold; *in fact, it will be highly accentuated because of certain capacities of machines (such as the speed of making computationally complex inferences) and the consequent expectation of U that the system use these capacities to generate its responses.* This is one major point I have attempted to make. The types of interactions I am concerned with are clearly narrow but I believe very useful. I am certainly not concerned with computer systems that may be considered as one's friendly conversational partners!

2. (S) There is no question that the responses generated by S based on the revised maxim of quality can be elaborate and convoluted. One can get the feeling that S is overcorrecting unnecessarily. S can, of course, trim its response by using additional pieces of knowledge, if available. For example, in Example 2, if S believes that the name is an extraneous description and is not relevant to overall goals of the user, and further that this is mutually believed by S and U, then S can drastically trim its "squaring away" response, thus giving the impression that S is avoiding the problem of correcting misconceptions. (I want to thank Candy Sidner for some valuable comments on this issue.) Hence, it is not the case that the revised maxim is not followed, but that the response is trimmed by S by concluding that an elaborate response can be dispensed with. Thus S's apparent avoidance of overcorrection is only due to a complex interaction of the revised maxim and some richer mutual beliefs. The main issue of asymmetry is not really affected by these considerations.

It might be worth pointing out that in practice, since it is not always an easy task to discern uniquely, from the interaction itself, some higher level goals of the user (unless these are given to the system *a priori*), it is not safe to trim the response from some partial identification of the higher level goals. Such a behavior is likely to cause some disparities in the mutual beliefs about these higher level goals requiring further complex squaring away responses. In practice, it might be better to let the system S adhere to the revised maxim and give the user the possibility of turning off S's response if U believes that it is not useful or relevant to him/her, a possibility that is usually not available in man–man interaction!

3. (M) My discussion of how surplus information should be incorporated is certainly very preliminary. My main purpose is to point out certain differences between the updatability requirements for different types of surplus information (e.g. pertaining to content or structure). It is quite possible that these distinctions will fall out of a theory of conversational relevance. The work of Sperber and Wilson (this volume) certainly suggests some possible approaches towards the treatment of surplus information. I have not looked into this aspect in any great detail as yet. M is right in pointing out that not all surplus information is equally relevant or interesting in a given context. However, this does

not blur the distinction between content and structure from the system's point of view. I am certainly not claiming here that notions such as "interestingness" are directly correlated to structure or content.

4. (S) I am definitely suggesting that the characterization of man–machine interaction discussed in my paper is a descriptive one and not a prescriptive one. Here there is clearly a disagreement. There would not be a point to my paper if this characterization is prescriptive.

On a lighter side:

5. (S,M) It is amusing to see that both S and M have taken me to task for being harsh on the machine by making it do things humans don't do. I am interested in computer systems that serve as helpful agents, and I want them to do the things they are good at and do them better and faster. Machines clearly are not good at everything humans do, and perhaps will never be so.

6. (S) Although Chomsky has interest in certain aspects of the theory of computation, I do not believe that he has ever shown any great interest or enthusiasm about building computer systems to do specific tasks! So I am a bit puzzled by the last sentence in S's remarks.

Chapter 5
Meaning Revisited*

Paul Grice

I'm going to talk informally about some topics connected with meaning. I have not in fact been doing a great deal of work on this subject during the last four or five years or so, although I have done some. And rather than saying something particularly new, I have the idea of putting one or two of the thoughts I have had at various times into some kind of focus, so that there might emerge some sort of sense about not merely what kind of views about the nature of meaning I am, or was, inclined to endorse, but also why it should be antecedently plausible to accept this kind of view. When I say "antecedently plausible", I mean plausible for some reasons other than that the view in question offers some prospects of dealing with the intuitive data: the facts about how we use the word "mean", and so on. So I will be digging just a little bit into the background of the study of meaning and its roots in such things as philosophical psychology; but I hope without any very formidable detail.

The main theme will be matters connected with the relation between speaker's meaning and meaning in a language, or word meaning, sentence meaning, expression meaning, and so on. In the course of this, I shall make reference to something like the definitions or analyses that I have previously offered; I do not guarantee that any that I use will be

---

* An earlier version of the first two sections was delivered as a talk to a colloquium organized by the Ontario Institute for Studies in Education and held in Toronto in March 1976.

quite the same, but this does not worry me because I am not here concerned with the details. It seems to me that with regard to the possibility of using the notion of intention in a nested kind of way to explicate the notion of meaning, there are quite a variety of plausible, or at least not too implausible, analyses, which differ to a greater or lesser extent in detail, and at the moment I am not really concerned with trying to adjudicate between the various versions.

The talk will be in three sections. In the first, I will try to sketch three kinds of correspondence which one might be justified in looking for, or even demanding, when thinking about thought, the world and language. I hope this will provide some sort of a framework within which to set views about meaning; it may in fact offer some sort of impetus towards this or that view. In the second section, which will again involve an attempt to fit things into a wider framework, I will provide some discussion of what I once called the distinction between natural and non-natural meaning. Here I am interested not so much in the existence of that distinction, which has now, I think, become pretty boringly common ground (or mutual knowledge), but rather in the relationship between the two notions, the connections rather than the dissimilarities between them. I shall announce the contents of the third section when I come to it; we'll keep it as a mystery package.

LANGUAGE, THOUGHT AND REALITY

The first of the three correspondences which one might expect to find, when thinking in largish terms about the relationships between reality, thought and language or communication devices, is a correspondence between thought and reality: what I shall call, for some kind of brevity, psychophysical correspondence. This has obvious connections with the general idea of truth in application to beliefs or analogous notions describing physical states. The point I want to get at is that it is not just that there *are* such correspondences, or that it is intuitively plausible to think there are, but rather that their presence is *needed*, or *desirable*, if one looks at the ways in which human beings and other sentient creatures get around and stay alive, as well as perhaps doing more ambitious things than that. This leads to a view, which I have held for some time, of a battery of psychological concepts which we use both about ourselves and about what one might think of as lower creatures, as having the function of providing an explanatory bridge between the appearance of a creature in a certain kind of physical situation and its producing certain sorts of behaviour.

For instance, suppose we have a creature C that is in the presence of a certain object, let's say a piece of cheese, and we get a situation in which the creature eats the object. In certain circumstances, we might want to invoke the contents of a psychological theory in order to explain the transition from the creature's being in the presence of the object to its eating it. The "bridge-work" which would be done in these terms might run somewhat as follows: put in a rather schematic and unrealistic way, which again does not worry me since I am not trying to provide a proper explanation, but merely a rough idea of what the pattern of a proper explanation would be.

First, let's suppose that the creature believes (or thinks, if it is not advanced enough to have beliefs) that the object is a bit of cheese, and that it also believes that the object is nearby. Secondly, let's suppose that the creature believes, or thinks, that cheese is something to eat; and thirdly, that the creature is hungry, that it wants to eat. All this looks relatively unexciting, just as it should. Then in virtue of what I would think of as a vulgar, vernacular, psychological law, the operation of which is what we can for these purposes think of the concepts of believing and wanting as being introduced to bring into play, we get our first psychological law for the creature or type of creature in question. This is that for any particular object X and for any feature F and for any activity or type of behaviour A, if the creature C believes that the object X both has the feature F and is nearby, or within reach, and that things of type F are suitable for activity A, then the creature wants to A with respect to the object X. In other words, the law harnesses the object to the type of activity.

Applying the law to the three initial premises given above, we reach a further stage: namely, that the creature C wants to eat the object X, that is, the piece of cheese. We might then invoke a second psychological law for this creature, this time a psychophysical law: that for any type of activity A, if a creature C, wants to A with respect to some particular object X, and if it is not prevented in one or another of a set of ways which might or might not be listable, then creature C does produce the activity A with respect to X. And with the application of the second law, we get to our final step, which is that the creature C eats the object X. We now have our explanation, a bridge between the initial situation, the creature's being in the presence of a piece of cheese, and the final behaviour, the creature's eating it.

The laws I have mentioned are vulgar laws. The kind of theory in which I think of them appearing would not be a specialist or formalized psychological theory, if indeed there are such things; I am perhaps not very comfortable with the word "theory" being applied to it. It would be the rough kind of system with which we all work, and the laws in it are to be thought of as corrigible, modifiable and *ceteris paribus* in character.

Now the creature C may be frustrated if certain psychophysical correspondences do not obtain. For instance, if C believes *wrongly* that the object in front of it is a piece of cheese, or thinks *wrongly* of cheese as being from its point of view something to eat, then at the very least, C may get indigestion when it consumes the object. For this reason, psychophysical correspondences are required (things like beliefs have to be true, and so on) for the operation of the psychological mechanisms which I have sketched to be *beneficial* to the creature in question.

In a similar way, if the creature's desire to eat the object is for some reason not fulfilled, the creature stays hungry. Here again we need some kind of correspondences, parallel to those between beliefs and reality, between desires, wants, states of will and so on, and reality. Desires, etc. need to correspond to reality in order to be fulfilled: that is, in order for the psychological mechanism to operate in a beneficial way.

Finally, if C is a rational or reflective creature (which I have not so far been assuming) it may recognize the kind of facts about itself that I have just sketched, may recognize that correspondences between psychological states and the world are in general required for the psychological mechanism to be useful, and may also recognize that subject to this proviso of correspondence, the psychological mechanism is conductive to survival or to the attainment of other of its objectives. If it recognizes all this, then it will presumably itself think of such correspondences as being desirable things to have around from its own point of view: that is, the correspondences will not only *be* desirable but will be regarded by C as desirable.

In the first place, then, we have psychophysical correspondences, and they seem to be the kind of things that one would want to have. But there are further correspondences too. There is, as it were, a triangle consisting of reality, thought and language or communication devices, and we now have, I hope, one hook-up, between thought and reality.

However, I think there is also a hook-up of a different kind, which would also be desirable, between thought and communication devices. This would again involve correspondences of a relatively simple and obvious kind, along the following lines.

First, the operation of such creatures as I have been talking about is at least in certain circumstances going to be helped and furthered if there is what one might think of as shared experience. In particular, if psychological states which initially attach to one creature can be transmitted or transferred or reproduced in another creature (a process which might be called *psi*-transmission), that would be advantageous. Obviously, the production of communication devices is a resource which will help to effect such transfers.

If one accepts this idea, then one could simply accept that for the process to be intelligible, understandable, there will have to be correspondences between particular communication devices or utterances on the one hand, and psychological states on the other. These correspondences may be achieved either directly, or (more likely) indirectly, via the *types* to which the particular utterances belong: the sentences which the particular utterances are utterances of, the gesture-types which the particular gestures are productions of, and so on. Whether direct or indirect, the correspondence would be between utterances or utterance-types on the one hand, and *types* of psychological states on the other, where these would include, for example, the belief-types to which the beliefs of particular people belong: not *Jones'* belief that such-and-such, but *a* belief that such-and-such.

If there exist these correspondences between utterances or utterance-types on the one hand, and psychological types on the other, we can say that it is in general, and subject to certain conditions, *desirable* for there to occur, in the joint or social lives or creatures of the kind in question, sequences of the following sort: a certain psychological state psi^1 in certain circumstances is followed by a certain utterance U, made in certain circumstances, which in turn, if the circumstances are right, is followed by a particular instance of a further psychological type psi^2, a state not now in the communicating creature but in the creature who is communicated to. And it might be a matter of desirability for psi^1 and psi^2 to be states of one and the same, rather than of different sorts, so that when these sequences psi^1, U, psi^2 occur, they involve utterances and psychological states between which these psycho-linguistic correspondences obtain.

Of course, transfers can occur without these correspondences obtaining. A creature may choose the wrong utterance to express its psychological state, and then there will probably be a misfire in the utterance, and the psychological state induced in the second creature will not be the same as the one present in the first. Alternatively, the first creature may operate all right, but the second creature may, as it were, misunderstand the device that was produced, and so pick up the wrong belief or desire, one that does not correspond to the utterance produced by the first creature.

The general condition, or at least the most salient general condition, for the desirability or beneficial character of transfers of this sort is connected with the obtaining of the first kind of correspondence. That is, if all these transfers were to involve the transmission of mistaken beliefs, it is not clear that one would regard this communication mechanism as beneficial, even if the appropriate psycholinguistic correspondences held. I do think it is in some sense inconceivable that all the transfers should involve mistaken beliefs, but at least such a state of affairs can be contemplated. So a general condition would be that soul-to-soul transfers, so to speak, are beneficial provided that the states transmitted are ones which correspond with the world.

It looks now as if we have got to a point at which we have in outline, presented in a sort of general, semi-theological way, a rough prototype of a notion of truth in application to beliefs and such-like things. That would give the first kind of correspondence. In the second case, we have what is at least a promising candidate for being a rough prototype of the notion of meaning, for it looks as though it is not unplausible to suggest that to explain, with respect to some particular utterance or utterance-type what type of psychological state it corresponds to, in such a way that transfers of this kind are characteristically a feature of creatures' lives, would be a first approximation to explaining the meaning of the utterances or utterance-types in question. We have thus hooked up all three corners: corner number one, reality, has been hooked up with corner number two, thought, and we have hooked up thought, corner number two, with language or communication devices, corner number three. This of course yields a derivative link between corner number three, utterances or sentences, and corner number one, reality, via the beliefs or other psychological states with which they are themselves connected. But it is perhaps also worth while to ask whether in addition to such an indirect connection between language and reality, one which proceeds through the intermediation of psychological states, there is an arguable possibility of a direct link: a direct line between language and reality as well as a line through thought. And I think it is at least arguable that there is, though of course one of a kind which we will have to harmonize with the ones that have already been introduced.

If I ask the question "What are the conditions for a specified belief (for instance a belief that snow is white) corresponding with the world?", I can give answers for individual cases without much difficulty. For instance, I can say that a belief that snow is white will correspond to the world just in case snow is white, and I can say that a belief that cheese is blue will correspond to the world just in case cheese is blue; and you can see perfectly well what the rather dreary routine is that I use in these particular cases. However, it has been noticed by philosophers that there are difficulties about explicitly generalizing the individual bits of communication of which I have just spouted one or two samples. That is because to generalize from them would presumably be to omit reference to the particular objects and the particular beliefs, and to state in general what the conditions are for beliefs corresponding to objects. That is to say, a general condition of correspondence between beliefs and the world would have to begin something like: "For any item which one believes, that item corresponds with the world if. . ."; but then how does one go on? In the particular cases, I had a sentence which I had cited or referred to in the antecedent on the left-hand side, which I then produced on the right-hand side; but since I have eliminated all reference to particular beliefs or sentences, I no longer have a sentence available to complete the general condition with.

It looks as if I should want to say something like: "For any item P, if one believes that P, then one's belief that P corresponds with the world just in case P". Unfortunately that involves difficulties, because by the ordinary account of quantification, I am talking about objects or items, so I might just as well use the letter x, characteristic of objects, and say: "For any item x, if x is believed, then x corresponds with the world just in case x". But that seems rather like producing the generalization that if any object x is a pig, then x: and that is not an intelligible form of statement, because "x" is not a variable for which one can substitute sentences. In fact, something seems to have got left out somewhere, and we have not got an intelligible specification of truth-conditions. Moreover, this is difficult to remedy, because without getting into tortures over shifts between thinking of propositions or propositional expressions as sometimes like names (with the form of *that*-clauses) and sometimes like sentences (the result of detaching the word "that" from these *that*-clauses), it is difficult to know what to do.

It looks as though, to avoid this difficulty, if I want to produce a generalization of the idea of correspondences between psychological states and the world which I have already in some sense provided for, I might well have to use some form like the following: "If a certain sentence S is an expression of a certain particular belief, then the belief which the sentence S expresses corresponds with the world just in case S is true". That is to say, to remedy this difficulty in generalization, I now bring into play a notion of truth in application to sentences, and I do this in order to have a way of stating generally the conditions for the correspondence of beliefs and the world. Thus, in trying to safeguard the characterization of what it is for beliefs to correspond with the world, I have introduced another correspondence, a correspondence between utterances or sentences and the world, signalized by the appearance of the word "true".

It looks, then, as if in order to achieve a characterization of the first kind of correspondence, between beliefs and the world, one has to make use of a parallel kind of correspondence between utterances or sentences and the world. Hence these latter correspondences may be not only possible but needed if one is to be able to state, in a general way, that correspondences of the psychophysical kind actually obtain.

However, though they may be required for expository purposes, as I have sketched, it might still be the case that in order to show that correspondences between sentences and the world were desirable, not just for purposes of theoretical exposition but from the point of view of creatures who operate with such utterances or utterance types, one still has to bring in the psychological states in specifying the conditions of suitability, desirability, or whatever. That is, it might be that one can certainly formulate or characterize some notion of direct correspondence between utterances and the world, and this might have a certain limited teleological justification because it is needed to provide a general way of expressing the conditions for other types of correspondence, but that if one wants to provide a more general teleological justification, one would need to make reference to beliefs and other psychological states. In other words, for a more general justification of the idea of truth in application to sentences, one might have to bring in all three corners, including the missing one.

NATURAL AND NON-NATURAL MEANING

I have now as it were smuggled in some sort of preliminary version of the kind of view about meaning which I have gone on record as holding; but that is qualified by the fact that I have also smuggled in versions of the kind of views that other people have gone in for too. Let me now try to advance the case a little further, in a way which might support my sort of view as opposed to certain other ones.

I do not think it is too controversial to advance the idea that there is a reasonably clear intuitive distinction between cases where the word "mean" has what one might think of as a natural sense, a sense in which what something means is closely related to the idea of what it is a natural sign for (as in "Black clouds mean rain"), and those where it has what I call a non-natural sense, as in such contexts as "His remark meant so-and-so", "His gesture meant that he was fed up", and so on (cf. Grice, 1957).

I have offered one or two recognition tests which might enable one to tell which of these, natural or non-natural meaning, one was actually dealing with in a given case. The tests were, roughly speaking, that the non-natural cases of meaning, cases which are related to communication, are what we might call non-factive, whereas the natural cases are factive. That is, anyone who says "Those black clouds mean rain", or "Those black clouds meant that it would rain", would presumably be committing himself to its being the case that it will rain, or that it did rain. However, if I say "His gesture meant that he was fed up", under an interpretation of a non-natural kind, one specially connected with what we think of as communication, then to say that does not commit you to his actually being fed up. I also noted that the specification of the non-natural meaning of items can be comfortably done via the use of phrases in quotation marks, whereas it would seem rather odd to say that those black clouds meant "It will rain": it does not look as if one can replace the *that*-clause here by a sentence in quotation marks.

Assuming for the moment that these tests are roughly adequate, what I want to do now is not to emphasize the differences between these cases, because that has already been done, but rather to look at what they have in common. Is this double use of the word "mean" just like the double use of the word "vice" to refer sometimes to something approximating to a sin and sometimes to a certain sort of instrument used by carpenters? One is pretty much inclined in the latter case to say that there are two words which are pronounced and written the same.

On general grounds of economy, I would be inclined to think that if one can avoid saying that the word so-and-so has this sense, that sense and the other sense, or this meaning and another meaning, if one can allow them to be variants under a single principle, that is the desirable thing to do: don't multiply senses beyond necessity. And it occurs to me that the root idea in the notion of meaning, which in one form or adaptation or another would apply to both of these cases, is that if x means that y, then this is equivalent to, or at least contains as a part of what it means, the claim that y is a consequence of x. That is, what the cases of natural and non-natural meaning have in common is that, on some interpretation of the notion of consequence, y's being the case is a consequence of x.

Of course one will expect there to be differences in the kind of consequence involved, or the way in which the consequence is reached. So what I want to do now is look to see if one would represent the cases of non-natural meaning as being descendants from, in a sense of "descendant" which would suggest that they were derivative from and analogous to, cases of natural meaning. I will also look a little at what kind of principles or assumptions one would have to make if one were trying to set up this position that natural meaning is in some specifiable way the ancestor of non-natural meaning.

In the case of natural meaning, among the things which have natural meaning, besides black clouds, spots on the face, symptoms of this or that disease, are certainly forms of behaviour: things like groans, screeches and so on, which mean, or normally mean, that someone or something is in pain or some other state. Thus special cases of natural meaning are cases in which bits of things like bodily behaviour mean the presence of various elements or states of the creature that produces them. In the natural case, the production of these pieces of behaviour, or at least the presence in those pieces of behaviour of the particular features which as it were do the meaning for one, is non-voluntary. Thus we have as a sort of canonical pattern that some creature X non-voluntarily produces a certain piece of behaviour α, the production of which means, or has the consequence, or evidences, that X is in pain. That is the initial natural case. Let us now see if we could in one or more stages modify it so as to end up with something which is very much like non-natural meaning.

The first stage in the operation I will call stage 1. This involves the supposition that the creature actually voluntarily produces a certain sort of behaviour which is such that its non-voluntary production would be evidence that the creature is, let's say, in pain. The kinds of cases of this which come most obviously to mind will be cases of faking or deception. A creature normally voluntarily produces behaviour not only when, but *because*, its non-voluntary production would be evidence that the creature is in a certain state, with the effect that the rest of the world, other creatures around, treat the production, which is in fact voluntary, as if it were a non-voluntary production. That is, they come to just the same conclusion about the creature's being in the state in question, the signalled state. The purpose of the creature's producing the behaviour voluntarily would be so that the rest of the world should think that it is in the state which the non-voluntary production would signify.

We then go to stage 2, in which not only does creature X produce this behaviour voluntarily instead of non-voluntarily, as in the primitive state, but we also assume that it is *recognized* by another creature Y, involved with X in some transaction, as being the voluntary production of a certain form of behaviour the non-voluntary production of which evidences, say, pain. That is, creature X is now supposed not only to simulate pain-behaviour, but also to be recognized as simulating pain-behaviour. The importation of the recognition by Y that the production is voluntary undermines, of course, any tendency on the part of Y to come to the conclusion that creature X is in pain. So, one might ask, what would be required to restore the situation: what could be added which would be an antidote, so to speak, to the dissolution on the part of Y of the idea that X is in pain?

A first step in this direction would be to go to what one might think of as stage 3. Here, we suppose that creature Y not only recognizes that the behaviour is voluntary on the part of X, but also recognizes that X *intends* Y to recognize his behaviour as voluntary. That is, we have now undermined the idea that this is a straightforward piece of deception. Deceiving consists in trying to get a creature to accept certain things as signs of something or other without knowing that this is a faked case. Here, however, we would have a sort of perverse faked case, in which something is faked but at the same time a clear indication is put in that the faking has been done.

Creature Y can be thought of as initially baffled by this conflicting performance. There is this creature as it were simulating pain, but announcing, in a certain sense, that this is what it's doing: what on earth can it be up to? It seems to me that if Y does raise the question of why X should be doing this, it might first come up with the idea that X is engaging in some form of play or make-believe, a game to which, since X's behaviour is seemingly directed towards Y, Y is expected or intended to make some appropriate contribution. Cases susceptible of such an interpretation I shall regard as belonging to stage 4.

But, we may suppose, there might be cases which could not be handled in this way. If Y is to be expected to be a fellow-participant with X in some form of play, it ought to be possible for Y to recognize what kind of contribution Y is supposed to make; and we can envisage the possibility that Y has no clue on which to base such recognition, or again that though some form of contribution seems to be suggested, when Y obliges by coming up with it, X instead of producing further play-behaviour, gets cross and perhaps repeats its original, and now problematic performance.

We now reach stage 5, at which Y supposes not that X is engaged in play, but that what X is doing is trying to get Y to believe or accept that X is in pain: that is, trying to get Y to believe in or accept the presence of that state in X which the produced behaviour, when produced non-voluntarily, is in fact a natural sign of, naturally means. More specifically, one might say that at stage 5, creature Y recognizes that creature X in the first place intends that Y recognize the production of the sign of pain (of what is usually the sign of pain), to be voluntary, and further intends that Y should regard this first intention as being a sufficient reason for Y to believe that X is in pain; and that X has these intentions because he has the additional further intention that Y should not merely have sufficient reason for believing that X is in pain, but should actually believe it.

Whether or not in these circumstances Y will not merely recognize that X intends, in a certain rather queer way, to get Y to believe that X is in pain, whether Y not only recognizes this but actually goes on to believe that X is in pain, would presumably depend on a further set of conditions which can be summed up under the general heading that Y should regard X as trustworthy in one or another of perhaps a variety of ways. For example, suppose Y thinks that, either in general or at least in this type of case, X would not want to get Y to believe that X is in pain unless X really were in pain. Suppose also (this would perhaps not apply to a case of pain, but might apply to the communication of other states) that Y also believed that X was trustworthy, not just in the sense of not being malignant, but in the sense of being as it were in general responsible, for example being the sort of creature who takes adequate trouble to make sure that what he is trying to get the other creature to believe is in fact the case, and who is not careless, negligent or rash. Then, given the general fulfilment of the idea that Y regards X either in general or in this particular case as being trustworthy in this kind of competent, careful way, one would regard it as rational for Y not only to recognize these intentions on the part of X, that Y should have certain beliefs about X's being in pain, but also for Y actually to pass to adopting these beliefs.

So far I have been talking about the communication of the idea that something is the case, for example that X is in pain or some other state, by means of a non-deceptive simulation on the part of the communicating creature of the standard signs or indices of such a state. But the mechanism that has been used, involving the interchange of beliefs or intentions of different orders, really does not require that what is taken as the communication vehicle should be initially a natural expression or sign of the state of affairs being communicated. If we now relax this requirement, we get to stage 6, the road to which may be eased by the following reflection, for which I am indebted to Judith Baker.

In relation to the particular example which I have been using, to reach the position ascribed to it in stage 5, Y would have to solve, bypass or ignore a possible problem presented by X's behaviour: why should X produce what is not a genuine but a faked expression of pain if what X is trying to get Y to believe is that X is *in pain*? Why not just let out a natural bellow? Possible answers are not too hard to come by: for example, that it would be unmanly, or otherwise uncreaturely, for X to produce *naturally* a natural expression of pain, or that X's non-natural production of an expression of pain is not to be supposed to indicate *every* feature which would be indicated by a natural production (the non-natural emission, for example, of a loud bellow might properly be taken to indicate pain, but not that degree of pain which would correspond with the decibels of the particular emission). This problem would not, however, arise if X's performance, instead of being something which, in the natural case, would be an *expression* of that state of X which (in the non-natural case) it is intended to get Y to believe in, were rather something more loosely connected with the state of affairs (not necessarily a state of X) which it is intended to convey to Y; X's performance, that is, would be suggestive, in some recognizable way, of the state of affairs without being a natural response of X to that state of affairs.

We reach, then, a stage in which the communication vehicles do not have to be, initially, natural signs of that which they are used to communicate; provided a bit of behaviour could be expected to be seen by the receiving creature as having a discernible connection with a particular piece of information, then that bit of behaviour will be usable by the transmitting creature, provided that that creature can place a fair bet on the connection being made by the receiving creature. Any link will do, provided it is detectable by the receiver; and the looser the links creatures are in a position to use, the greater the freedom they will have as communicators, since they will be less and less restricted by the need to rely on prior natural connections. The widest possible range is given where creatures use for these purposes a range of communication devices which have no antecedent connections at all with the things that they communicate or represent, and the connection is simply made because the knowledge, or supposition, or assumption, of such an artificial connection is prearranged and foreknown. Here one can simply cash in, as it were, on the stock of semantic information which has already been built into creatures at some previous stage.

In some cases, the artificial communication devices might have certain other features too, over and above the one of being artificial: they might, for example, involve a finite number of fundamental, focal, elementary, root devices and a finite set of modes or forms of combination (combinatory operations, if you like) which are capable of being used over and over again. In these cases, you will have, or be near to having, what some people have thought to be characteristic of a language: namely, a communication system with a finite set of initial devices, together with semantic provisions for them, and a finite set of different syntactical operations or combinations, and an understanding of what the functions of those modes of combination are. As a result of this, you generate an infinite set of sentences or complex communication devices, together with a correspondingly infinite set of things to be communicated, as it were.

So, by proceeding in this teleological kind of way, we seem to have provided some rationale both for the kind of characterization of speaker's meaning which I went in for long ago, and also for the characterization of various kinds of communication systems, culminating in things which have features which are ordinarily supposed (more or less correctly, I would imagine) to be the features of a fully developed language. I say that we *seem* to have provided a rationale; for there is, I think, a large residual question of a methodological kind. My succession of stages is not, of course, intended to be a historical or genetic account of the development of communication and language; it is a myth designed, among other things, to exhibit the conceptual link between natural and non-natural meaning. But how can such a link be explained by a *myth*? This question is perhaps paralleled, as was recently suggested to me, by the question how the nature and validity of political obligation (or perhaps even of moral obligation) can possibly be explained by a *mythical* social contract. While the parallel may be suggestive and useful, one might be pardoned for wondering how much more it does besides match one mystery with another. But that is a problem for another day.

THE MYSTERY PACKAGE

Well, this is the mystery package. First, a small anecdote. My sometimes mischievous friend Richard Grandy once said, in connection with some other occasion on which I was talking, that to represent my remarks it would be necessary to introduce a new form of speech act, or a new operator, which was to be called the operator of *quessertion*. It is to be read as "It is perhaps possible that someone might assert that . . .", and is symbolized as follows: ?-; possibly it might even be iterable. Everything I shall suggest here is highly quessertable. I shall simply explore an idea; I do not know whether I want to subscribe to it or not. In what follows, then, I am not to be taken as making any ground floor assertions at all: except for the assertion that something is quesserted.

The general idea that I want to explore, and which seems to me to have some plausibility, is that something has been left out, by me and perhaps by others too, in the analyses, definitions, expansions and so on, of semantic notions, and particularly various notions of meaning. What has been left out has in fact been left out because it is something which everyone regards with horror, at least when in a scientific or theoretical frame of mind: the notion of value.

Though I think that in general we want to keep value notions out of our philosophical and scientific enquiries (and some would say out of everything else) we might consider what would happen if we relaxed this prohibition to some extent. If we did, there is a whole range of different kinds of value predicates or expressions which might be admitted in different types of case. To avoid having to choose between them, I am just going to use as a predicate the word "optimal": the meaning of which could of course be more precisely characterized later.

The reason why I am particularly interested in this general idea is that my own position, which I am not going to try to state or defend in any detail at the moment, is that the notion of value is absolutely crucial to the idea of rationality, or of a rational being. There are many ways in which one can characterize what it is to be a rational being. Some of them may turn out to be equivalent to one another in some sense: they may turn out to apply to exactly the same cases. However, it may be that even though they are equivalent, there is one that is particularly fruitful from a deductive-theoretical point of view. I have strong suspicions that the most fruitful idea is the idea that a rational creature is a creature which evaluates, and that the other possible characterizations may turn out to be co-extensive with this, though in some sense less leading. I don't know whether it follows from this, but at any rate I think it is true, that all naturalistic attempts at the characterization of rationality are doomed to failure. Value is in there from the beginning, and you can't get it out. This is not something to be argued about here, but it should give some indication of the kind of murky framework in which I shall now start to operate.

It seems to me that there are two different problems connected with meaning in which questions of value might arise. I call them the minor problem and the major problem. The minor problem has to do with the relation between what, speaking generally, I may call word meaning and speaker meaning. It seems plausible to suppose that to say that a sentence (word, expression) means something (to say that "John is a bachelor" means that John is an unmarried male, or whatever it is) is to be somehow understood in terms of what particular users of that sentence (word, expression) mean on particular occasions. The first possible construal of this is rather crude: namely, that usually people do use this sentence, etc., in this way. A construal which seems to me rather better is that it is conventional to use this sentence in this way; and there are many others.

Now I don't think that even the most subtle or sophisticated interpretation of this construal will do, because I don't think that meaning is essentially connected with convention. What it is essentially connected with is some way of fixing what sentences mean: convention is indeed one of these ways, but it is not the only one. I can invent a language, call it Deutero-Esperanto, which nobody ever speaks. That makes me the authority, and I can lay down what's proper. Notice that we are immediately arriving at some form of evaluative notion: namely, what it is proper to do.

The general suggestion would therefore be that to say what a word means in a language is to say what it is in general optimal for speakers of that language to do with that word, or what use they are to make of it; what particular intentions on particular occasions it is proper for them to have, or optimal for them to have. Of course, there is no suggestion that they *always* have to have those intentions: it would merely be optimal, *ceteris paribus*, for them to have them. As regards what is optimal in any particular kind of case, there would have to be a cash value, an account of why this was optimal. There might be a whole range of different accounts. For example, it might be that it was conventional to use this word in this way; it might be that it was conventional among some privileged class to use it in this way—what some technical term in biology means is not a matter for the general public: it's a matter for biologists; it might be, when an invented language is involved, what is laid down by its inventor. However, what you get in every case, as a unification of all these accounts, is the optimality or propriety of a certain form of behaviour. That concludes my discussion of the minor problem.

The major problem in which questions of value arise has to do not with attempts to exhibit the relation between word meaning and speaker meaning, but with attempts to exhibit the anatomy of speaker meaning itself. At this point, my general strategy was to look for the kind of regresses which Schiffer and others have claimed to detect concealed beneath the glossy surface of my writings on meaning: infinite and vicious regresses which they propose to cast out, substituting another regressive notion, such as mutual knowledge, instead; raising somewhat the question as to why their regresses are good regresses and mine are bad ones.

However, as I tried, by looking at Schiffer, to disentangle exactly what the alleged regresses are, I found it almost impossible to do so. That is, someone who alleges an infinite regress ought surely to provide a general method for generating the next stage of the regress out of the previous one, and I could see no general way of doing this: the connections between one stage and another seemed to be disparate. That is not to say that there is no way of doing this. I used to think when talking to Schiffer that there was one, and that I understood it, but now I don't.

However, since the actual nature of the regress, or regressive accusation, does not matter very much, what I have done is to invent my own, which I will call a pseudo-Schiffer regress; and so far from trying to make it leaky or creaky at the joints, on the contrary, I would like it to be a strong as I can make it, and if it is not strong enough, I am going to pretend that it is.

The regress can be reconstructed along the following lines. One might start with the idea that when some speaker S utters some sentence to a hearer A, meaning by it that p, he does this wanting A to think 'p'. That is, at Stage 1 we have "S wants A to think 'p' ", where p represents the content of A's thought or intended thought. However, for reasons that came up long ago, having to do with the distinction between natural and non-natural meaning, we cannot stop at Stage 1. We have to proceed to Stage 2, at which we get "S wants A to think "p, on the strength of the idea that S wants A to think 'p' " "; and so on.

We have now reached a curious situation, in that there is a certain sort of disparity between what S wants A to think: namely "p, on the strength of S wanting A to think that p", and the accounts that are given so to speak in the sub-clause of this as to what it is that S wants A to think. That is, S wants A to think not just "p", but "p on the grounds that S wants A to think that p"; but when we are stating what the grounds are, what A is supposed to think, we find that he is only supposed to think "p". In other words, what we specify A as intended to think of as the reason for thinking "p" is always one stage behind what the speaker envisages as the reason why he wants A to think "p".

We thus arrive at something of the form "S wants A to think 'p, because S wants A to think "p, because S wants . . ." ' "; and so on. We put in the extra clause in order to catch up, but we never do catch up, because by putting in the extra clause we merely introduce another thing to catch up with. It's like moving from Stage 1 to Stage 2: we start with Stage 1, we add the move from Stage 1 to Stage 2, but by the time we get to Stage 2, the place we have to get to is Stage 3, and so on.

I have chosen this regress because it is rather colourful, but it is not the only one I could have used. What I am looking for is an infinite regress which combines the two following characteristics: first, like all infinite regresses, it cannot be realized: that is, a completion, a situation in which S has an intention which is infinitely expanded in this kind of way, cannot actually exist; and secondly, the idea that it should exist is a desideratum. That is, what I am looking for is a situation in which a certain highly complex intention is at one and the same time logically impossible and also desirable. That is not in itself, it seems to me, an unreasonable goal: it certainly can happen that things are logically impossible but desirable, and if it does, I can make use of it.

The pattern of analysis which I would now suggest as the primary interpretant for speaker's meaning would be that S is in that state with respect to whatever he wishes to communicate or impart (p) which is optimal for somebody communicating p. It then turns out that when you cash the value of what it is that is optimal, you find that the optimal state is a state that is in fact logically impossible. That in itself seems to me to be not in the least objectionable so far, although there are some points that would have to be argued for. The whole idea of using expressions which are explained in terms of ideal limits would seem to me to operate in this way. The ideal limits might not be realizable in any domain, or they might be realizable in certain domains but not in the domain under consideration; for instance, the fact that they are not realizable might be contingent, or it might be non-contingent. It might be for one reason or another (let's pretend for simplicity) that there cannot be in the sublunary world any things that are strictly speaking circular. Nevertheless, that does not prevent us from applying the word "circular" in the sublunary world, because we apply it in virtue of approach to, or approximation to, the ideal limit which is itself not realized. All we need is a way of so to speak measuring up actual particulars against the unrealizable quality of the perfect particular. Indeed, maybe something like this is what Plato went in for.

It seems to me that the notion of knowledge might be explicable in this way. This is a notion which might be, is conceivably, realizable in a certain domain but not in others. Here we look to the people in the past who have suggested that the standard, or crucial, feature of knowledge is that if you know something, you can't be wrong. Some people then went on to say that it follows that the only things we can know are necessary truths, because there, in some sense of "can't", we can't be wrong; and there are various familiar objections to this. Now I might want to say that those people are right, if what they meant was that *strictly speaking* the only things that can be known are necessary truths. However, that does not restrict us to supposing that people who talk about knowing other things are using the word "know" improperly: all it requires is that there should be some licence to apply the word non-strictly to things which in some way approach or approximate to the ideal cases.

It is not my business on this occasion to suggest exactly, or in any detail, what the demands for approach or approximation might be. I will only say that, whatever they are, they ought to be ones which justify us in *deeming* certain cases to satisfy a given ideal even though they do not, in fact, strictly speaking exemplify it; just as in Oxford on one occasion, there was a difficulty between an incoming provost and a college rule that dogs were not allowed in college: the governing body passed a resolution deeming the new provost's dog to be a cat. I suspect that crucially, we do a lot of deeming, though perhaps not always in such an entertaining fashion.

Let me summarize the position we have now reached. First, on this account of speaker-meaning, as a first approximation to what we mean by saying that a speaker, by something he says, on a particular occasion, means that p, is that he is in the optimal state with respect to communicating, or if you like, to communicating that p. Secondly, that the optimal state, the state in which he has an infinite set of intentions, is in principle unrealizable, so that he does not *strictly speaking* mean that p. However, he is in a situation which is such that it is legitimate, or perhaps even mandatory, for us to deem him to satisfy this unfulfillable condition.

Finally, there is the question of how this relates to the regresses which people have actually found: regresses, or prolongations of the set of conditions, which actually exist. Certain ingenious people such as Strawson and Dennis Stampe, and ending up with Schiffer, who moves so fast and intricately that one can hardly keep up with him, have produced counter-examples to my original interpretant in an analysis of meaning, counter-examples which are supposed to show that my conditions, or any expansion of them, are insufficient to provide an account of speaker meaning. The alleged counter-example is always such that it satisfies the conditions on speaker meaning as set forward so far, but that the speaker is nevertheless supposed to have what I might call a sneaky intention. That is, in the first and most obvious case, his intention is that the hearer should in fact accept p on such and such grounds, but should *think* that he is supposed to accept p not on those grounds but on some other grounds. That is, the hearer is represented, at some level or other of embedding, as having, or being intended to have, or being intended to think himself intended to have (or . . .), a misapprehension with regard to what is expected of him. He thinks he is supposed to proceed in one way, whereas really he is supposed to proceed in another. I would then want to say that the effect of the appearance of a sneaky intention, the function that such a sneaky intention would have in the scheme I am suggesting, would simply be to cancel the licence to deem what the speaker is doing to be a case of meaning on this particular occasion: that is, to cancel the idea that this is to be allowed to count as a sublunary performance, so to speak, of the infinite set of intentions which is only celestially realizable.

In a way, what this suggestion does, or would do if it were otherwise acceptable, is to confer a rationale upon a proposal which I actually did make in an earlier paper, to the effect that what was really required in a full account of speaker meaning was the *absence* of a certain kind of intention. This may very well be right, but the deficiency in that proposal was that it gave no explanation of *why* this was a reasonable condition to put into an account of speaker meaning. I think, if we accepted the framework I have just outlined, this arbitrariness, or *ad hocness*, would be removed, or at least mitigated.

Chapter 5

Comments

Comments on Grice's Paper

S. D. Isard

I would like to discuss one or two theoretical points from Professor Grice's paper, and then offer an example, due to my colleague Dr R. A. Boakes, of a mechanism which might be said to derive non-natural meaning from natural meaning in animals other than man, and which bears at least a superficial similarity to the mechanism suggested by Prof. Grice.

Let us begin, however, with Prof. Grice's concern to justify on teleological grounds the existence of correspondences between utterance types and the world. I wonder if this might not be taking the problem the wrong way round. Prof. Grice seems to be taking for granted that there should be spoken language, and asking why it seems to have this "extra" property, while I think that the basic puzzle is how we have come to be uttering sentences in the first place, and that any solution must surely involve their potential for referring to the world.

Furthermore, as I will try to show below, Prof. Grice's account of the way in which sentences are needed to mediate between psychological states and states of the world can be viewed as explaining this potential, as providing a pre-linguistic creature with something to say, once we remark that the mediating sentences needn't necessarily come from a language that anyone speaks. Any abstract formal language would appear to serve the purposes of the argument.

The account strikes me as roughly model-theoretic in spirit, since we have a language independently interpretable in two separate domains: the world, and the domain of the creature's beliefs; and the correspondence that we seek between the two domains is just that some selection of sentences that we are interested in should turn out true under both interpretations.

Note that no other sort of similarity between the two domains is postulated. They don't have to "look alike", or be made of the same kind of stuff. Also, the systems for matching sentences against them, for determining truth or falsity with respect to them, can turn out to be radically different. For instance, there are psychologists whose views I will caricature by saying that they think our heads are stuffed full of inscriptions of sentences. "Interpretation" of a sentence with respect to such a belief system might amount to nothing more than discovering whether it is among those inscribed.

Now it seems to me that is just in case we feel, on the basis of good evidence or bad, that a creature's mental make-up affords an independent interpretation of sentences that can also be applied to the outside world, i.e. that it has an internal representation of the world, that we want to say that the creature has beliefs. We attribute beliefs to Prof. Grice's cheese-eating creature C, because we find it indulging in a relatively complex form of behaviour which seems most economically explained by an ability to "think about", to represent internally, pieces of cheese. In other words, we suppose that the creature has some sort of mental representation of the world with respect to which the sentence "That's a piece of cheese over there" might turn out to be true from time to time, although we do not necessarily suppose that the creature itself is capable of producing or understanding spoken utterances.

So a language, at least in an abstract sense, is logically necessary as a bridge between the outside world and anything we would be willing to call beliefs. And if some subset of the abstract language is translatable into a *spoken* language, it will follow that the utterance types of the spoken language can be interpreted in the outside world. This seems to me to be pretty much the situation we find ourselves in. We speak languages which are capable, on the whole, of expressing our thoughts. How we have come to speak them, rather than just thinking in them, is not something that I will speculate on here, but what would have been distinctly odd, and in real need of teleological justification, would have been for us to develop spoken languages uninterpretable with respect to the world, and hence incapable of expressing our beliefs about the world.

Moving on to Prof. Grice's "rough prototype of the notion of meaning", we find the role of utterances characterized as aiding in the transmission of a psychological state from one creature to another, and the meaning of a given utterance type related to the psychological state characteristically transmitted. I think it most important, if the prototype is ever to be successfully refined, to remove the assumption that utterances induce in the hearer the *same* state that provoked them in the speaker. That is plainly false even for rather basic cases like "I am hungry", or "I am afraid". What is induced in the hearer is not in general the state (hunger, fear) experienced by the speaker, but instead a state of knowledge, or belief, that *someone else* is hungry or afraid, which is not at all the same thing. The case of fright is complicated by the fact that in expressing my fright to you, I may well hope that knowledge of my state will somehow make you frightened as well, perhaps because I want you to act against whatever danger I perceive. But if I tell you that I am hungry in order to obtain your help in getting food, my plan won't normally depend on making you hungry too.

This relates to the further point that the non-natural meaning attached to a sign by the mechanism that Prof. Grice outlines in his second section may be entirely different from the natural meaning that the sign started with. The meaning can easily undergo a sea-change from expressing the state of the utterer to eliciting the characteristic response of the hearer. For instance, a baby might cry because its stomach hurts, and as a result of the crying, its parents might pick it up and feed it. If the parents later perceived the baby to be "faking" a cry, in the manner suggested by Prof. Grice, I submit that their most natural inference would not be that it was in pain anyway, but rather that it wanted to be picked up or fed.

Finally, I am led to the work of Dr Boakes, in which we see something at least analogous to Prof. Grice's proposed mode of progression from natural to non-natural meaning, but since we are dealing with pigeons, the role played by beliefs and rational thought remains uncertain at best. The point of departure for Boakes' study (reported in Boakes and Gaertner, 1977) was the demonstration by Bastian (Evans and Bastian, 1969; see also Wood, 1973) of a form of communication between dolphins. Two dolphins were placed in adjoining tanks in such a way that they could hear each other, but neither could see what was going on in the other tank. In the tank of one of the dolphins, a light would occasionally appear, either steady or flashing. In the tank of the other dolphin, there were two paddles. The experimenter had arranged that if the dolphin with access to the paddles pushed the *left* paddle after a *flashing* light had appeared in the other tank, both dolphins would receive a fish. Similarly, a press on the *right* paddle after a *steady* light would produce a reward. In either case, a press on the wrong paddle would produce nothing for either dolphin. After a reasonably long training period, the dolphins arrived at a point where they received their fish nearly every time either kind of light went on. Evidently, the dolphin who was capable of seeing the lights was somehow reacting differently to the two sorts of light, and the other dolphin was using these reactions to guide its paddle pushing.

Bastian did not suggest a specific mechanism through which the dolphins might have developed their system of signals, but Boakes thought that he saw one, and furthermore one that made only minimal assumptions about the learning abilities of the animals involved. In particular, his idea made no appeal to the apparently superior intelligence of dolphins. He therefore tested his theory by repeating the dolphin study, but using pigeons pecking at keys in place of dolphins pressing paddles. He also changed the choice of lights from steady *vs* flashing to red *vs* green. He found that with sufficient practice, the pigeons also reached a state where they got their reward almost every time.

Boakes' mechanism is based on four assumptions:
(a) That the pigeon doing the pecking, i.e. the one that has to receive signals from the other, will initially show some preference for one or the other of the keys that it is presented with. This is commonly found to be the case in animal experiments.
(b) That if the probability of reward associated with a red light is different from that associated with green, then the pigeon looking at the lights, the sender of signals, will come to behave differently in the presence of the two sorts of light.
(c) That the receiver will be capable of noticing and acting on the above differences in the sender's behaviour.
(d) That responses of the sender pigeon to the lights can be modified as a result of their consequences for the pigeon.
Boakes then proposes the following sequence of events:

The receiver initially develops a preference for, say, the right-hand key (assumption (a)), thus getting food for both pigeons roughly half the time. Consequently, the colour associated with the right-hand key, say green, now predicts food for the sender, while the other colour, red, does not. Assumption (b) leads to a difference in the sender's reaction to the two colours. In the case of pigeons, this is commonly manifested by pecking at whatever signal predicts the arrival of food.

Once this has started to happen, the receiver can begin to notice (assumption (c)) that a peck to the right when the sender is pecking produces food, but that it fails to produce food when the sender is not active. Eventually, this leads to pecking to the left when the sender does nothing, which does produce food.

At this stage, the pigeons are getting food more than half the time, and the probability of food associated with the green light is no longer so much greater than that associated with red, from the point of view of the sender. This can lead the sender to begin pecking to both colours, consequently confusing the receiver and producing a decline in performance, noted in Boakes' study. However, after a time, assumption (d) will act to suppress the counter-productive pecking to red, and performance will stabilize at a high level.

It is, of course, difficult to say that the activities of these pigeons involve "meaning", natural or non-natural. There is, nevertheless, an analogue to Prof. Grice's progression from natural to non-natural use of communication devices in that what is originally a "natural", spontaneous activity: getting excited over the prospective arrival of food, is brought under control and indulged in when it is useful, but not otherwise.

Furthermore, if we take an enormous leap and try to interpret this experiment in human terms, perhaps by imagining two humans with the intention to communicate performing a similar exercise, we are led back to the previous observation that the non-natural meanings derived are not the same as the original natural meanings. "Oh, boy, food!" becomes "It's the green light this time" from the point of view of the sender, while from the point of view of the receiver, we have initially mysterious activity becoming "Press the left one".

In conclusion, then, let me repeat that I think Prof. Grice might do well to decouple his device for deriving non-natural meanings from the idea that communication is transmission of psychological states. Things are more complex than that, even among pigeons.

Comments on Grice's Paper

Annabel Cormack

Professor Grice has introduced a welcome note of sanity into our discussions by talking about utility (or benefit), and correspondence to reality, with respect to language and beliefs. I have some minor quibbles, and a more substantial reservation about his exposition.[1]

The first quibbles relate to the "thought and reality" connection: this mouse and the chalk or cheese in front of it. What I want to know is whether the connection Professor Grice has drawn is due to Darwinian selection, or merely to Grice's own rationality. So what I shall do is to attempt to construct a mouse (a mechanical mouse, perhaps) which fails to relate its thoughts to reality correctly, yet is not thereby disadvantaged.

We need to assume that the satisfaction of a "want" is beneficial to the creature at an appropriate time. Grice's correspondence would obviously fail to benefit the species if the only genuine want were to commit suicide. So the "want" we use is a combination of that in "that plant wants watering", or "that mouse wants feeding", with that in "that mouse wants to be fed". I'll come back to wanting.

At the other end of the chain, Grice has imputed to the mouse two thoughts (or beliefs). For example, that x is cheese (A), and that cheese is edible (suitable for eating, suitable for partially satisfying a want of food), (B). Why do we have the two steps, and not simply that the creature thinks x is edible? Well, let us simply suppose, as seems to me natural here, that the creature has sensory capacities which make it capable of distinguishing cheese from chalk with a fair degree of accuracy (1); and that it is capable of learning somehow by teaching or experience, that cheese and other things are edible, but that chalk and other things are not; but it may perhaps sometimes forget this lesson, or fail to apply it for some reason, (2). The capacity in (1) is obviously beneficial, but that is not the point. The point is that such a capacity is a prerequisite to our being able to say of the creature, "It thinks this is cheese".

I assume also that the reasoning is not interesting if there is no possibility of making a mistake, of getting things wrong; so we need more. For suppose the creature is capable of discriminating objects just by colour. Now we show it white chalk under an unnatural yellow light, and it eats it. Well? Did it make a mistake in assigning the lump to "cheese", or did it make a mistake in assigning all "yellow lumps" to "edibles", having correctly assigned the stuff to "yellow lump"? It is not clear that the question makes sense in the absence of alternative criteria which distinguish chalk and cheese. We get no further by postulating further direct sensory criteria: we need another want. The suitability of chalk for drawing on blackboards will do, if the creature wants to do that. I shall take it then that the creature *is* sufficiently elaborate that it is proper to impute thoughts about class-membership to it as in (1); from which it follows that some thoughts as in (2) will also be needed.

We can now try the first move at getting the connection between thought and reality wrongly arranged. Here, I assume Grice's two psychological laws to be valid. Suppose the creature thinks (wrongly) that arsenic is good for drinking; and thinks (wrongly) that x is arsenic. Is not the second error beneficial, in view of the first? The answer is, no, it can't be, given that we have correctly characterized the creature as distinguishing arsenic as opposed to say, water. For I have argued that it is only when the same classes are pressed into use for alternative wants that we are entitled to assume the classification at all. So it follows that unless there is a matching error in the B-type belief connected with the other want, an error of classification cannot be everywhere beneficial. Furthermore, matching errors throughout the system are impossible, because again we would lose the independence of criteria which justifies our asserting that the creature does classify, and that the classes are as we have described them: "cheese", not "yellow lump".

It appears then, that provided the wants are such that their satisfactions are of equal value to the individual (or species), then it is beneficial for the creature to get its classification "right". What, then, of the case where the wants are unequal in importance to survival: *then* could it be that particular errors are beneficial? It is pretty obvious that some mistakes *are* beneficial, but the general argument shows that it is not possible to describe a creature such that *all* errors, or errors in general, are beneficial. The description does not make sense, or lacks any justification as to its own correspondence with the purported reality. There just *is not* classification, unless it is largely correct classification.

Can I alternatively make a creature for whom it is beneficial that its beliefs do not coincide with reality by giving it different psychological laws? Suppose we try changing the second, psychophysical, law. Instead of the creature doing A with respect to x (say, eating x) if and only if it both wants to and is not prevented from doing so; suppose that under those circumstances, it does not do A, but rather it does do A with respect to x just when it does *not* want to, and is not prevented. I construct then an entirely perverse creature. It eats when it is not hungry, and fails to eat when it is hungry. It may not survive long. But even so, it had better get its "x is cheese" and "cheese is edible" facts right than not. It is the thought "I am hungry" that it would be advantageous to get wrong; the thought "I want to eat". This was not one of the thoughts that Grice allotted to the creature. And it is not, indeed, interesting, if one has any remotely operational criterion or definition of "want". For the creature is not behaving as if it did want to do A; its behaviour and postulated state is such that I think it is not proper to describe it as wanting to do A. (The sense of "want" which is missing is the "desire" sense.)

Let us try instead to change the first law. The creature thinks x is cheese; the creature thinks cheese is suitable for eating; the creature wants (desires and needs) to eat; but in this state, the creature perversely fails to wish to eat x. We'll give it the converse too: if it thinks x is something unsuitable for eating, then it *will* want to eat x. This creature is such that it is beneficial for it to take as edible that which is not, and conversely.

Only, now we are in the same position with respect to the classification "edible" as we were with "cheese" in the first attempt inversely to correlate belief and fact. What grounds could there be for supposing that our labels edible, inedible corresponded to the two classes postulated? We should have some sort of independent evidence. The arguments will run much as before: whether the classification is independent, or whether there is other use of the classes, it must be better for the classification to be correct, or correct where it matters; but it is we, making the description, who decide what to call the classes and hence in some sense the correctness of any particular act of classification on the creature's part.

There are conceivable circumstances under which even a mechanical mouse might properly be said to act in this perverse way, however. Suppose that some non-essential piece of behaviour is correlated with thinking x is an instance of cheese: say the mouse twitches its tail, or its heartbeat increases, or certain neurons are activated. Imagine a population of mechanical or natural creatures, with various bits of non-useful behaviour like this. Then if in the population there is one mouse with aberrant behaviour, it just might be simpler (and even correct?) to describe it as being wrongly wired for the psychological law, than to describe it as producing the non-essential behaviour patterns for states other than those for which the general population produces those behaviours. But this creature must be exceptional.

What we have, overall, then, is that we have creatures whose behaviour is well or badly adjusted to the environment in which they find themselves. A sufficiently badly adjusted creature will have natural selection tending to eliminate his kind. As to the well-adjusted creature: if we choose to describe what goes on in his mind with our vocabulary, then it would normally be perverse of *us* to set up our description in such a way that we postulate an irrational psychological law and a consequent advantage in error of classification; and presumably a rational creature would feel the same. Similarly, it would be perverse of us, and contradictory for an operationalist, to postulate wholesale cancelling errors in classification, or a misclassification to cancel a perverted second psychological law. The correlation between thought and reality is a product of human (or rather, Gricean) rationality, not of Darwinian selection; a conclusion that I think will not surprise Professor Grice.

Given that the creature works according to internal laws, then it will be advantageous for it to make consistent decisions with respect to class-membership, with respect to any item relating directly to a need. There will be an evolutionary push towards adequate and hence probably consistent discrimination. But when it comes to more elaborate beliefs, only indirectly connected with needs, or connected with needs that are not important to survival, then there is likely to be too much play in the system for any lack of correspondence between thought and reality to show up clearly (what else am I hoping for!), so that no suggestion that belief needs to be corrected may reach the rational creature, no evolutionary push be exerted to select one kind of hard-wiring rather than another. I cannot find it in me to trust that the thoughts of, say, economists will naturally tend to coincide with reality.

My last quibble is to do with non-natural meaning as a descendant of natural meaning. Professor Grice has set this up using as a heuristic a double use of *mean*. My complaint is that if play is being made with *mean*, it might as well be done properly. If we look at the range of uses of *mean*, we find a whole class of occurrences, related to those Professor Grice used, as in

I don't have any sugar. That means I can't make buns

We can have

My being hungry means my hand shakes

as well as

My hand shaking means I am hungry

So if a unifying strand is to be found among these uses of *mean*, it cannot lie in some relation between on the one hand a sign, and on the other, a natural or non-natural "meaning". What all have in common perhaps is that on the basis of the first thing given, one would predict the second. It is too strong, to say that the second is some kind of consequence of the first.

I come now to my more serious reservation about Professor Grice's story. The story does not of course rely in any essential way on a double use of *mean*. That was only introduced in order to direct us to consider how it might be that some signals are readily associated with some messages. The story continues, developing non-natural signalling systems and some of the associated conversational principles, from this basis. But it stops short of telling us how a genuine language system, an articulated and productive system, could have developed from the simple signalling system. We are left with what might be relatively weak correlations between language-signs and reality, via the thoughts. And what has happened to the distinction drawn elsewhere by Professor Grice, between sentence-meaning (literal meaning) and speaker's meaning (utterance-meaning)? Grice has endowed his creatures with the sort of pragmatic principles, such as an intention to co-operate and an ability to accommodate to new uses of signals, that are needed in explaining divergencies between literal meaning and utterance meaning. But given the correlation urged between utterances and reality, we might expect to find sentence-meaning sandwiched between the two, so that sentence-meaning too would exhibit correspondence with reality, and indeed a description of the reality-type would give the truth-conditions of the sentence.

However at stage 1, Grice's story depends on the creature's ability to simulate and deceive: he can exaggerate, tell lies for effect. And if the recipient too understands this, as he must at stage 2 of the story, then there must already be a semantics/pragmatics distinction. The listening creature needs to know first what the natural and non-natural meaning of the signal is, and secondly whether it has occurred inadvertently, or is being used properly or deviantly (say, deceptively, ironically, or indeed in some other way such as for telling entertaining stories). With discrete signals, it seems plain that proper use must predominate over any particular nonstandard use, otherwise the signal will become debased, or change its meaning. So we might say that on balance, there would have to be correspondence between the signal and reality, so that sentence-meaning and utterance-meaning for the signals would have to be identical most of the time. But when it comes to language, to genuine articulated language where there is not just a message and an unanalysed signal, but a system for constructing new signal-sentences out of units which do not themselves constitute messages, then I think there need not be this overall correspondence between signal-sentence and reality. There are other, different constraints on the system.

Let me construct an example, to see just what might go on in a simple signalling system. Suppose there is a natural sign of fear, which can be simulated. Let us suppose that this sign has come to be used co-operatively to mean "danger", and that the response to danger is to run away. Now suppose a creature simply wants his approaching friend to leave him alone, and uses this same signal to achieve his ends. How do we describe this use? If we distinguish sentence-meaning from utterance-meaning, then there are three possibilities. In every case, the creature *meant* his approaching friend to go away. First, he could have achieved this by telling a lie. Then the utterance-meaning and the sentence-meaning are both "danger". Or he may manage to indicate to his friend that he is not intending to mislead, but that the message must be construed other than in the normal way, as in the utilization of natural signs for non-natural meanings. If this is successful, then we may say either that there is now a new sentence-meaning for the sign, "go away", or that sentence-meaning and utterance-meaning diverge through the application of pragmatic principles. There is the further possibility that I had no justification for assuming the sign meant "danger" in the first place: it meant "go away" all along.

As far as I can see, Professor Grice has offered no direct way of distinguishing these positions. All these kinds of possibilities are needed in order to explain the development of the system. That there might be conventions applying, or things which it is "generally optimal to do" with a word, or I presume, a sentence, does not seem to me to help. For obviously, it is generally necessary to apply pragmatic principles in the interpretation of any utterance; we cannot pretend that in general, utterances must be interpreted literally. In the simple signalling system, it would be more realistic to suppose that there was no semantics, than that there was no pragmatics. The line between the two can be drawn more or less arbitrarily, here.

It seems to me that in order to explain the necessity for a distinction between semantics and pragmatics, in order to be able to separate in a principled way sentence-meaning from utterance-meaning, we need quite different kinds of stories. Professor Grice has made no use of the articulation of language: he merely mentions after he has reached stage 6, that the communication devices might have other features, combinatory ones. I am convinced that it is the existence of units which are used in more than one combination, and in new combinations, that forces us to distinguish sharply between sentence-meaning and utterance-meaning. It is the compositionality of meaning which gives us the contrast between an absolute correlation of sentences with truth conditions (subject of course to all sorts of complications which I trust are not relevant to the main point), and an approximate, sufficient-for-overall-benefit, kind of correlation between utterance-meaning, and truth or reality. All of Professor Grice's stories apply simply to unanalysed signals; explanations appropriate to language proper, to an articulated compositional system, will need to refer to those essential properties of language.

NOTE

1. I suppose I should add that I am by no means convinced as to the benefits of offering myths as explanations, and that my first reaction on being told these stories was one of anger. However, I would like to thank Professor Grice for some enjoyable conversations; if I remain unenlightened that is my fault entirely.

REFERENCES AND CITATION INDEX*

Austin, J. L. (1962). "How to do things with words". Oxford University Press, Oxford. (*20, 34*).

Bach, E. and Partee, B. H. (1980). Anaphora and semantic structure. *In* "Papers from the Para-session on Pronouns and Anaphora" (J. Kreiman and A. Ojeda, eds), pp. 1–28. Chicago Linguistics Society. (*148, 154, 172*).

Bach, K. and Harnish, R. M. (1979). *Linguistic communication and speech acts.* MIT Press, Cambridge, Mass. (*4, 12, 19, 34, 36*).

Bar-Hillel, Y. and Carnap, R. (1953). Semantic Information. *British Journal of the Philosophy of Science* **4**, 147–157. (*99*).

Bickerton, D. (1975). Some assertions about presuppositions and pronominalisation. *In* "Papers from the parasession on functionalism" (R. E. Grossman *et al.*, eds), pp. 24–35. (*150, 152*).

Boakes, R. A. and Gaertner, I. (1977). The development of a simple form of communication. *Quarterly Journal of Experimental Psychology* **29**, 561–575. (*248*).

Bobrow, D. and Winograd, T. (1977). An overview of KRL, a knowledge representation language. *In* "Cognitive Science 1". pp. 3–46. (*114*).

Boden, M. (1977). "Artificial intelligence and natural man". Harvester, Hassocks. (*210*).

Bolinger, D. (1979). Pronouns in discourse. *Syntax and Semantics* **12**. Academic Press, London and New York. pp. 289–309. (*150, 152, 154*).

Bouton, L. F. (1970). "Antecedent-contained proforms". C.L.S. **6**, pp. 154–167. (*149*).

Brody, M. (1979). "Infinitives, relative clauses and deletion". Unpublished mimeo, U.C.L. (*146*).

Cantrall, W. R. (1971). "Viewpoint, reflexives and the nature of the noun phrase". Mouton, The Hague. (*154*).

Charniak, E. (1976). Inference and Knowledge. *In* "Computational Semantics" (Charniak and Wilks, eds) North-Holland, Amsterdam. pp. 129–155. (*114*).

Chomsky, N. (1965). "Aspects of the theory of syntax". MIT Press, Cambridge, Mass. (*4*).

Chomsky, N. (1975). Questions of form and interpretation. *Linguistic Analysis* **1.1**, 75–109. (*167, 174*).

Chomsky, N. (1976). Conditions on rules of grammar. *Linguistic Analysis* **2.4**, 303–351. (*164, 165*).

* (Numbers in parentheses refer to where reference works are cited in this volume.)

Chomsky, N. (1977). "On *wh*-movement". *In* "Formal Syntax" (P. Culicover, A. Akmajian and T. Wasow, eds), Academic Press. London and New York. pp. 71–132.(*167*).

Chomsky, N. (1979). Government-binding: Pisa Lectures, mimeo. (*166*).

Chomsky, N. (1980a). On binding. *Linguistic Inquiry* **11**, 1–46. (*150*).

Chomsky, N. (1980b). *Rules and Representations*. Columbia University Press, New York. (*103, 155*).

Clark, E. V. and Clark, H. H. (1979). When nouns surface as verbs. *Language* **55**, 767–811. (*1*).

Clark, H. H. (1977a). Bridging. *In* "Thinking: readings in cognitive science" (P. N. Johnson-Laird and P. C. Wason, eds), Cambridge University Press, Cambridge. (*57*).

Clark, H. H. (1977b). Inferences in comprehension. *In* "Basic processes in reading: perception and comprehension" (D. Labesge and S. J. Samuels, eds), Erlbaum, Hillsdale, N.J. (*125*).

Clark, H. H. (1979). Responding to indirect speech acts. *Cognitive Psychology* **11**, 430–477. (*1*).

Clark, H. H. and Carlson, T. B. (1980). "Who are speech acts directed at?" Paper presented at Stanford Conference on Pragmatics, Asilomar, July, 1980. (*21, 22, 36, 59*).

Clark, H. H. and Carlson, T. B. (forthcoming). Context for comprehension. *In* "Attention and performance IX" (J. Long and A. Baddeley, eds), Erlbaum, Hillsdale, N.J. (*62, 63, 68*).

Clark, H. H. and Marshall, C. R. (1981). Definite reference and mutual knowledge. *In* "Elements of Discourse Understanding" (A. K. Joshi, I. Sag and B. Webber, eds), Cambridge University Press, Cambridge. (*xii, 1, 5, 6, 40, 57, 63, 67, 79, 85, 98, 123, 183*).

Cohen, D. and Yemini, Y. (1979). Protocols for dating coordination. In *Proceedings of the Fourth Berkeley Conference on Distributed Data Management and Computer Networks*. (*36*).

Cohen, L. J. (1971). Some remarks on Grice's views about the logical particles of natural language. *In* "Pragmatics of Natural Languages" (Y. Bar-Hillel, ed.), Reidel. (*203*).

Cohen, P. R. and Perrault, C. R. (1979). Elements of a plan-based theory of speech acts. *In* "Cognitive Science 3", pp. 197–212. (*1*).

Donnellan, K. (1966). Reference and definite description. *Philosophical Review* **75**, 281–304. (Reprinted in "Semantics" (D. Steinberg and L. Jakobovits, eds), Cambridge University Press, 1971.) pp. 100–114. (*26, 41, 184, 187*).

Evans, G. (1980). Pronouns. *Linguistic Inquiry* **11**, pp. 337–362. (*168*).

Evans, W. E. and Bastian, J. (1969). Marine mammal communication: social and ecological factors. *In* "The Biology of Marine Mammals" (Y. T. Anderson, ed.), Academic Press, New York and London, pp. 425–475. (*248*).

Foss, D. J. and Jenkins, C. M. (1973). Some effects of context on the comprehension of ambiguous sentences. *Journal of Verbal Learning and Verbal Behaviour* **12**, 577–589. (*106*).

Fraser, B. (1971). "An examination of the performative analysis". Indiana University Linguistics Club. (*39*).

Fromkin, V. (ed.) (1973). *Speech Errors as Linguistic Evidence*. Mouton, The Hague. (*96*).

Gazdar, G. (1979). *Pragmatics: Implicature, Presupposition and Logical Form*. Academic Press, London and New York. (*58*).

Grice, H. P. (1957). Meaning. *Philosophical Review* **66**, 377–388. Reprinted in "Semantics" (D. Steinberg and L. Jakobovits, eds), C.U.P. 1971, pp. 53–59; and in "Philosophical Logic" (P. Strawson, ed.), O.U.P., London 1967. (*xii, 12, 34, 125, 231*).

Grice, H. P. (1967). William James Lectures. Unpublished. (*xiii, 71*).

Grice, H. P. (1968). Utterer's meaning, sentence-meaning, and word-meaning. *Foundations of Language* **4**, 225–242. (Reprinted in "The Philosophy of Language" (J. Searle, ed.), O.U.P., London 1971, pp. 54–70.) (*12, 19, 58, 125*).

Grice, H. P. (1975). Logic and Conversation. *In* "Syntax and Semantics: Speech Acts, Vol. 3" (P. Cole and J. L. Morgan, eds), Academic Press, London and New York. pp. 41–58. (*xiii, 71, 107, 125, 190, 202, 210*).

Grice, H. P. (1978). Further Notes on Logic and Conversation. *In* "Syntax and Semantics 9: Pragmatics" (P. Cole, ed.), Academic Press, London and New York, pp. 113–128. (*71*).

Grinder, J. and Postal, P. M. (1971). Missing Antecedents. *Linguistic Inquiry* **2**, 269–312. (*144*).

Grosz, B. (1978). "The role of focus in task oriented dialogues", Technical Report, Stanford Research Institute, Menlo Park. (*181*).

Hankamer, J. (1973). Unacceptable Ambiguity. *Linguistic Inquiry* **4**, 17–68. (*144*).

Harder, P. and Kock, C. (1976). *The Theory of Presupposition Failure*. Akademisk Forlag, Copenhagen. (*4*).

Higginbotham, J. and May, R. (1979a). Crossing, Markedness, Pragmatics. (to appear in "A theory of markedness in generative grammar" (A. Belletti, L. Brandi and L. Rizzi, eds). Proceedings of the 1979 GLOW Colloquium, Pisa, Scuola Normale Superiore. (*xiv, 133, 134, 137, 140–143, 145, 149, 151, 156, 160, 165, 168, 175*)

Higginbotham, J. and May, R. (1979b). Questions, quantifiers and crossing, mimeo. (*170*).

Hintikka, J. (1962). "Knowledge and belief". University Press, New York. (*40*).

Hintikka, J. (1973). Are logical truths tautologies? *In* "Logic, Language Games and Information", O.U.P., Oxford. pp. 150–173. (*99*).

Hobbs, J. R. (1979). Coherence and Coreference. *Cognitive Science* **3**, 67–90. (85).

Hobbs, J. R. and Robinson, J. (1977). "Why ask?", Technical Report, Stanford Research Institute, Menlo Park. (*181*).

Jackendoff, R. (1972). *Semantic interpretation in generative grammar*. MIT Press, Chicago. (*150*).

Jacobson, P. (1977). The syntax of crossing coreference sentences. Doctoral dissertation, University of California Berkeley (1979—IULC). (*142, 145, 179*).

Jefferson, G. (1972). Side sequences. *In* "Studies in Social Interaction" (D. Sudnow, ed.), The Free Press, New York. (*95*).

Johnson-Laird, P. N. and Garnham, A. (1980). Descriptions and discourse models. *Linguistics and Philosophy* **3**, 371–393. (*41*).

Johnson-Laird, P. N. and Wason, P. C. (1970). A theoretical analysis of insight into a reasoning task. *Cognitive Psychology* **1**, 134–148. (*56*).

Joshi, A. K. (1978). A note on partial match of descriptions. *Proc. Second Workshop on Theoretical Issues in Natural Language Processing.* Urbana-Champaign, Illinois. (*192*).

Joshi, A. K. and Weinstein, S. (1981). Control of inference: Role of some aspects of discourse structure:—centering. (To appear in: *Procs. 7th International Joint Conference on Artificial Intelligence. Vancouver*) (*197*).

Kaplan, S. J. (1979). Cooperative responses from a portable natural language data base query system, Ph.D. dissertation, University of Pennsylvania, Technical Report, April, 1979. (*181, 186*).

Karttunen, L. and Peters, S. (1975). Conventional implicature in Montague grammar. *Proceedings of the first annual Berkeley Linguistics Society.* pp. 266–278. (*1, 63*).

Kasher, A. (1977). "Foundations of philosophical pragmatics". *In* "Basic Problems in Methodology and Linguistics" (R. E. Butts and J. Hintikka, eds), Reidel. (*205*).

Katz, J. (1972). "Semantic Theory". Harper and Row, New York. (*123*).

Kempson, R. and Cormack, A. (1981). Ambiguity and quantification. *Linguistics and Philosophy* **4**, 259–309. (*36*).

Kripke, S. (1977). Speaker reference and semantic reference. *Midwest Studies in Philosophy* **11**, 255–278. (*187*).

Kuno, S. (1972). Functional sentence perspective. *L.I.* **3**, 269–320. (*150, 152*).

Langacker, R. W. (1969). On pronominalisation and the chain of command. *In* "Modern Studies in English" (D. A. Reibel and S. Schane, eds). Blaisdell, pp. 160–186. (*150*).

Leech, G. (1976). Metalanguage, pragmatics and performatives. In *Georgetown University Round Table on Languages and Linguistics* (C. Rameh, ed.). Georgetown University Press. pp. 81–98. (*154*).

Lewis, D. K. (1969). *Convention.* Harvard University Press, Cambridge, Mass. (*xii, 1, 2, 3, 8, 63, 64, 68*).

Linde, C. (1979). Focus of attention and the choice of pronouns in discourse. *In* "Syntax and Semantics 12: Discourse and Syntax" (T. Givón, ed.). Academic Press, New York and London. pp. 337–354. (*122*).

Loftus, E. F. (1979). The malleability of human memory. *American Scientist* **67**. (*197*).

Loftus, E. F., Miller, D. G. and Burns, H. J. (1978). Semantic integration of verbal information into a visual memory. *Journal of Experimental Psychology* **8**, No. 1. (*197*).

Lyons, J. (1977). "Semantics", 2 Vols. C.U.P., Cambridge. (*151*).

Marslen-Wilson, W. and Tyler, L. K. (1980). The Temporal Structure of Spoken Language Understanding. *Cognition* **8**, 1–71. (*106*).

May, R. (1979). "Movement and Binding", manuscript, The Rockefeller University, New York. (*165*).

Mays, E. (1980). "Failures in natural language systems: application to data base query systems", *Proc. International Joint Conference on Artificial Intelligence.* Stanford: August 1980. (*181, 186*).

McCarthy, J. (1979). Unpublished manuscript, Stanford University, Stanford. (*9*).

McCawley, J. (1979). Presupposition and Discourse Structure. *In* "Syntax and Semantics II: Presupposition" (C-K. Oh and D. Dinneen, eds), Academic Press, London and New York. pp. 371–388. (*76, 79*).

McKeown, K. R. (1980). "Natural language generation: generating explanations about the structure of a data base", *Proc. International Joint Conference on Artificial Intelligence*, Stanford, August, 1980. (*181*).

Meringer, R. and Mayer, K. (1978). *Versprechen und Verlesen: Eine psychologische-linguistiche Studie*. Goschen, Stuttgart, 1895. Reissued with an introduction by A. Cutler and D. A. Fay in *Amsterdam Studies in the Theory and History of Linguistic Science 11: Classics in Psycholinguistics, Vol. 2.* John Benjamins, Amsterdam. (*96*).

Metzing, D. (ed.) (1980). *Frame Conceptions*. De Gruyter, Berlin. (*116*).

Newmeyer, F. (1980). *Linguistic Theory in America: The first quarter-century of transformational generative grammar*. Academic Press, London and New York. (*xi*).

Nunberg, G. (1979). The non-uniqueness of semantic solutions: Polusemy. *Linguistics and Philosophy* **3**, 143–184. (*1*).

Perrault, C. R. and Cohen, P. R. (1981). Inaccurate reference. *In* "Elements of Discourse Understanding" (A. K. Joshi, I. A. Sag and B. L. Webber, eds), Cambridge University Press. (*183, 184, 187*).

Postal, P. M. (1972). An invisible performative argument. *Foundations of Language* **9**, pp. 242–245. (*145*).

Prince, E. (1980). "A comparison of left-dislocation and topicalisation in discourse", manuscript. (*197*).

Reinhart, T. (1976). "The syntactic domain of anaphora". Unpublished Ph.D. dissertation, M.I.T. (*172*).

Reinhart, T. (1979). Syntactic domains for semantic rules. *In* "Formal Semantics and Pragmatics for Natural Languages" (F. Guethner and S. Schmidt, eds), Reidel. (*172*).

Reinhart, T. (forthcoming). Pragmatics and Linguistics: an analysis of sentence topics. *Philosophica* (forthcoming). (*197*).

Rescher, N. (1966). "The Logic of Commands", Routledge and Kegan Paul, London. (*53*).

Rieger, C. (1975). Conceptual memory and influence. *In* "Conceptual Information Processing" (R. Schank, ed.), North-Holland, Amsterdam. pp. 157–288. (*114*).

Ross, J. R. (1967). On the cyclic nature of English pronominalisation. In *To Honour R. Jakobson*. Mouton, pp. 1669–1682. Reprinted in D. Reibel and S. Schane (eds), *Modern Studies in English* (1969). Prentice-Hall. pp. 187–200. (*150*).

Ross, J. R. (1969). "Guess who". *In* Papers from the 5th Regional Meeting of the Chicago Linguistic Society, Chicago (R. Binnick, A. Davison, G. Green and J. Morgan, eds), pp. 252–286. (*144*).

Ross, J. R. (1970). On declarative sentences. *In* "Readings in English Transformational Grammar" (R. Jacobs and P. Rosenbaum, eds), Prentice-Hall. pp. 222–272. (*38, 154*).

Sag, I. (1977). Deletion and logical form. Indiana University Linguistics Club. (*145, 162, 167, 174*).

Schegloff, E. A. (1972). Notes on a conversational practice: formulating place. *In* "Studies in Social Interaction" (D. Sudnow, ed.), The Free Press, New York. (*95*).

Schelling, T. (1960). *The strategy of conflict*. Harvard University Press. Cambridge, Mass. (*2*).

Schiffer, S. R. (1972). "Meaning". Clarendon Press, Oxford. (*xii, 1, 3, 12, 16, 36, 38, 40, 63, 64, 67, 68, 85*).

Searle, J. R. (1969). "Speech Acts", Cambridge University Press. (*10, 12, 34, 46, 52*).

Searle, J. R. (1975). A taxonomy of illocutionary acts. In *Language, Mind and Knowledge, Minnesota Studies in the Philosophy of Science, vol. III* (Keith Gunderson, ed.), University of Minnesota Press, pp. 344–369. Also in J. R. Searle, *Expression and Meaning: Studies in the Theory of Speech Acts*. Cambridge University Press, pp. 1–29, 1979. (*10, 33, 46*).

Smith, N. and Wilson, D. (1979). *Modern Linguistics: The results of Chomsky's revolution*. Penguin Books, Harmondsworth. (*xi, 68*).

Sperber, D. and Wilson, D. (1981). Irony and the Use-Mention Distinction. *In* "Radical Pragmatics" (P. Cole, ed.), Academic Press, London and New York, pp. 295–318. (*71*).

Sperber, D. and Wilson, D. (forthcoming). "Language and Relevance: Foundations of Pragmatic Theory". (*72*).

Stalnaker, R. (1974). Pragmatic Presuppositions. *In* "Semantics and Philosophy" (M. K. Munitz and P. K. Unger, eds), New York University Press, New York, pp. 197–214. (*63*).

Stalnaker, R. (1978). Assertion. *In* "Syntax and Semantics 9: Pragmatics" (P. Cole, ed.), Academic Press, New York and London. pp. 315–332. (*1*).

Vergnaud, J-R. (1974). French Relative Clauses. Doctoral dissertation. M.I.T., Cambridge, Mass. (*145*).

Wasow, T. (1979). Problems with pronouns in transformational grammar. *In* "Syntax and Semantics 10". Academic Press, London and New York. pp. 199–222. (*150*).

Wilks, Y. (1972). "Grammar, Meaning and the Machine Analysis of Language", Routledge, London. (*114*).

Wilks, Y. (1975a). A preferential, pattern-seeking, semantics for natural language inference. *Artificial Intelligence* **6** (*114, 116, 118, 119, 121, 122*).

Wilks, Y. (1975b). An intelligent analyzer and understander for English. *Comm. A.C.M.* **18**. (*114, 115*).

Williams, E. (1977). Discourse and logical form. *Linguistic Inquiry* **8**. pp. 101–139. (*144, 145*).

Wilson, D. and Sperber, D. (1981). On Grice's theory of conversation. (To appear in "Conversation, speech and discourse" (P. Werth, ed.), Croom Helm, London. (*71, 107*).

Wood, F. G. (1973). "Marine Mammals and Man: The Navy's Porpoises and Sea Lions". R. B. Luce, Washington. (*248*).

Yemini, Y. and Cohen, D. (1979). Some issues in distributed processes communication. *In* Proceedings of the 1st International Conference on Distributed Computer Systems. (*36*).

Index

Proper names are entered only if they are mentioned in the text without reference to any particular bibliographical citation. A citation index is included in the References.

A

Aboutness, 194
Absorption, 178
a–c dependency, xiv, 135–139, 144, 149, 156–157, 159, 162, 175
Acquisition (of language and knowledge), 41, 43, 109
Addressee, 2, 10–13, 15, 19–23, 25–35, 39, 42–44, 46–50, 53, 59, 63, 66, 76, 80, 96, 98, 108, 116, 124, *see also* individual recognition assumption, eavesdroppers, participants
   attributive, 26–31, 33–34, 44
   indefinite, 24–26, 28–30, 34, 48, *see also* reference
Adjunct model, 29–30
Adjustable joint acts, *see* joint acts
Alphabetic variance, 162–163, 167
Ambiguity, xi, 71, 83, 91–92, 104, 109, 130, 162–163, 231, *see also* disambiguation
Anaphora, xiv, 79, Ch. 3 *passim*
Anaphoric dependency, 135–137, 140–141, 143–145, 148–155, 159, 163, 168, 178
Anaphoric expansion, xiv, 142–143, 145–146, 149, 158, 159, 169, 176, 179
Anaphors (non-linguistic), 146, 149–151, 153–154, 157–158, 168, 173–174
and elimination, 102
and introduction, 90, 103, 109
Apologies, 53, 56, *see also* speech acts
Appropriateness, *see* relevance
Assertion, 1, 35, 57
Asymmetry (principle of), 135–141, 144, 175–177
Atom (planetary model of), 113
Attention, 74, 77, 106, 108–109, 116
Attribution, 33
Attributive NP's, 24, 26, 33, 41, *see also* addressees (attributive)

B

Bach & Harnish, 58
Bach-Peters sentences, 150
Backward pronominalisation, 152, 174, *see also* circular readings
Bacon, Sir F., 52
Baker, J., 235
Belief, 224–230, 233–235, 246–248, 251–254

Belief (*contd*)
  common (or joint), 8–10, 15–17,
    31, 34–36, 127, 215
  hearers', 1–36, 186
  vs knowledge, 3, 8, 36, 39, 182, 196
  mutual, xii–xiii, xv, 3–9, 15, 20,
    55–57, 61, Ch. 4 *passim*
    definition of, 5, 8, 182
    grounds for, 5–7, 10
    relative strength of, 6
    structure of, 182, 194–195
    mutual belief induction schema,
      xii, 5–6, 18, 183
  shared, 1–2, 6
Binding (double), 171
Binding (proper), 143, 162, 173–174,
  179, *see also* quantifiers
Boakes, R. A., 246, 248
Bridging, 57, 225, *see also* inference

C

Canonical speech act, *see* speech act
  (canonical)
c-command, 142–143, 146, 148–149,
  172, 177–178
Chain of inference, *see* inference chain
Chain (anaphoric), *see* anaphoric de-
  pendency
Chain (referential), *see* referential de-
  pendency
Cheese, 225–226, 247, 251–254, *see
  also* mice
Chomsky, xi, 206–208, 210, 221
Circular readings, xiii–xiv, Ch. 3
  passim
Circularity principle, 137–139, 160–
  161, 175, 178
Clarification (dialogue), 183–186,
  194, 196, 212–213, *see also* mis-
  conception
Classification, 251–254
Clause-mates, 154
Cleft sentences, 167
Coherence (principle of), 85

Co-indexing, 148–151, 153, 155, 156
Collective requests, *see* requests (collective)
Command, 150, 152, *see also* c-com-
  mand
Commands, 10, 20, 31, 33, *see also* directives
Common ground, 56–57, 63, 65–66,
  70, 76–78, 98, 124, 126–127, 128
Communication, xiii, 1, 36, 40–42,
  57, 61, 68, 107, 128, 181, 212,
  215, 224, 227, 229, 231, 235–236,
  241–242, 248–250, 257
Community membership, *see* copre-
  sence heuristics
Competence, xi, xiv–xv, 100
Complement construction, 150–151
Compositional dependency, 135–
  137, 140–141, 144–145, 148–149,
  154, 158, 178
Compositionality (of meaning), 257
Comprehension, 61–63, 65–72, 75–
  78, 80–81, 84–85, 91, 93, 96, 100,
  106, 111–112, 124, 126, 129–131
Computers, 36, 202, 206, 210, 221, *see
  also* man-machine interaction
Conditionals, 47, 53, 202, 229
Conjunction introduction, *see and* introduction
Consciousness, 56
Consequence (logical), 232, 255
Constant (referential), 160 *see also*
  pronouns
Constraints, *see* processing constraints
Context, xi, 29–30, 50–51, 61–62, 65–
  85, 88, 92–95, 98–99, 103, 105–
  107, 113, 115, 120–121, 128, 134,
  150, 155, 160, 170–171
  augmented, 89, 92, 95, 110, 116
  incidental, 62
  intrinsic, 62–63
Contextual implication, 51, 73–79,
  80–83, 88, 101–107, 110, 119,
  121, 124–127, 129–130
Contradiction, 114, 135–136

Convention, 1, 44, 63, 67–68, 207, 209, 238–239

Conversational implicature, 76, 80, 108, 126, 202

Conversational maxims, *see* maxims (of conversation)

Cooperative behaviour, xv, 181–184, 190, 192, 195, 205, 211, 214–215, 218–219, 256, *see also* rational coordination

Co-operative principle, xv, 71, 124–125, 127, 128, 131, 200, 202–205, 207, 210

Copresence heuristics, 6–7, 9, 41, 64–65, 84

Co-reference, 135, 148, 150–154, 159, 164–165, 167–168, 171–172, 178, *see also* referential dependency

Crossing dependency, *see* circular reading, coreference, referential dependency

Cultural copresence, *see* copresence heuristics

D

Deception, 233, 235, 248, 255–256

Deductive inference, *see* inference (deductive)

Deeming, xv, 36, 242–243

Definite descriptions, 26, 40–41, 57, 120, 163–164, 167, 172, 216, *see also* attributive NP's

Deictics, xv, 79, 134, 139, 145, 187

Dependency, *see* a-c dependency, anaphoric dependency, compositional dependency, referential dependency

Desire, 225–228, 240, 251–253

Deutero-Esperanto, 239

Directives, 10–12, *see also* speech acts

Disambiguation, xi, 69, 75, 89, 91, 93, 105–106, 108, 113, 122, 130, 138–139, 145, 160, 175–176, *see also* ambiguity; relevance (principle of)

Discourse, 40, 42, 93, 95, 123, 148, 152–155, 157, 181, 194–195, 201

Discourse grammar, 142, 144–145, 148–149, 150, 161–162, 176–179, *see also* sentence grammar

Disjunction introduction, 90, 101–102

Distributive requests, *see* requests (distributive)

Divination, 84–85

Dolphins, 248–249

Donnellan, K., 216

Drive reduction, 42

Duet, *see* violin duet

E

Eavesdroppers, 18–19, 21–22, 31, 39

Economic theory, 74, 98, 204–210

Elementary illocutionary act, *see* illocutionary act (elementary)

Elementary informative (e-informative), *see* informative (e-informative)

Elementary request, *see* requests

Errors (speech), *see* speech errors

Essential condition, *see* felicity conditions

Evans, G., 170

Evolution, 207–208, 254

Existential quantification, 173, *see also* quantifiers

Exophoric anaphora, *see* anaphora (non-linguistic)

Expansion, *see* anaphoric expansion

Expectation (mutual), 181, 191, 201, 219

Experience (shared), 227

Eye-gaze, 32–33

F

Felicity conditions, 10–13, 24

Figurative speech, 71

Finiteness (of grammars), 141
Firing squad, 20
Focus, 122, 155, 195
Four card problem, 56
Friction, 157

G

Gestures, 32–33, 227
Grammar (rules of), 134
Grandy, R., 237
Gravitation, xiv, 157
Grice, P., xiii, xv, 20, 23, 36, 50, 56, 71, 73, 80, 99, 107, 111, 124–127, 131, 190, 200–210, 211–213, 215

H

Hayek, F., 208
Hearer, *see* addressee, eavesdroppers, participant
Hearer uptake, 54–56
Hearers' belief, *see* belief (hearers')

I

Ideal limits, 241
Identity, 156, 162, 167
Ignorance, xv, 40–45
Illocutionary acts, xii, 11–12, 15, 18–23, 25, 28, 31, 33–34, 42, 53, *see also* speech acts
   addressee directed, 21, 23, 25, 28, 42
   canonical, 28, 31
   complex, 12, 34
   elementary, 12, 23
   participant directed, 21
Implicature (conversational), *see* conversational implicature
Indefinite addressee, *see* addressee (indefinite)

Indefinite reference, *see* reference (indefinite)
Indexing, 156, 162, *see also* co-indexing
Indirect speech acts, *see* speech acts (indirect)
Individual recognition assumption, 12, 23
Inductive inference, *see* inference (inductive)
Inference, 4–6, 18–19, 39, 41, 51, 57, 61–62, 69–70, 72, 78, 80, 90, 97, 100, 103, 112, 113–115, 118, 125–126, 146, 190–191, 214, 219
   contextual, *see* contextual implication
   deductive, 119
   inductive, 5, 63–65, 119
   intended, 79
   non-trivial, 72–73, 75, 88–90, 92, 97, 99, 101–104, 109, 114
   trivial, 72, 90, 102
Inference chain, 114–116, 119, 121
Infinite regress, *see* regress (infinite)
Information (old *vs* new), 152, 195
Information (surplus), 182, 192–195, 197, 218, 220
Informatives, xii, 14–15, 18–23, 26–35, 38, 42–44, 46, 49–50, 52–55, 58–59, *see also* illocutionary acts
   e-informatives, 14–17, 22, 27, 36
   j-informatives, 15–18, 20–23, 25–28, 32, 34, 36, 42–43, 49
   partial, 36
Informative first hypothesis, 22, 26, 27, 34
Informative hypothesis, 22
Informee, *see* participants
Innateness, 206–208
Intentions (speaker's), 10, 12–13, 19–20, 22, 24, 26, 34, 36, 43, 50–51, 54–56, 58, 66, 75, 78, 81–82, 84, 92, 96, 98, 114, 125–126, 128, 224, 233–235, 239, 241–243, 256, *see also* m-intentions
Intentions (sneaky), 242–243

Intonation, 112
Island constraints, 191

J

Joint acts, 1–4, 8–11, 14–16, 19–20, 23, 26, 28–29, 35–36, 43, 49, *see also* firing squad; quintet; violin duet
Joint informatives (j-informatives), *see* informatives (j-informatives)

K

Knowledge (*vs* belief), *see* belief (*vs* knowledge)
  common, 1, 3, 8–9, 42, 44, 85, 113
  encyclopaedic, xiii, 76, 88, 94, 108, 116, 123, 182, 192–193, 241, 248
  mutual, xii–xv, 6, 36, 38–39, 40–42, 44, 50–51, 56–58, 61–71, 82, 84–85, 88, 94, 98, 114, 127, 131, 182, 211–212, 239
Kripke, S., 212, 216

L

Language, 224, 226, 228–229, 236, 246–247, 251, 255–256, 257
  foreign *vs* native, 68, 70
Law (vulgar, psychological), 225–226
Least effort hypothesis, 114–115
Leftness constraint, 142, 160, 163–167, 174, 177
Legal language, 69
Lewis, D., 3, 4, 5, 36
Lexical relatedness, 153
Linguistic copresence, *see* copresence heuristics
Literal meaning, 71, 181, 257
Logic, 72–73, 89–90, 99, 101–103, 119, 203

Logical connectives, 202–203
Logical form, 141, 143, 148–150, 156, 159–174, 176–177
Logical impossibility, 240–241

M

m-intention, 19–21, 23, 29, 36, 50–51, 53, 58, 124–126, 128–131, *see also* intention (speaker's)
Man–machine interaction, xv, Ch. 4 *passim*
  information-seeking, 190, 201
Man–man interaction, xv, 190–191, 195, 200–202, 205–206, 211, 215, 218–220
Manner (maxim of), *see* maxims (of conversation)
Maxims (of conversation), xiii, xv, 71, 73, 80, 99, 107, 111, 125–126, 128, 182, 189–191, 195, 201–204, 206–210, 211–213, 220, *see also* cooperative principle
Meaning, Ch. 5 *passim*
  linguistic, xv, 223, 238–239, 255–257
  literal, *see* literal meaning
  natural *vs* non-natural, xv–xvi, 224, 231–237, 240, 248, 250, 254–257
  speaker's, xv, 12, 19–20, 40, 63, 67, 124–125, 130, 223, 236, 238–239, 241–242, 255–257
Memory, 62, 64, 66, 76, 88–89, 93, 97–98, 108, 116, 197
Mention (*vs* use), 138
Mice, 251–254, *see also* cheese
Misconception, 183–186, 188, 190, 200, 211, 213–215, 217, 220, 242–243, *see also* clarification (dialogue)
Model theory, 246
Modularity, 103
Mystery package, 237
Myths, 237, 257

N

Neologisms, 1
Nishiyama, Y., 109
Non-linguistic anaphors, *see* anaphors (non-linguistic)
Non-sequitur, 100, 119
Non-trivial implication, *see* inference (non-trivial)

O

Obligation, 237
one anaphora, 173
Optimal(ity), *see* value
Overhearing, *see* eavesdroppers

P

Paranoid interpretation, 83, 118
Participants, 21–25, 31–32, 34–35, 40, 42, 48, *see also* addressee; eavesdroppers
Participant hypothesis, 21
Perception, 106, *see also* processing
Performance, xi–xii, 100
Performatives, 38, 58, 154
Physical copresence, *see* copresence heuristics
Pigeons, 248–250
Plato, 241
Possessive pronouns, *see* pronouns (possessive)
Pragmatics, xi–xv, 47, 58, 61–62, 88, 100, 107–109, 120, 126, 128, 130–131, 133–134, 137–139, 148, 157, 159–161, 168–176, 178, 194, 196, 205, 255–257
Precede, 150, 152
Presuppositions, 1, 156, 211
Processing and processing constraints, 4, 69, 74–78, 83, 88–89, 91–98, 99, 100, 102, 105–109, 111, 113–116, 119, 121, 131, 191, 206, 217

inferential, 105
resource limited, 114
Productivity, 74
Pronouns, 118–122, 134, 137, 139–140, 142–146, 148, 151–152, 154, 157–158, 159–160, 162–166, 169–172, 175–177
possessive, 172, 178
reflexive, 154
resumptive, 191
Proper names, 79, 120, 137–138, 151–152, 172, 214
Propositional content condition, *see* felicity conditions
psi-transmission, 227–228, 247, 250
Psychological limits, *see* processing constraints
Psychological realism, 41, 63–64, 93, 102
Psychophysical correspondence, 224, 226, 230

Q

Quality (maxim of), *see* maxims (of conversation)
Quantifiers, 99, 135–136, 141, 145, 159, 161–162, 164, 166, 171–172, 174, 229
Quantifier extraction, 162, 163, 167
Quantifier raising, 136, 145–146, 163–167, 179
Quantity (maxim of), *see* maxims (of conversation)
Quessertion, 237
Questions, 10, 169, *see also* directives
Question-answer systems, Ch. 4 *passim*
Quintet, 8–9
Quotation, 231

R

R-intention, *see* m-intention

Rational coordination (principle of), 205, 206
Rationality, 238, 248, 251, 254
Reality, 224, 226, 228–230, 246–247, 251–253, 255–256
Redundancy, 115
Reference, xi, 1, 40, 57, 66–67, 69–71, 79, 108, 118–122, 134, 139, 145, 160, 170, 175, 184, 187, 196, 212, 214–216, 246, *see also* coreference
    inaccurate, 184, 214–216, 218
    indefinite, 24–26, 28–30
Referential dependency, 134, 137, 139–142, 148, 153–155, 157, 160, 162, 168, 170–174, 175–176, 178
Reflexive pronouns, *see* pronouns (reflexive)
Regress (infinite), xii, xv, 3–5, 8, 36, 39, 41–42, 57–58, 63, 98, 239–240, 242
Relative clauses, 170–171, 173
Relevance, xiii, xv, 47, 50, 70–85, 88–100, 101–110, 111–112, 113–116, 119–122, 124–127, 128–131, 160, 186, 202–203, 217–218, 220
    degrees of, xiii, 74–75, 81–82, 84, 91–92, 104, 108–109, 115, 119, 124, 126
    infinite, 90, 110
    principle of, 75–76, 80, 84, 88–89, 105, 107, 110, 111–112, 116, 120–121, 126–127, 129, 131
Repair, 81
Requestees, *see* addressee
Requests, 10, 12–14, 17–18, 21, 28–35, 39, 42–44, 46–56, 59, 183–184, *see also* directives; illocutionary acts
    canonical, 31–33
    collective, 11, 13–17, 22–30, 38, 42, 49, 54–55
    distributive, 11, 13–14, 16–18, 24–27, 29–31, 54
    elementary, 12, 18, 25, 42
Ross, J. R., 58

S

Sacred texts, 77, 99
Santa Claus, 215
Saying, 125
Schiffer, S. R., 4, 5, 36, 58, 239, 242
Searle, J., 20, 23, 46, 47, 56, 58, 59, 126
Selection (natural), 207, 251, 254
Selection restrictions, 138, 145
Semantic representation, 140–141, 143–144, 148–150, 153–154, 171, 256–257
Sentence grammar, 135, 143, 145–146, 148, 162, 176–179, *see also* discourse grammar
Sexual preoccupation, 84
Shops and shop-keepers, 204, 207–209
Side-sequences, 95
Single-target criterion, 12, 15
Skinner, B. F., 210
Sloppy identity, 176, *see also* identity
Smith, Adam, 204, 215
Sparck-Jones, K., 115
Speaker's intention, *see* intention (speaker's)
Speaker's meaning, *see* meaning (speaker's)
Speech acts, xii–xiii, 1, 7, 10–11, 14, 17, 24, Ch. 1 *passim*, 237, *see also* directives; informatives; illocutionary acts; quessertion
    canonical, 1, 10, 23, 31–35
    indirect, 1, 31, 39, 58
Speech errors, 96
Squaring away, 182–184, 187–193, 195–197, 201, 220
Stampe, D., 242
Stoppard, T., 85
Storage, *see* memory
Strawson, P., 242
Sub-VP anaphora, 174, 179, *see also* VP anaphora
Suicide, 251

Supposition (mutual), 56–57, 61, *see also* belief (mutual)
Surface structure, 163, 166
Synonymy, 173, 179
Syntax, 148–149, 167, 172

T

Target as agent criterion, 12–13, 23, 47, 49
Target condition, 142–143, 145
Taste, 104
Text linguistics, 116, 120–121
Thought, 224–229, 240, 247, 251–252, 254–255
Topic, 194–195
Trace theory, 160–167
Trivial implication, *see* inference (trivial)
Truth, xii, 48, 52, 224, 228–230, 241, 255, 257
    necessary, 241

U

Unique identification, 187, 192, 196, 213, 217
Universal quantification, 162, 167, 174, *see also* quantifiers
Updating (of knowledge base), 188, 193–195, 197, 217

of content, 194
structure, 194
Uptake, *see* hearer uptake
Utility, 251
Utterance, 227–228, 230, 240, 246, 257
Utterance meaning, *see* meaning (speaker's)

V

Value, 237–239, 242, 257
Variable, 135, 141–143, 145, 159–160, 162, 166–167, 169–170, 174, 176–178, 229
    free, 134, 142
vel introduction, *see* disjunction introduction
Verb anaphora, 162, *see also* VP anaphora
Verb deletion, 179
Violin duet, 2–4, 7–9, 15
VP anaphora, 136, 139, 160–163, 167

W

Wanting, *see* desire
wh movement, 167
wh phrase, 142–143
wh question, 169
Wittgenstein, L., 116
World, *see* reality